The Californios

The Californios
A History, 1769–1890

HUNT JANIN *and*
URSULA CARLSON

McFarland & Company, Inc., Publishers
Jefferson, North Carolina

Recent works of interest and from McFarland
The California Campaigns of the U.S.–Mexican War, 1846–1848 by Hunt Janin and Ursula Carlson (2015); *Mercenaries in Medieval and Renaissance Europe* by Hunt Janin and Ursula Carlson (2013); *Rising Sea Levels: An Introduction to Cause and Impact* by Hunt Janin and Scott A. Mandia (2012); *Trails of Historic New Mexico: Routes Used by Indian, Spanish and American Travelers through 1886* by Hunt Janin and Ursula Carlson (2010); *The University in Medieval Life, 1179–1499* by Hunt Janin (2008); *Islamic Law: The Sharia from Muhammad's Time to the Present* by Hunt Janin and André Kahlmeyer (2007); *Claiming the American Wilderness: International Rivalry in the Trans-Mississippi West, 1528–1803* by Hunt Janin (2006); *The Pursuit of Learning in the Islamic World, 610–2003* by Hunt Janin (2005; softcover 2006)

Library of Congress Cataloguing-in-Publication Data

Names: Janin, Hunt, 1940– author. | Carlson, Ursula, 1943– author.
Title: The Californios : a history, 1769–1890 / Hunt Janin and Ursula Carlson.
Description: Jefferson, North Carolina : McFarland & Company, Inc., Publishers, 2017. | Includes bibliographical references and index.
Identifiers: LCCN 2017043123 | ISBN 9781476663036 (softcover : acid free paper ∞)
Subjects: LCSH: California—History—To 1846. | California—History—19th century. | California—Ethnic relations. | Spain—Colonies—America—History. | Frontier and pioneer life—California.
Classification: LCC F864 .J29 2017 | DDC 979.4/04—dc23
LC record available at https://lccn.loc.gov/2017043123

British Library cataloguing data are available
ISBN (print) 978-1-4766-6303-6
ISBN (ebook) 978-1-4766-2946-9

© 2017 Hunt Janin and Ursula Carlson. All rights reserved

No part of this book may be reproduced or transmitted in any form or by any means, electronic or mechanical, including photocopying or recording, or by any information storage and retrieval system, without permission in writing from the publisher.

On the cover: *Padron*, oil on canvas, 29.2 × 24.5 cm, James Walker, 1818–1889, circa 1885 (UC Berkeley, Bancroft Library)

Printed in the United States of America

McFarland & Company, Inc., Publishers
 Box 611, Jefferson, North Carolina 28640
 www.mcfarlandpub.com

To Professor Richard Griswold del Castillo,
whose deep knowledge of *Californio* life
has helped to make this book possible

In old days there was not a hotel in California, and it was considered a grievous offense even for a stranger, much more for a friend, to pass by a ranch without stopping. Fresh horses were always furnished, and in many cases on record when strangers appeared to need financial help a pile of uncounted silver was left in the sleeping compartment, and thus were given to understand they were to take all they needed. The money was covered with a cloth, and it was a point of honor not to count it beforehand or afterwards. It was "guest silver," and the custom continued until its abuse by travelers compelled the native Californians to abandon it.

Charles Howard Shinn
(American writer, 1852–1924)
The Century Magazine
December 1890

Table of Contents

Preface: Alta California and the *Californios*	1
Introduction: *Californios* Under Three Flags	5
1. Taking Possession of Alta California: The Portolá Expedition	13
2. The Naval Department of San Blas	17
3. Missions and Missionaries	20
4. Ranchos	25
5. Presidios and Soldiers	41
6. Pueblos and Their Inhabitants	46
7. A Pirate Attack on Monterey	50
8. The Old Spanish Trail	54
9. *Californio* Men and *Californio* Women	60
10. Foreigners in Alta California	73
11. Governing the *Californios*	82
12. *Californios* in the U.S.-Mexican War of 1846–1848	94
13. Land Titles	99
14. Kaleidoscope of *Californio* Events	107
15. Mariano Guadalupe Vallejo	116
16. The Eclipse of the Old *Californio* Order: From Rancho to Barrio	124

17. Opinions on the *Californios* and Their Works	144
18. Three Young *Californio* Women	153
Conclusion: Six Calamities of *Californio* Life	158
Annotated Chronology, 1510–1890	161
Appendix 1: Notes on California Ports, 1769–1850	166
Appendix 2: Rancho Camulos	171
Appendix 3: Jo Mora on the *Nuqueo*	173
Appendix 4: An Interview with the *Californio* Bandit Tiburcio Vasquez (1835–1875)	175
Appendix 5: A Recipe for *Puchero,* a *Californio* Meat Stew	178
Chapter Notes	181
Bibliography	191
Index	199

Preface:
Alta California
and the *Californios*

Before the Gold Rush of 1848–1858, Alta (Upper) California—i.e., what is now the state of California, in contrast to the southern region known as Baja, or Lower, California—was only a simple and very isolated cattle frontier without any close parallel among the many other frontiers familiar to the United States. It was, however, the home of a unique and exceptionally colorful group of men and women known as the *Californios*.

One of the coauthors' interest in them dates from 1950, when at the age of 10 he received as a Christmas present Jo Mora's vividly-illustrated work entitled *Californios*, which had been published the year before. The book you now have in your own hands is the final result of that gift: it, too, is an introductory survey of the *Californios* and of their way of life.

It focuses on the 121-year period between 1769, when the Spanish first began to settle Alta California, and 1890, when the historian, ethnologist, editor, and compiler Hubert Howe Bancroft (1832–1918) published the last volume of his magisterial seven-volume *History of California*. Bancroft had moved to San Francisco in 1852 to sell books. He was so successful in this calling that in 1868 he resigned from business and devoted himself entirely to writing, publishing, and collecting historical works. Today he is still such an important source on the history of the *Californios* that here he will often be cited simply as "Bancroft."[1]

The most important parts of this book are arguably the first-hand accounts from contemporary men and women. Since the *Californios* themselves did not write much about their own ways of life, most of what we do know about them comes from other sources. Some of the longer paragraphs in the accounts quoted here have been subdivided for ease of reading but the texts themselves have not been changed except for minor editing. They are presented here in their original (if often translated) form and are quite invaluable because they are the real words of real people. As such, they are the best way to bring the *Californios* alive for modern readers who may know little or nothing about them.

An important caveat is necessary here: great care is needed when reading these accounts. Much of the extensive historiography produced by foreigners during the 19th century depicted *Californios* as lazy, cowardly, and incompetent in most fields.[2] The underpinnings of this pervasive school of thought are the deep-seated clashes of values between Anglo-American and Latin American culture. These clashes draw on a wide range of very strong feelings, for example, the Protestant distrust of Catholicism; the Puritan dedication to unremitting hard work, popularly known as the "Protestant Ethic"; the American belief in Manifest Destiny, which will be described; the Americans' distaste for rich foreign aristocracies; and the Anglo-Saxon fear of any mixing of the races.[3]

On the other hand, the limited historiography produced by the *Californios* themselves (most of it written after they had lost the U.S.-Mexican War in 1848), usually praises their warmth, their generosity, their ranching skills, and their dedication to their extended families. The modest goal of these memoirs was to leave to posterity a range of narratives that highlighted the virtues of their own society and might help to balance the scales against the far more numerous criticisms directed by foreigners against Mexican culture and society.[4]

A few definitions are needed now. "*Californio*" is a broad term in historic and regional Spanish that came into widespread popular use in Alta California in the 1820s during the flourishing of the first generation of California-born Mexicans. It can variously refer to:

1. A Spanish-speaking, Roman Catholic person who was born in Alta California between 1769, when the first Spanish colonies were founded there, and 1848, when the Treaty of Guadalupe Hidalgo ended the U.S.-Mexican War and forced Mexico to surrender Alta California, which was then a territory and department of Mexico, to the United States.

2. The early immigrants who moved to Alta California from other parts of Mexico or from other Spanish-speaking lands.

3. The descendants of *Californios*, including those who were married to other *Californios*.

4. The children of non–Spanish-speaking immigrants who married Spanish speakers, learned Spanish, converted to the Catholic faith, and

often became naturalized Mexican citizens after Mexico became independent of Spain in 1821.

It must be stressed here that the Indians of Alta California[5] were never considered to be *Californios*, nor were the non–Spanish-speaking foreigners.

At their best, the *Californios* themselves were described by many foreigners as being a good-looking, happy, vibrant, improvident people. By profiting from the forced labor of large numbers of captive local Indians, they managed to carve out and maintain for themselves a remarkable seigneurial and patriarchal way of life, based on raising cattle along parts of the coast and in some of the valleys of Alta California. Many traces of their culture are still visible and are still much admired in California today.

The prosperity of these rancheros rested entirely on the continued and undisputed ownership of their land, namely, their ranches, which usually covered four square miles (2,560 acres) but could cover up to thirty square miles (19,200 acres).[6] As they gradually lost control of their ranches, however, they also lost the high economic and social status to which they had become accustomed. Many of them were then reduced to taking subsistence-level jobs or fell into abject poverty. The "decline of the Californios," to use historian Leonard Pitt's apt phrase, was a long, slow, and painful process that will be discussed in a later chapter.[7]

Alta California lay on the far fringes of the Spanish empire and its historical geography is complicated. It was initially a province and territory of the Spanish Viceroyalty of New Spain; later, it became a territory and department of newly-independent Mexico. There is no evidence that the Spaniards or the Mexicans ever crossed the Sierra Nevada mountains when they ruled California.[8] Thus they never established any settlements beyond the southern and central coastal areas of what is now the state of California, although they always asserted that large areas lying east of the Sierra Nevada mountains and San Gabriel mountains were, in some vague and non-demarcated way, also part of Alta California.

The Americans had long wanted Alta California to become part of the United States so that their country would then extend from the Atlantic all the way to the Pacific. For example, as early as 1758 an American almanac predicted that "[American] Arts and Sciences will change the Face of Nature in their Tour from Hence over the Appalachian Mountains to the Western Ocean."[9] It was not until 1850, however, that this dream was finally realized—when California joined the United States as the 31st state and the remaining segments of Mexican rule in Alta California became all or parts of the states of Arizona, Nevada, Utah, Colorado, and Wyoming.

Taken as a whole, the goal of this book is to present a brief, fair-minded, balanced account of the lives and times of the *Californios*—an account that aims at being both concise and comprehensive. Chapters vary considerably in length: the longer ones address topics where more details are needed to give the reader a clear understanding of what was going on. An annotated chronology describes some of the key historical events between 1510 and 1890. Five appendices add background and details to the text. Endnotes have been used very generously, both for attribution and to expand on points mentioned in the text itself.

Our warm thanks are due now to the following men and women who have provided helpful comments and corrections. They include, in random order, Richard Griswold del Castillo, San Diego State University; Judith Rascoe, a film script writer; Alan Rosenus; David J. McLaughlin, California Mission Resource Center; Pat Ragains, University of Nevada, Reno; Ken Sullivan, Western Nevada College, Carson City, Nevada; Albert M. Camarillo, Stanford University; Alexander King, former California Director of the Old Spanish Trail Association; Jeff Lanzman, Colton Hall Museum, Monterey; and Glenn Farris, a historical archaeologist who studies the history of the Russians in Alta California.

Any errors or shortcomings in this book, however, are of course the authors' responsibility alone.

Introduction: *Californios* Under Three Flags

These three flags were, respectively, those of Spain (1769–1821), Mexico (1821–1848), and the United States (1848 to the present). Many of the key events of these eras are chronicled in much greater detail in the pages that follow, but here it may be useful to offer a brief overview of each of them.

Spain's last colonial undertaking in the New World was the occupation of California, which lay on the far fringes of the Spanish empire. The *Californios* owed most of their own way of life to Spanish culture, i.e., their language, ranching practices, religion, and social structure. Indeed, the very name "California" comes from a Spanish novel, *Las Sergas de Esplandián* (*The Labors of the Very Brave Knight Esplandián*), which was published in 1510 in Seville by the Spanish author Garci Rodríguez Ordóñez de Montalvo. This novel was well known to the Spanish explorers of the New World. In it, Montalvo assured his readers (spelling as in the translation):

> Know ye that on the right hand of the Indies there is an island called California, very near the Terrestrial Paradise [i.e., the Biblical Garden of Eden] and inhabited by black women without a single man among them and living in the manner of Amazons. They are robust of body, strong and passionate in heart, and of great valor. Their island is one of the most rugged in the world with bold rocks and craigs. Their arms are all of gold, as is the harnesses of the wild beasts which, after taming, they ride. In all the island there is no other metal.[1]

In 1542 Juan Rodríguez Cabrillo, armed with a commission from Viceroy Antonio de Mendoza, was the first European to sail along and explore the California coast. However, the actual Spanish settlement of Alta California did not begin until 1769, i.e., after Spain had learned from its ambassador in Moscow that the Russians, who were busy harvesting fur seals in Alaskan waters, now planned to extend their hunts further south, i.e., into the waters off Alta California.

The Russian involvement in this region came about due to expeditions of exploration and discovery undertaken by the Russians in 1725–1729 and 1733–1742 under the orders of Peter the Great, who wanted to make his country more modern and less isolated.[2] The Spanish decided that they must quickly occupy California themselves to prevent it from falling into the hands of the Russians.[3]

In 1768, two influential Spanish officials—*visitador general* [inspector general] Gálvez, whose remarkable determination and abilities led to the founding of Alta California and Viceroy de Croix—had put forward persuasive reasons for such an occupation. They wrote:

> Many dangers can be averted which now threaten us, by way of the South Sea [i.e., the Pacific Ocean], from certain foreign powers who now have an opportunity and the most eager desire to establish a colony in the harbor of Monterrey, or at some of the many harbors which have already been discovered on the western coasts of this New World…. The Russians have been gaining an intimate knowledge of the navigation of the Sea of Tartary [the Gulf of Tartary divides the Russian island of Sakhalin from mainland Asia]; and … they are now, according to some very credible and well-grounded statements, carrying on the fur trade on a continent or perhaps an island [the reference here is to Alaska] which, it is estimated, lies at the distance of only eight hundred leagues [about 2,080 miles[4]] from the western coast of the Californias [i.e., Baja California and Alta California], which run as far as Capes Mendocino and Blanco.[5]

At the same time, the Spanish were also worried, though not quite to the same extent, that the British and the French had designs on California, too. Although all these fears would ultimately prove to be groundless, they alarmed the Spaniards to such an extent that what was termed a "sacred expedition" would be launched by Spain to occupy Alta California before any other power could do so.

The Spanish decided that California could best be settled by establishing a very loosely-linked but mutually-supporting chain of small military, religious, and civil institutions there. These were, respectively, the presidios (garrisoned forts), the 21 Roman Catholic missions, and the pueblos (towns).

The tiny port of Monterey was judged by the Spanish, with a good deal of poetic license, to be "truly the most advantageous [place] for protecting the entire west coast of California and the other coasts of the southern part of this continent against any attempts by the Russians or any northern nation."[6] Monterey would therefore become the capital of Alta California, the location of its Custom House (now considered to be the oldest public building in California), and the only official port of entry for goods coming into Alta California. Its population varied from a low of about 202 people in the early 1790s to a high of about 400 people (many of them soldiers) in 1796.[7]

As will be discussed in the next chapter, beginning in 1769 with an overland expedition from Loreto, Baja California led by the former governor of Baja California Gaspar de Portolá, who was accompanied by the indefatigable missionary friar Junípero Serra, the Spaniards did begin to colonize Alta California, albeit only very lightly. In the process, they saw San Francisco Bay for the first time: before this, it had never been sighted from the sea by any passing ship because of the frequent fogs.

Close to the Alta California coast, the Spanish would initially build four presidios: San Diego, (1769), Monterey (1770), San Francisco (1776), and Santa Barbara (1782). They would also build 21 missions in Alta California between 1769 and 1823, which would ultimately employ 142 friars who would baptize tens of thousands of Indians to make them, at least nominally, Roman Catholics. The missions, however, were never owned by the friars themselves: the lands they occupied on a temporary basis initially belonged to the king of Spain and then later, after Mexico became independent, to the Mexican government.

In their heyday before the missions were secularized (that is to say, before they were seized by the Mexican government in the 1830s), their land holdings were extensive, to say the least. Land grants were usually measured in square leagues, i.e., a unit of measure that was a square, one Spanish league on each side, and that totaled approximately 4,428 acres. The median size of a grant was 2.3 square leagues, or about 10,184 acres.[8]

Mission San Fernando initially had over 50 square leagues, i.e., nearly 350 square miles; Mission San Juan Capistrano had even more. In 1822, Mission San Diego reported that its lands stretched 13 leagues to the south, 17 leagues to the east, and 7 leagues to the north. In that same year, Mission Santa Barbara estimated its own land holdings at about 28 square leagues, or close to 122,000 acres.[9]

The missions were often protected by a handful of "leather jacket" soldiers (so named because of the six-or-seven-layer deerskin jackets they wore to deflect Indian arrows) and were administered by a small number of Franciscan friars, aided by a few *Californio* men and women. The actual work force for the missions consisted of roughly 15,000 Indians, who lived in and who worked under conditions often approaching outright slavery.[10]

The bloody and long-fought Mexican War of Independence, which extended from 1810 to 1821, finally ended the rule of Spain in its Viceroyalty of New Spain.[11] Thus, in 1821 Alta California became part of newly-independent Mexico. The next 27 years, i.e., up to the end of the U.S.-

Mexican War in 1848, formed, in retrospect, the high-water mark of the *Californio* experience. (In overview, the U.S.-Mexican War of 1846–1848 can be summarized by saying that it involved closely-linked undertakings by American forces both on land and at sea. These included the campaign in northern Mexico; the war in New Mexico and California; naval and Marine Corps operations; and the march on Mexico City and the Treaty of Guadalupe Hidalgo.)

Four momentous economic and social changes took place in Alta California during this period[12]:

1. Independent Mexico repealed the restrictive Spanish laws that had prevented foreign trade. As a result, foreign ships could now begin to trade legally with Alta California. (See Appendix 1 on Notes on California ports, 1769–1850.)

2. The 21 missions were secularized between 1833 and 1836 and became churches without any extensive lands attached to them. The former mission-controlled lands, which totaled about 1,000,000 acres and were located in some of the best agricultural and grazing regions of Alta California, were confiscated by the Mexican government and were then distributed to *Californios* and their extended families. Some former missions remained in use as Catholic churches; others were simply abandoned and were allowed to fall into ruin.

3. The greatest single impact of secularization was that it opened up for the *Californios* enormous tracts of prime cattle-raising land—just as world markets for cattle products were beginning to boom. Until the 1820s, Latin America had been the main supplier of beef products, but political instability there now forced traders to find other sources of supply.[13] The *Californios* used their new ranches to profit from the hide and tallow trade. In this business, Americans sailed up to 18,000 miles around Cape Horn to bring finished goods and merchandise from Boston to trade with *Californios* for the hides and tallow generated by their vast herds of semi-wild cattle.

Tallow was rendered beef fat. Indian laborers, often women, carved the fat from the carcass of a freshly-killed animal and boiled it in big vats. When the fat cooled, it would solidify into chunks of tallow, which could be used to make soap and candles.[14] It has been estimated that between 1800 and 1847 Alta California produced roughly 5,000,000 hides and 10,000,000 *arrobas* of tallow (1 *arriba* = about 25 pounds).[15] Some of their horns were made into buttons. Most of the meat was left to rot or be consumed by grizzly bears and other wild animals.

4. The downside of the secularization of the missions, however, was that it left the Indians themselves with no place to live and to work. For the vast majority of them, trying to return to their ancestral way of life was quite impossible because that way of life had long vanished. Most of them therefore became *vaqueros* (cowboys), unskilled part-time laborers, or were simply unemployed.

The third and last flag to fly over the *Californios* was that of the United States.

Mexico's politicians and military leaders understood full well that the American doctrine of Manifest Destiny, i.e., the belief that Americans were somehow "destined"—divinely or otherwise—to control all of what is now the territorial United States, put Mexico in very grave danger of losing its western lands in any war with its far more powerful northern neighbor.

These same politicians and military leaders also clearly understood, however, that to surrender any Mexican territory to the United States—that is, before Mexico was defeated in battle by the Americans—would be a political death sentence for them. Thus, although it was clearly an act of folly, Mexico's leaders decided that to hang onto power themselves and to continue to enjoy the rewards of high office, they had no choice but to go to war.

They pursued this folly even in the face of the gravest misgivings from their own side about Mexico's prospects in such a war. For example, Luís Cuevas, Bernardo Couto, and Miguel Atristain—the three Mexican negotiators who in 1848 signed, on behalf of Mexico, the Treaty of Guadalupe Hidalgo ending the U.S-Mexican War—realized that the war had been lost "the day the first shot" was fired. (Before and during the war, for example, Alta California had no Mexican naval defenses whatsoever.) This was their considered opinion:

> The singular circumstances of our being owners of remote and distant territories (like the Californias) which we were unable to preserve once the war was declared and without a powerful navy of any kind on which to rely, should have prevented us from trying our luck by the use of arms.[16]

Not surprisingly, during the course of the war the Mexicans were totally defeated by the Americans, whose officers and troops were far better armed, better trained, and better disciplined. The end result was that in the terms of the 529,000-square mile Mexican Cession (part of the Treaty of Guadalupe Hidalgo of 1848), Mexico was forced to surrender to the United States the present-day states of California, Nevada, Utah, most of

Arizona, about half of New Mexico, about a quarter of Colorado, and a small section of Wyoming. The Americans thus became the new masters of and, to a limited extent, the occupiers of what is now the state of California. It was by far the most valuable chunk of the Mexican Cession.

Perhaps surprisingly, however, this dramatic shift in sovereignty did not have any immediate or major impacts on the lives of most *Californios* themselves. Previous Mexican governments had been politically unstable, corrupt, and rarely long-lasting. Moreover, they had usually ignored or exploited the *Californios*, making no effort to earn their trust or loyalty. Not surprisingly, many of the *Californios* therefore had no confidence in their own central government. Not a few of them even believed that rule by the Americans could only be an improvement over what they had experienced before.

Such putative "pro–American" sentiments gained strength as it became evident that most of the American occupiers of California were in fact behaving themselves tolerably well. They generally kept the peace and never tried to impose any significant changes on the social, economic, and religious status quo they had inherited as a result of winning the U.S-Mexican War. Nevertheless, two profound and unforeseen changes did occur that were beyond the control even of the powerful American occupiers.

First, in 1848 gold was discovered in the foothills of the Sierra Nevada mountains. The chief gold-bearing region, famously known as the Mother Lode, was in places nearly 4 miles wide and was 120 miles long. The Gold Rush quickly ushered into California a tidal wave of energetic, ambitious, well-armed newcomers. Gold was their primary objective but many of them also wanted land, i.e., the vast, unfenced, undefended ranchos of the *Californios*.

As a direct result of the Gold Rush, a great deal of land-grabbing and violence would occur in Northern California. It must be noted here that "Northern California" is not a formal geographic designation. Although California's north-south midway division is located near San Francisco, this term is used now to refer to all of the state's northernmost 48 counties. However, since there is no precise geographic term for the northernmost ranchos located near the present-day city of Chico (which is on the northern edge of the Sacramento Valley, close to the foothills of the Cascade Range to the north and the Sierra Nevada mountains to the east), "Northern California" will perforce be used here to refer to them.

That said, it must also be noted that the prosperous pastoral life of Southern California itself would continue much as before until a later period. (The absence of gold there, coupled with the shortage of water, made this an unattractive region for miners and farmers alike: it was best suited to cattle-raising.) By the 1870s, however, times had changed, and many of the *Californios* living in the southern part of the state would now be impoverished, too.

Second, after the U.S.-Mexican War, Congress passed legislation that called into question the legal validity of the land titles on which the more than 800 *Californio* ranchos, and thus *Californio* prosperity itself, ultimately rested.[17] These and related changes would slowly but inexorably destroy the traditional *Californio* way of life.

Indeed, by 1890 (when this book ends) the transformation process was well-advanced. By then, the life-styles of most of the descendants of the original *Californios* were not all that different (excepting their fluency in Spanish, their family solidarity, and their adherence to the Catholic Church) from those of most of the other citizens living in California under the American flag.

1

Taking Possession of Alta California
The Portolá Expedition

Given Spain's long-running dominance in the New World, including California, it is important to sketch out here some of its historical background.

After Columbus "discovered" the West Indies in 1492 when looking for a western sea route from Europe to Asia, imperial competition between Spain and Portugal for mastery of the newly-found lands of the non–Christian world went into high gear.[1] Spain quickly claimed the entirety of North America under the terms of the bull (i.e., papal document) *Inter Caetera* (1493). To divide the unexplored world between Spain and Portugal, Pope Alexander VI drew an imaginary north-south line, pole-to-pole, running near the mid–Atlantic islands of the Azores and Cape Verde.

The Pope gave the Spaniards all the lands to the west of that line and the Portuguese all the lands to the east. However, Portugal strenuously protested because this bull meant that it would not be able to claim Brazil. The next year, to clarify their respective boundaries for exploration and colonization, the Spanish and Portuguese therefore drew up the Treaty of Tordesillas (1494). This agreement defined the boundary as a straight line, pole-to-pole, located 370 leagues (about 962 miles) west of the Cape Verde islands. The English, however, did not accept such papal grants: Queen Elizabeth specifically refused to recognize the pope's authority to hand over the New World to the Spanish as their fief.

The explorer Hernán Cortés gave the name *Nueva España* (New Spain) to the territories he had won for Spain in his 1521 conquest of Mexico. The Viceroyalty of New Spain, headquartered in Mexico City, exerted political control (in theory, at least), not only over what is now Mexico but also over large chunks of the Pacific coastal region; the Southwest; the Gulf of Mexico coastal region; and Greater Florida, which included Florida and parts of seven other southern states.[2]

The first significant Spanish step regarding California itself came in 1768, when a royal order by King Carlos III directed that Upper California be occupied by Spaniards to keep it out of the hands of the Russians, who were harvesting sea otters for their rich fur—not only in Alaskan waters but also, it was rumored, even off the California coast itself. *Visitador-general*, i.e., Inspector General, Gálvez and Viceroy de Croix therefore drafted a plan, which was quoted here earlier, to protect Spanish interests in California.

Captain Gaspar de Portolá founded the California settlements of San Diego and Monterey, discovered San Francisco Bay, and became the first governor of Alta California. Spanish objectives in California at this time were three-fold: to counter a perceived Russian threat; to build another mission north of San Diego; and, over time, to fill in the territory between Monterey and San Diego with additional missions.[3]

In 1769, accompanied by Father Serra and other hardy souls, Portolá left Baja California on an overland journey towards San Diego, where the first of California's 21 missions (San Diego de Alcala) was established.[4] Three diaries of the Portolá expedition of 14 July 1769 to 24 January 1770, written respectively by Portolá himself, by the Ensign and engineer Miguel Constansó, and by the Franciscan missionary Fray (Friar) Juan Crespi, each give day-by-day descriptions of their travels from San Diego to San Francisco and back again. (Spelling as in the translation.)

Portolá began his diary with these words:

> Diary of the journey that Gaspar de Portolá, captain of dragoons of the España Regiment, Governor of the Californias, made by land to the ports of San Diego and Monterey..., having been appointed commander-in-chief of this expedition by the Most Illustrious Don Joseph de Galvez [sic], in virtue of the viceregal powers which had been granted to him by His Excellency [i.e., the Viceroy]. The expedition was composed of thirty-seven soldiers in leather jackets with their captain, Don Fernando de Rivera; this officer was sent in advance with twenty-seven soldiers and the Governor [followed] with ten men and a sergeant.[5]

This expedition was trying to find Monterey Bay, which the earlier explorer Sebastián Vizcaíno had over-enthusiastically depicted being an excellent harbor. The going was very hard for Portolá and his party, however, and on 11 May 1769 he wrote in his diary:

> I set out from Santa Maria, the last mission to the north, escorted by four soldiers with Father Junípero Serra, president of the missions, and Father Miguel Campa.

1. Taking Possession of Alta California

This day we proceeded for about four hours with very little water for the animals and without any pasture, which obliged us to go farther in the afternoon to find some. There was, however, no water.[6]

The next day, he added: "The 12th we proceeded over a good road [probably a path used by the Indians] for five hours and halted at a place called La Ponza de Aqua Dulce. No water."[7]

Portolá's initial quest for Monterey Bay ended in an embarrassing failure. As Father Crespi, the diarist and chaplain of this expedition explained, despite their most strenuous efforts Portolá and his men were quite unable at that time to locate

the port of Monterey so celebrated and so praised in their time by men of character, skillful, intelligent, and practical navigators [i.e., by Vizcaíno] who came expressly to explore these coasts by order of the king.[8]

The probable reason for Portolá's failure here was that he did not understand that when the frequent fogs obscured the Santa Cruz shoreline, the choppy waters of Monterey Bay itself when seen from the land (it was in fact little more than an open roadstead, not a protected harbor) looked much like the Pacific Ocean close to the shore. Viewed from the sea by Vizcaíno, however, it must have looked more like a possible port.

In any case, Portolá was not a man to give up easily and soon concluded that Monterey must be further north. He therefore proceeded in that direction, but when he got to Half Moon Bay (about 25 miles south of San Francisco) in November 1769, he recognized, from Vizcaíno's descriptions, the Farallon Islands (a group of small islands and sea stacks located 30 miles outside the Golden Gate, which would later become a base for Russian sea-lion hunters and sealers), Point Reyes, and Drake's Bay. He thus realized that he was now too far north. This mistake, however, turned out to be a blessing in disguise.

When he sent Sergeant José Francisco Ortega and a small party of men up into the coastal hills to see what they could find, they reported that from Sweeney Ridge, a 1,200-foot hilltop overlooking what is now the town of Pacifica, they could see an enormous bay. Crespi wrote:

About one in the afternoon [on 4 November 1769] we set out to continue the journey, following the beach to the north. We then entered the mountains, directing our course to the northeast and from the summit of a peak we beheld the great estuary or arm of the sea, which must have a width of four or five leagues [about 10.4 to 13 miles], and extends to the southeast and south-southeast.[9]

Crespi said that this body of water was so big that "doubtless not only all the navies of our Catholic Monarch, but those of all Europe, might lie within the harbor."[10] As the best natural harbor along the North American Pacific coast, San Francisco Bay would be an excellent base for further Spanish exploration and settlement.

Portolá returned to San Diego in 1770 but then he headed northward again and this time he managed to find Monterey Bay. There he built a presidio in order "to occupy the port and defend us against attacks from the Russians, who are about to invade us."[11]

However, expeditionary travel in Alta California was never easy, and Portolá recorded that at the end of each day's travel he ordered that one of the weak, old baggage mules be killed and cooked for food. He and his men were so ravenous that they ate the mule meat "like hungry lions." Indeed in 12 days they ate 12 mules and rode into San Diego "smelling frightfully of mules."[12]

Finally, having at last discharged all his assignments successfully, Portolá went back to Baja California and was appointed governor of the city of Puebla. He later returned to Spain.

By taking possession of Alta California, the Portolá expedition paved the way for the region's gradual colonization by Spain. In 1773, there were only two presidios, five missions, and about 70 Spaniards in Alta California, but all this was about to change. Portolá's travels, buttressed later by those of Juan Bautista de Anza's expeditions of 1774–1776, established what would eventually become an overland route from Mission San Diego de Alcalá in Southern California north to Mission San Francisco Solano in Sonoma.

This route would turn into a 650-mile-long track known as El Camino Real ("The Royal Road," also called "The King's Highway") and would make it possible for Franciscan friars and for Spanish soldiers and ranchers to establish and maintain a string of 21 missions and a lucrative cattle-ranching economy in Alta California.

2

The Naval Department of San Blas

The Naval Department of San Blas was vital to the success of the Spanish colonial effort in the Californias. At a time when virtually no organized civilian infrastructure existed there, only San Blas was able to ship badly-needed supplies both to the missions and to the presidios.[1]

Its story begins in 1768. That year, José de Gálvez, the *visitor general* (inspector-general) of New Spain, supervised the founding of a shipyard and naval depot at San Blas in what is now the Mexican state of Nayarit. San Blas is located on Mexico's west coast about 60 miles north of present-day Puerto Vallarta. So closely was San Blas associated with Alta and Baja California that the new port became known as "San Blas de Californias."

This port was not only a depot for shipping goods to the north but also soon became a shipbuilding center and a commercial area of some importance in its own right. As the missions of California increased in prosperity and as a moderate surplus of goods accumulated in Alta California itself, San Blas became the destination of all the products leaving California via legal trade channels. It also served as an arrival point for furs from the Pacific Northwest, for agricultural products from California, and as an administrative center through which many of the Spanish personnel going to and coming from Alta California were obliged to pass. Moreover, the syndics of the missions (the syndics were the representatives of the missions); the military supply officer of the California presidios; the commissary officer of the Spanish Naval Department; and other commercial agents all made San Blas or the nearby city of Tepic their headquarters.[2]

Spain had recently learned from its ambassador in Moscow that Russia was intensifying its activities along the North American coast. Fearing that Russian advances across Siberia into Alaska and further south would pose a grave threat to California, the Spanish crown wanted to strengthen New Spain by reorganizing its defenses and finances there. As a result, Gálvez was given broad authority to thwart any Russian expansionist designs.

Gálvez decided that the best and easiest way for Spain to counter the perceived Russian threat was to establish its own settlements in Alta California. An early step in this process was to occupy the port of Monterey. Thus at a meeting held in San Blas on 16 May 1768, he and other senior Spanish officials agreed that, among other things,

> there be made ready at once [at San Blas] all the necessary supplies of provisions, rigging, sails, and whatever else is thought useful and indispensable to be put aboard ... two new brigantines which are to undertake the voyage to the harbor of Monterey....³

As a nautical aside, it can be noted here that in the first half of the 18th century the term "brigantine" referred not to a vessel but to her rigging. A brigantine was a two-masted vessel: her foremast was square-rigged, while her mainmast was rigged with a fore-and-aft mainsail, square topsails, and possibly topgallant sails as well.

However, the first two ships assigned to San Blas were not brigantines but the packet boat *San Carlos* (discussed below) and the vessel *El Principe*. Gálvez ordered that four new vessels be built, one of which—the schooner *Sonora*—was later sailed to Alaska. In Spanish and Mexican California, a schooner, or *goleta*, was a small, two-masted vessel about 100 feet long whose shallow draft made it ideal for coastal exploration.

After the San Blas conference, Gálvez proceeded to Alta California to take personal charge of organizing the exploration and settlement of the region. It was agreed that the exploration phase would consist of five parts under the overall command of Portolá: two parties were to travel by land, two by sea, and an additional supply ship was to follow. The first vessel to depart was the *San Carlos*, which left La Paz on 9 January 1769. The second ship was the *San Antonio*, which arrived in San Diego on 11 April 1769. The third vessel, the *San José*, was lost at sea with all hands.

With San Diego itself now lightly occupied, Portolá decided to push on overland to Monterey. The extract below is from the diary of the expedition's engineer, Miguel Constansó and describes how the overland expedition set out from San Diego on 17 June 1769. Constansó makes an interesting and unexpected point about this trip, writing that

> ... the pack animals themselves constitute the greatest danger on these journeys and are the most dreaded enemies—though without them nothing could be accomplished. At night, and in a country they do not know, these animals are very easily

frightened. The sight of a coyote or a fox is sufficient to stampede them, as they say in this country. A bird flying past is likely to frighten them and to make them run many leagues, throwing themselves over precipices and cliffs, defying human efforts to restrain them.[4]

San Blas also became the base for Spanish expeditions to the Pacific Northwest. From 1789 to 1795, it was responsible for establishing and maintaining the Spanish post at Nootka Sound and Fort San Miguel, both located in British Columbia on Vancouver Island. Indeed, for about 20 years in the late 18th century, San Blas was one of the busiest ports and shipbuilding centers on the Pacific coast, even rivaling Acapulco, the eastern terminus of the trans-Pacific Manila galleon convoy.

Between 1798 and 1810, however, San Blas went into a rapid decline.[5] Historically, this port and Alta California had been linked by very strong political, economic, and religious bonds. The viceroyalty of New Spain had shipped to Alta California not only food, implements, tools, and church vestments, but also the Franciscan friars needed to staff the new missions and towns there. Such inputs from San Blas were for a long time the key way for Spain to sustain this remote province, but as Alta California became more prosperous and more independent, San Blas began to count for less and less. In its place, beginning in 1798, there arose a new growth industry, i.e., smuggling along the Pacific Coast, which was conducted (illegally, of course) by American, English, Russian, and other foreign ships.

Although trading with foreigners in California was technically illegal at this time, it would become so essential to the gradual development of Alta California that, eventually, it was quietly condoned by the Mexican authorities. It therefore continued virtually unchecked and, indeed, it increased significantly after 1810—when as a result of persistent political instability and guerrilla fighting in Mexico itself, the supply ships from San Blas to Alta California stopped coming altogether. Smuggling and, later, officially-sanctioned trade took their place.

3

Missions and Missionaries

The Spaniards began building missions as the first step in their colonization of Baja and Alta California, beginning in Baja California in 1697.[1] They believed that they had a religious responsibility in both Californias to "convert the heathen" to Catholicism and to integrate them, by force if necessary, into the lowest rung of Spanish culture as unpaid workers.

In Alta California, they also wanted to occupy the land to keep the Russians away. Thus in 1772, by order of the Viceroy of New Spain, the Territory of Alta California was assigned as a missionary project to the friars of the Regular Order of San Francisco de Assisi, more commonly known as the Franciscans. None of the Franciscan friars were *Californios*. Since a great deal has already been written about the missions of Alta California (the Library of Congress alone holds more than 1,000 books on this subject), the comments offered here must be seen only as a very brief introduction to a topic that has attracted much scholarly and popular attention over the years.

Under Serra's very firm and energetic leadership, the friars took possession of this Territory and established their first mission, San Diego de Alcalá, on 16 July 1769. Between 1769 and 1823, it would be followed by 20 other missions, strung out for about 650 miles along the coast of Alta California—ranging from San Diego in the south to Sonoma in the north. (Sonoma is located about 35 miles north of San Francisco Bay.)

They were all sited to be as close as feasible to water, arable land, and centers of Indian population. They had to be easily accessible by land and, where possible, by sea as well. Since there were few external sources of supply for the key items they needed (it took a long time for goods to get from the Spanish naval base at San Blas on the Pacific coast of mainland Mexico to Alta California), the basic hope of each mission was to become as self-sufficient as possible and as quickly as possible.

3. Missions and Missionaries

Over time, and under the able, devoted "hands-on" leadership of the friars, the hard work of the Indian laborers, and the contributions of a small but dedicated *Californio* staff, the missions became a remarkable success story *in agricultural terms*. Whether they were also a success story *in cultural and social terms* is a very different and, indeed, a very controversial question. It is beyond the scope of this book, but the following points can safely be made about the missions.

Wheat, corn, barley, and beans were raised. Fruit trees were cultivated. Grapes were grown and were fermented to make wine and brandy, both for sacramental religious use and to trade for other products. Cattle ranching and sheep raising were major activities. By 1800 the herds of cattle in Alta California totaled 187,000 animals, of which 153,000 were in the pastures of the missions.[2] By 1805, there were also more than 130,000 sheep, most of them owned by the missions. The total crop production of 19 missions was almost 60,000 *fanegas* (bushels), that is, about 720,000 Imperial bushels, or 3,330,000 liters, of wheat, corn, barley, and beans.[3]

Measured by the amount of productive land it held, its agricultural output, the size of its livestock herds, and the numbers of its Indian workers, the largest and richest mission was clearly San Luis Rey. Its buildings covered more than six acres; indeed, one European visitor said of it in 1827: "In the still uncertain light of dawn, this edifice has the aspect of a palace."[4] Known as the "King of the Missions" and now a National Historical Landmark, San Luis Rey is located in Oceanside, California.

The Indians came to the missions for various reasons. Sometimes they were enticed by offers of free food. At other times, they simply may have wanted to side with the Spanish and the *Californios*, who were not only the most heavily-armed force in the Californias but who also claimed to have a direct relationship with a god more powerful than any Indian deity. In later times, however, Indians were sometimes hunted down on horseback like wild animals and were captured with lariats: riding and lassoing were skills that *Californio* men had honed from early boyhood and for which they were justifiably famous.

On 3 December 1859, for example, the Los Angeles *Star* gave a graphic account of these skills in an article reporting on a two-day *recogida* (i.e., a roundup of horses) held on William Workman's Rancho La Puente, a 49,000-acre spread located in the southern San Gabriel Valley. The article said:

> The feats of horsemanship performed by the Californians were astonishing; but the facility and precision with which the "lasso" was thrown could scarcely be credited

by those who have not witnessed such experts. The animal aimed at was secured whether in the band or running full speed over the plain; and that, too, by the neck or limb at the fancy of his pursuer.[5]

With such expert riders and ropers at hand to capture him if he tried to escape, almost the only way an Indian could be sure of leaving a mission after he had entered it (voluntarily or otherwise), was "feet-first," i.e., as a corpse. If he fled, he would be pursued and would be punished most severely when caught.

As mentioned earlier, the missionaries were often assisted by a few *Californios*. For example, the Bancroft Library, which is named after the celebrated historian, compiler, and editor Hubert Howe Bancroft, has a touching photo of Eulalia Pérez (1768–1878). She was reported to have been more than 100 years old at that time. Born in Loreto, she devoted her life to helping others as a widow, midwife, head cook, *llavera* (wardress, i.e., chief housekeeper), teacher, and supervisor of various shops at Mission San Gabriel in what is now Los Angeles County.[6]

Her life is important because her supervisory capacity positioned her, first, on equal footing with men who were initially her superiors, and ultimately, warranted her position as their overseer. Secondly, she is significant because of her personality: she was a tough, independent, sure-minded woman never lacking in self-esteem.

In her very old age, Eulalia still retained a sprightly, youthful, and affectionate sense of humor. In Mexican villages, all the passages of life, e.g., births, marriages, and deaths, were marked by fiestas or by other ceremonies. As a young girl in Loreto, Eulalia had been a fine singer and dancer. She must have played active roles in many such events and was justly proud of her participation in the village's heritage.

She was interviewed in 1877 by Thomas Savage, one of Bancroft's writers. Born in Havana, Cuba in 1823, where his New England father was a merchant, he grew up speaking both English and Spanish fluently. He began working for Bancroft in 1873 and did such a fine job that Bancroft later wrote of him:

> For many years, Mr. Savage was my main reliance on Spanish-American affairs.... With good scholarship, ripe experience, and a remarkable knowledge of general history, he brought to the library strong literary taste, a clear head, and methodological habits.[7]

At the end of the interview, Eulalia asked Savage to tell her his first name. He said to her, in Spanish, that it was Tomás (Thomas). She then spontaneously bid farewell to him by reciting, in Spanish, these concluding and (here paraphrased) lines from an old song from her Loreto days:

Tomasito, I wish that someone could describe my sorrow to you, so that—so lovingly—you could ease my suffering with your love. My intention is never to offend you, but always to have blind passion for you, knowing the great happiness and tender tranquility with which you surrendered your soul and your heart to me.[8]

The missions were so successful in agricultural terms that, over time, they would come to control huge herds of cattle, which would become the most valuable product of Alta California. (A dried cattle hide would later become known as "a California banknote.") In the mid–1820s, the missionaries and their *Californio* and Indian helpers were instrumental in founding the Alta California hide and tallow trade.

In this lucrative business, which was so admirably described by Richard Henry Dana, Jr., in his popular, influential book *Two Years before the Mast* (1840), American and British companies signed contracts with the missions and with ranchers to buy their hides and tallow. The companies loaded and shipped them in vessels trading up and down the Alta California coast. This was truly the golden age of the *Californios* and will be examined in some detail in later pages.

The missions also controlled about 8 million acres of potentially very valuable land in Alta California.[9] Indeed, the missions acquired most of the desirable land along what would gradually become El Camino Real, the main travel artery of the region. Ironically, however, their very success here led to their own destruction.

As soon as the revolutionaries who had worked so hard to free Mexico from Spanish rule finally came to power themselves, they demanded that the missions be secularized. In addition to wanting independence from Spain, they had long coveted the rich lands of the missions. No more than 30 private land grants had been made before the independence of Mexico in 1821, but now it was the revolutionaries' own turn. They were not slow to demand these lands for themselves, for their extended families, and for their friends.

Prior to the American conquest of California in July 1846, Mexican governors had made approximately 750 land grants in order to stimulate economic development and to reward prominent *Californio* families.[10] Secularization, i.e., the confiscation and privatization of these lands, began in earnest in 1834, with the ostensible goal of turning over some of the mission lands, perhaps as many as half of them, to the Indians who worked them. The *Californios*, however, had no intention of giving these lands to the Indians, so the result was entirely foreseeable. Due to endemic corruption and administrative slight-of-hand, virtually all of the desirable mission lands soon ended up in the hands of well-connected *Californios* and their relatives. Most of the missions were pillaged and were left in ruins. The Indians themselves were left empty-handed and without any support from the missionaries, who were now deprived of the agricultural and other assets of the missions and could dispense only religious consolation.

The relationships between the missionaries and the *Californios* could be warm and close. This was not surprising in a frontier land where the Catholic Church played a dominant role in everyday life. Guadalupe Vallejo was a nephew of General Mariano Guadalupe Vallejo (1807–1890), who was such a pivotal figure in the *Californio* story that a full chapter will be devoted to him later in this book.[11] For his own part, Guadalupe Vallejo had this to say in an article he wrote in 1890 on "Ranch Mission Days in Alta California":

> A Spanish lady of high social standing tells the following story, which will illustrate the honor in which the Mission fathers were held:
> Father Majin Catala, one of the missionaries early in the century, was held to possess prophetic gifts, and many of the Spanish settlers, the Castros, Peraltas, Estudillos, and others, have reason to remember his gift. When any priest issued from the sacristy to celebrate mass all hearts were stirred, but with this holy father the feeling became one of absolute awe. On more than one occasion before his sermon he asked the congregation to join in prayers for the soul of one about to die, naming the hour. In every case this was fulfilled to the very letter, and that in cases where the one who died could not have known of the father's words…
> [Father Catala] was one of the most genial and kindly of the missionaries, and he surprised all those who had thought that every one of the fathers was severe. He saw no harm in walking out among the young people, and saying friendly things to them all. He was often known to go with young men on moonlight rides, lassoing grizzly bears, or chasing deer on the plain. His own horse, one of the best ever seen in the valley, was richly caparisoned, and the father wore a scarlet silk sash around his waist under the Franciscan habit. When older and graver priests reproached him, he used to say with a smile that he was only a Mexican Franciscan, and that he was brought up in a saddle. He was certainly a superb rider.[12]

The mission era of Alta California ended with the final sale and lease of mission property in May 1845. Leonard Pitt, an authority on the decline of the *Californios*, put it very well:

> The dethronement of the padres elevated the rancheros and introduced a new social order based on their authority. More than eight hundred of them shared in the carving up of 8 million prime acres…. Land in parcels up to 11 leagues [i.e., a little over 48,712 acres] could be had practically for the asking by those with the right connections or with a record of civil or military service. Some families obtained several great adjoining parcels and thus prevailed over 300,000 acres or more.[13]

Since this great sea-change was the making of the *Californios*, it now needs to be discussed at some length in the next chapter.

4.

Ranchos

In their heyday in 1848, there were about 455 huge ranches in Alta California that, in total, embraced some 8,600,000 acres. They averaged nearly 19,000 acres each. At these, the ranchero and his family were at the top of the economic and social ladder, from which pinnacle they directed their extensive staffs of skilled workers, e.g., mayordomos (managers), vaqueros, leather craftsmen, blacksmiths, and female servants.[1] Most of the hard repetitive work, however, was done by large numbers of marginally-trained Indians. There were many smaller and poorer ranches, too, but it was the big ranches that have always attracted the most popular and scholarly attention.

Historically, grants of Baja California land given to deserving Spanish soldiers, both to reward them personally and to encourage young men to join the military service, date from 1768 and 1769. It was then that the *visitador general* (inspector general) of New Spain, José de Gálvez, first granted grazing permits to soldiers, but he never gave away the land itself because, technically, it still belonged to the king of Spain. This distinction, however, was always more fictional than real; once granted, these ranchos were universally understood, in practice, to have become the private property of the grantee, his family, and his descendants, to be used as they saw fit.

In the 1780s, Governor Pedro Fages followed this precedent by granting ranch lands in Southern California to veterans. In a report to his superior officers in Mexico City in 1784, he explained his reason:

> The cattle are increasing in such manner, that is necessary in the case of several owners to give them additional lands; they have asked me for some *sitios* [places] which I have granted provisionally, namely to Juan José Domínguez who was a soldier in the presidio of San Diego and who at this moment has four herds of mares and about 200 head of cattle on the river below San Gabriel, to Manuel Nieto for a similar reason that of la Zanja on the highway from said Mission along by the oak tree, and to the sons of the widow Ignacio Carillo on that deep creek contiguous to the foregoing....[2]

The grants Fages made were indeed generous. Juan José Domínguez became the owner of the 48,000-acre Rancho San Pedro, the first Spanish land grant in Alta California. José María Verdugo received the 36,403-acre Rancho San Rafael. Manuel Nieto was given the 167,000-acre Los Nietos ranch, which would eventually be subdivided into five big ranchos for his extended family. Later governors followed the lead of their predecessors, with the result that about 30 grants were eventually made in Alta California under Spanish rule.

It should be noted here that since the Spanish and the Mexican governments had paid nothing at all for these lands, they could well afford to distribute them free of charge to whomever they liked. Writing in 1863 about the Mexican land grant policy (which was essentially identical that of to its Spanish predecessor), John Hittell, an American commentator, explained that

> the public land was granted not by the acre, as in the American states, but by the square league…. The government granted away its land willingly, and without compensation; no pay was required; the only condition of the grant was that the grantee should occupy the land, build a house on it, and put several hundred head of cattle on it. Whenever he promised to comply with these conditions, he could get any piece of public land, of eleven square leagues or less, for which he might petition. It was a grand Mexican homestead law; and the chief complaint about it was by the government, that the number of applicants for grants was not greater.[3]

There were two reasons why only about 30 land grants were made by the Spanish. The first was that there were simply not many *Californios* who had the necessary practical skills and the military, social, or financial credentials to be entrusted with huge properties. The second reason was that a large part of the best land was already under the control of the missions, who very much wanted to maintain their hold on it so that—in theory at least, and at some indeterminate point in the very distant future—they could pass it on to their wards, the Mission Indians. Ultimately, Spanish and Mexican land grants would extend all the way north from what is now the U.S.-Mexican border to the city of Chico. The Mission Indians, however, would never get any land of any value.

A typical Spanish petition and grant ran along the following lines. In 1784, Manuel Pérez Nieto, a soldier at the presidio of San Diego, petitioned Governor Fages in these words, which Nieto, being illiterate, must have dictated (punctuation and spelling are as in the original):

> Sir:
>
> Manuel Perez Nieto, soldier of the Royal Presidio of San Diego, before Your Worship with the greatest and due honour, appear and say: That in attention to the fact

that I have my herd of horses as well as of bovine stock at the Royal Presidio of San Diego, and because they are increasing and because I have no place to graze them, and likewise because I have no designated place, I request Your Worship charity that you be pleased to assign me a place situated at three leagues distance [about 7.8 miles] from the Mission of San Gabriel along the road to the Royal Presidio of San Carlos de Monterey named La Sanja, contemplating, Sir, not to harm neither a living soul, principally the Mission of San Gabriel, nor even less the Pueblo of the Queen of the Angeles. I humbly request of Your Worship's superior government that it see fit to decide as I have requested, for if it is so, I shall receive a gift, and shall consider myself most favored; and therefore:

To Your Worship I humbly beg and request that you be pleased to decide along the tenor of my petition or as it may be to your superior pleasure, and I swear by all 'the necessary and that this my petition is not done in malice, nor least of all to injure any one, and not knowing how to sign I made the sign of the Cross.

Governor Fages approved the petition in a marginal note attached to the petition itself. It read:

San Gabriel, October 21, 1784

I grant the petitioner the permission of having the bovine stock and horses at the place of La Sanja, or its environs; provided no harm is done to the Mission San Gabriel nor to the Pagan Indians of its environs in any manner whatsoever; and that he must have someone to watch it, and to go and sleep at the aforementioned Pueblo.

Pedro Fages[4]

Legal private ownership of these lands was formally transferred to the grantees under Mexican law after Mexico became independent from Spain in 1821.[5] The total number of grants for ranchos was approximately 484, although some families had more than one ranch.[6] The largest single land grant of that era was probably Governor Manuel Micheltorena's El Tejon grant of 97,617 acres, in what is now Kern County, California, to José Antonio Aguirre and Ygnacio del Valle in 1843.

It is important to understand that at this point Alta California was only very lightly populated. Writing in 1842, the French diplomat Count Eugene de Mofras put its area at 500,000 square miles and estimated that there were then only about 4,000 native-born *Californios* living there, plus about 1,000 Americans, Europeans, and others, for a total of some 5,000 people.[7]

In 1845, Alfred Robinson, an American businessman, judged that the total non–Indian population was about 8,000 people. He said that whereas there had been over 30,000 Indians when he first came to Alta California in 1829, only 10,000 of them were still left. He attributed their precipitous decline chiefly to the secularization of the missions, which had cast the Indians adrift without any of the material and cultural resources they would need to survive in the new, post-missionary, environment.[8]

By 1846, it has been estimated that the population density of Alta California was then only one person per 26 square miles. About 25,000 people were thought to be living there, e.g., 10,000 "whites," i.e., Caucasians; 5,000 "semi-civilized Indian," i.e., Mission Indians; and 10,000 Indians living on their own, outside the purview of the Mexican government.[9]

Mexico's Secularization Act of 1833 rang down the curtain on the mission era and ushered in the golden age of the ranchos. Indeed, the frontier of Alta California soon became the setting for great upward economic and social mobility by some of the best-connected *Californio* families.

To stimulate the economic development of Alta California—and, more importantly, to enrich themselves in the process—*Californio* families began set up huge ranches for themselves and their relatives, not only along the coast but also inland along the Sacramento-San Joaquin Valley. Spain had only made about 30 land grants between 1784 and 1821, but between 1833 and 1846 the Mexican government handed out about 770 land grants to well-connected *Californio* families. These grants were not based on any formal land surveys that would accurately establish and reflect property lines, but rather on very crude freehand drawings known as *diseños* ("designs").

It must be remembered here, however, that the art of surveying large tracts of lands by means of a rectangular survey is purely an American invention. The surveying system of the United States is ultimately based on the Land Act of 1796, which was entitled "An Act Providing for the Sale of Lands of the United States, in the Territory north-west of the River Ohio and Above the Mouth of the Kentucky River."

This rectangular survey system stood in sharp contrast to the surveys being done at the same time in Europe. The British form of land grants, for example, was much like the system used in Spanish and Mexican grants. A property was described by its boundaries, e.g., "bounded on the east by Smith's fence, on the west by the River Thames, on the north by the Conley Estate, and on the south by the lands of Squire Jones."[10]

The *diseños* of the California land owners, for their part, frequently identified streams or other small landmarks that were always subject to natural or man-made changes, so in surveying terms they were inherently very unreliable. The boundary lines of the grant of the 36,000-acre Rancho San Rafael, for example, used this colorful but imprecise language:

> Beginning at a place on the river called Porciuncula [this was later known as the Los Angeles River], about ten miles up the said River from the city, where the water for the city is taken from the river, thence following up the river Northerly to the point

of the Mountain, then easterly passing by a swamp to the steep Mountain, thence in a Southern direction to a dry creek, thence along said dry creek to the Place of beginning.

The mountain which is reached following up the river is where the principal head waters of the river take their rise. From this Mountain the line runs in an Easterly or North Easterly course & strikes the place called Cerrito Colorado. From this place the line runs in a direct course to the Arroyo Seco, or Dry Creek, leaving the Canada [a small local river] within the boundary. The cross that is above the swamp is the boundary.[11]

Moreover, as an 1849 report put it, these *diseños* "frequently contain double the amount of land included in the grants; and even now very few of these grants have been surveyed or their boundaries fixed."[12] As if all this were not enough, many land claims also overlapped. Relying on rough drawings to depict their boundaries would prove to be a fatal mistake for many ranchers.

Four of the best contemporary insights into *Californio* culture and land usage are those provided by José del Carmen Lugo (1813—c. 1870), José Andrés Sepúlveda (1803–1875) Antonio Francisco Coronel (1817–1894), and Pío Pico (1801–1894)—virtual contemporaries who all experienced many of the same economic and social realities.

Lugo, a wealthy *Californio* rancher in the Los Angeles area who was also very much involved in public affairs, was born in Los Angeles and grew up on San Antonio Rancho. In 1839, he began to develop 250,000 acres in the San Bernardino and Yucaipa valleys and was granted Rancho San Bernardino in 1842. During the U.S.-Mexican War, he led a *Californio* militia. After the war, the American military governor of California appointed him as the first *Californio alcalde* of Los Angeles.

In 1837, Sepúlveda was granted Rancho Cienega de las Ranas, which encompassed present-day Irvine and San Joaquin Hills in Orange County, California. In 1842 he was also given Rancho La Bolsa de San Joaquin, which encompassed present-day Newport Bay and its estuary. Together these two ranches totaled 48,803 acres and were known as Rancho San Joaquin. Sepúlveda himself was famous for his hospitality, flashy clothes, and daring bets.

Coronel was born in Mexico City, came to Alta California with other family members in 1834 as part of the Híjar-Padrés colony (organized in the vain hope of taking over some of the secularized mission lands), and was granted a rancho in 1846. During the U.S-Mexican War, he was a Captain in the Mexican Artillery. After the war he served as the first Los Angeles County Assessor; as Mayor of Los Angeles; as a city councilman; and, finally, as the California State Treasurer.

Pico was the grandson of a soldier who had been part of Juan Bautista de Anza's 1775–1776 colonizing expedition that made its way from Culiacán, Mexico to San Francisco. Pico himself twice served as governor of Alta California. His extensive landholdings (more than half a million acres) made him a very rich man but like so many other *Californio* ranchers whose hospitality and generosity became the stuff of legend, in the end he could not pay the interest on the mortgages he had signed to finance his extravagant lifestyle. At the age of 93, Pico died in near-poverty in 1894 at the home of his daughter in Los Angeles.[13]

These four men deserve to be cited here in some detail because of the unique insights they can provide into a long-vanished *Californio* way of life. The following comments, which have been condensed, paraphrased, and edited, are drawn from four contemporary first-hand sources, namely, Lugo's *The Life of a Rancher*; Penelon's portrait of Sepúlveda; Coronel's *Tales of Mexican California*; and Pico's *Narración Historica* (*Historical Narrative*), which Pico dictated to Bancroft's interviewer Thomas Savage at Los Angeles in 1877.[14]

Wherever possible, the cadences and phrases of the English translations of their Spanish accounts have been retained here. These accounts follow Savage's lead by letting the *Californios* speak for themselves.

Lugo begins by saying that at 8:00 p.m. every day his entire family knelt in prayer, reciting the rosary and other special prayers, each person addressing the saint of his or her name. Husband and wife slept in the same room, nearly always in the same bed. Boys slept in the galleries outside in the open air; girls slept inside the house.

At 3:00 a.m., the entire family was summoned to prayers. After this, the women went to the kitchen and began such domestic tasks as sweeping, cleaning, and dusting. The vaqueros went to the fields to herd cattle and look after the horses. The cows were milked by men, women, or Indian servants. The women and servants made small, hard, flat cheeses; bigger cheeses; butter; curds; and a mixture made from some of the above to eat with beans. This work lasted until 7:00 a.m. or 8:00 a.m., after which the women were busy cooking, sewing, or washing.

The rancheros supervised Indian workers who spent the day in the fields, preparing the ground for sowing seeds, bringing in wood, etc. Some ranchers planted cotton, some hemp, and others planted both. Rice, corn, beans, barley and other grains, squash, watermelons, and cantaloupes were grown. Grapes, pears, apples, pomegranates, peaches, nectarines and other fruits were also cultivated.

On a small and relatively poor ranch, the house was built of rough timber roofed with tules, i.e., rushes, and rarely had more than two rooms. One room served as the entry and living room, the other as a sleeping room. If the family was large, these rooms were divided. Many of these houses had a door faced with sheepskin, cowhide, or horsehide. No door had a lock or key, nor was it necessary to close it on the outside because there was no one who would enter to steal, and there was nothing there worth taking. If family members were going to be away for several days, they would take with them their one thing of value, namely, a little chest of clothes, some bedding, and a cot.

Richer families had some furniture, e.g., a table, a long bench, and a few little stools with whalebone seats. Outside the house on each side of the door there were adobe benches. (An adobe brick is a composite material made of earth mixed with water and an organic material such a straw or dung.) Adobe was used, too, for stoves in the kitchen. For breakfast, the wealthy usually had Spanish chocolate made with milk or water, plus bread, tortillas, and wheat or corn porridge with butter. Poor people had to eat early so they could get to work, and usually had milk with pinole (parched corn, ground and mixed with sugar) or only toasted or parched corn.

The rich dined later and often had a solid breakfast of roasted or dried meat[15] with chilies, onions, tomatoes, and beans. (*Californio* cooks used chili with such a generous hand that many foreigners simply could not eat the food served to them because it was so heavily spiced.) This hearty breakfast was a sensible idea because the *Californios* would not eat again until 4:00 or 5:00 p.m. in the afternoon.

Meals were generally eaten in the kitchen beside the fire. Not many families had ceramic plates; most people used clay bowls shaped like plates. Only a few families had metal forks and spoons; most people used utensils made of horn. Each man, however, always carried a long-bladed steel knife in a scabbard, which was thrust inside the garter on his right leg. He used this knife to cut his food and, in an emergency, as a weapon. More commonly, however, people simply scooped up a portion of, say, meat and beans with a piece of tortilla, and popped it into their mouths.

José María Amador, formerly a presidio soldier but now a prosperous man, gave Thomas Savage, during a June 1877 interview, a more detailed account of *Californio* meals. At his own home, the well-to-do people there began with a light breakfast from 6:00 a.m. to 7:00 a.m. This included either chocolate (to drink) or sweetened *atole de pinole* (gruel made by boiling ground corn) made with milk. Amador added that his family milked 60 cows each day to make cheese.

After this light breakfast came the main breakfast, about one hour later. It consisted of cooked beef and cooked Mexican-style beans, accompanied either by bread or corn tortillas.

At the noon meal, each of Amador's sisters would get a small glass of wine from their mother. The main dish was rice or noodle soup, a pot of boiled beef with vegetables, and beans. Sometimes there was dessert cheese or sweet breads for dessert. After this meal, the men would get a small glass of *aguardiente* (liquor distilled from herbs, flowers, or fruit) from Spain. Amador told Savage that "this was the way of living of almost every family of means."

Supper, served between eight and nine o'clock at night, included beans and beef cooked in a Chile sauce, and a little wine.

Amador said that "the poor would eat whatever they could." In the towns, before going out to milk the cows, boys eight years old or older would skewer young ears of very soft white corn and toast them over an open fire. They would then put the kernels into a container and, with milk from the first cow they had milked, consume them. This was the common breakfast for the poor.

At the noon meal, family members would sit on the bare floor, on whalebone, or on a box made of wood. This meal would consist of boiled corn or wheat with hot water, lard, salt, and chilies added. For dessert there would be cheese and, sometimes, a bit of sugar.

At night, they would have cooked or roasted meat, beans, corn *atole*, and *migas* (crumbs of bread or tortillas fried in a pan, with lard, salt, and pepper). They did not drink wine or *aguardiente* because these were too expensive, especially the latter.[16]

Whether the *Californios* were well or poorly fed, however, their government demanded that they all comply with the doctrines and practices of the Catholic Church. Except for the sick, all had to attend Mass every Sunday and on every holy day. At Eastertime, adults had to confess their sins, receive the Holy Sacrament, and take part in reciting the catechism. In return, they received a document from the friar saying that they had complied with the precepts of the Church for that year.

Lugo added that by 1821 or 1823 there were such great numbers of wild horses that they began to eat the pasturage reserved for the *Californios'* riding horses. As a result, the government decided to have a general slaughter of these wild horses. Corrals were built; *vaqueros* drove both wild and tame horses into them; and lancers, supervised by rancher owners, were stationed at exit gates through which only one horse could pass at a time. When no rancher claimed a given horse, that animal was speared to death.

4. Ranchos

The hides were stripped from the carcasses and were staked out on the ground (to prevent shrinkage) and dried in the sun. Hides and tallow were then hauled to San Pedro, the little port of Los Angeles, by wooden *carretas* (carts) slowly pulled by yoked oxen. Each cart could carry 50 hides. The wheels of these carts were entirely made of wood and were only more or less round. They did not have an iron rim; indeed, no iron at all was used in making them. The hides and tallow were sold to the ships that called at San Pedro on their coastal runs for the hide and tallow trade.

Don José Andrés Sepúlveda is best remembered today because of a famous portrait of him painted in about 1856 by the French artist Henri Joseph Penelon. Working in Los Angeles by 1853, Penelon was a painter and daguerreotype photographer at a time when photography was only about 10 years old and Los Angeles had only four photographers for a city of about 2,500 people.

Penelon's portrait captures perfectly the conspicuous consumption so beloved by upper class *Californios* when they could afford it. The portrait shows Sepúlveda riding Black Swan, a mare he had imported from Australia. In 1852 Sepúlveda matched this mare against Pío Pico's then-unbeaten horse Sarco in a nine-mile race. The two men wagered $25,000 and 1,500 head of livestock (calves, heifers, and horses) on the outcome. Black Swan won the race and was later retired to El Refugio, the elaborate adobe home and ranchlands that Sepúlveda bought from Domingo Yorba, another *Californio* grandee, in about 1854.

A central feature of the portrait is Black Swan's very ornate saddle. Made of black leather, the saddle and all its accoutrements were lavishly embroidered with silver thread, while the bridle was decked out with silver inserts. Strapped to the saddle where it would be under Sepúlveda's left leg and easy to draw is a fine sword with a shiny brass (or perhaps even a gold-encrusted) handguard, carried securely in a decorated sheath.[17]

Coronel, for his part, made some revealing comments. When the colony of which he was part arrived in Alta California, the total population there, excluding those who were not Indians, was no more than 5,000 people. The education of the inhabitants consisted only of exposure to Catholic doctrines. These were taught by the missionaries, who also taught one or two youngsters how to write, added Coronel, "after a fashion." In the presidios there were only a few *Californios* with a little more than primary school education. However, even this modest amount of learning was due to external factors, i.e., to military officers who lived in the presidios but who had been educated elsewhere; to merchants and others who had arrived by ship; and to educated families who had come from elsewhere in Mexico.

Coronel said that in Alta California there were very few people who could read or write. Even after the arrival of a few well-educated people, education there remained at a low level. The women learned even less because they had been convinced (presumably by their mothers) that book-learning was bad for girls. As a result, they could barely read, let alone write. But in spite of their lack of education, said Coronel, *Californio* ladies were very moral, diligent, clean, charitable, hospitable, and dedicated to their household duties.

He mentioned that a traveler could go up to any house in Alta California, confident that he could stay as many days as he liked and pay nothing at all for shelter, bed, food, and even for horses to continue his journey. Mothers were very protective of their daughters; as a result, travelers met only the men of the family.

Coronel noted that the men busied themselves almost exclusively with livestock, but this meant that they only worked hard at certain times of the year, e.g., for roundups, branding, or slaughtering. Hides and tallow were their income as well as their coinage, i.e., a hide was jokingly known as a "California banknote." The *Californios* did not do much farming themselves because they could usually buy grain from the missions. As the missions declined and their production dwindled, however, more farming became necessary.

The men, continued Coronel, initially were much like their Spanish ancestors: that is to say, they were inflexible, upright, honorable, imperious men whose word, without any documents or witnesses to back it up in a court of law, was good for any amount of money. Their inflexible character, however, began to erode as a more liberal and relaxed social structure gradually arose. In any case, upper class *Californio* men never had to work.

Indeed, Juan Bandini (1800–1859), a member of the *Californio* gentry, said in 1828 that most of the men of the gentry "did nothing" at all.[18] Except for supervising cattle roundups, they had never worked a day in their whole lives and did not plan ever to do so in the future. Bandini elaborated on their characters as follows:

> Nature gave the Californians high talents, frankness, and simple manners. They were hospitable, and were capable of making great sacrifices to aid the afflicted. I do not believe there is one of the many white men [i.e., the *Californios*] who professes a trade; their occupation is tending stock, some small cultivation, and idling.[19]

To historians today it is clear that an extremely important social value for the *Californios* was an unquestioning respect for the head of the family. This was true to such an extent that parents still lorded it over their married sons and daughters, who had no choice but to submit meekly to

4. Ranchos

parental chastising. Daughters had very little choice of husbands. Young married couples lived with one or the other set of parents and helped with the work.

Today, all the *Californios* might be described as having been, figuratively speaking, members of one vast extended family, knitted together by ties of custom and of law. Writing in 1834, a French visitor to Alta California found that

> being almost all related to each other, they live in great intimacy. There is no difference of rank among them. One who has become rich by his industry is neither admired nor envied by anyone. Theft is extremely rare. Murder is without example [i.e., it never occurs].[20]

By the standards of our own time, women's work was harder, longer, and arguably more important than men's. They were in charge of the kitchens, made all their and the family's clothes, and had to comb the men's hair each day and tie it up (*Californio* men traditionally wore long hair, tied at the rear into a pigtail). Many women also baked bread, made candles and soap, and some even brought in the harvest and threshed the grain.

The most important item for any *Californio* man was his lariat. This was made of four or six rawhide strips half an inch wide, carefully plaited and worked by hand until it was perfectly flexible. When not needed, it was tied to the back of the saddle; when in use, it hung from the pommel. As mentioned earlier, a man's knife was also of first importance. A *serape* (a narrow blanket worn by men or tied to the saddle) kept him warm when ranch worked required him to spend the night outdoors. If he had to go on a campaign to fight Indians, he wore a long padded leather coat of up to seven layers, which covered him from neck to knee and which would deflect arrows. His usual weapons in such a campaign were an old flintlock shotgun, which was more useful than a rifle on the *Californios'* frontier because it could fire a much wider variety of lead projectiles, e.g., small pellets (birdshot), large pellets (buckshot), or a solid ball. He may have carried a lance or a pair of pistols as well. Each man also had "a good Spanish blade," i.e., a sword, from Toledo, although this was more a mark of high status than a practical weapon.

One of the most successful *Californios* was Pío Pico (1801–1894), who was Governor of Alta California from 1845 to 1845 and then again in 1853.

From an early age, he was a good businessman. In 1821, for example, at the age of 20 he built a shack in San José made of hides and wooden stakes. Inside it he placed a big box that served as a counter. On the box he put two small glasses for the strong liquor known as *aguardiente* and one big glass for drinking water. He charged customers one *real* (12 ½ cents) for half of a small glass of *aguardiente* and two *reals* for a full glass of the liquor.

He soon noticed, however, that he was not making very much money by using such small glasses, so he hit upon a creative solution:

> ... I had the idea of using a cattle horn. I cut about a third of it and put in a false wooden bottom. I coated the inside generously with tallow and added another bottom of tallow, besides the one made of wood. This naturally took up much space and diminished the quantity of aguardiente it could hold.
>
> The old drinkers were fooled, thinking that the horn contained more than it did, and they always asked not to be served in a small glass but in the horns, and with this they cheated themselves...
>
> Even though there was no lack of aguardiente in the northern missions, this article was scarce for general use, and if anyone from the south brought some aguariente up there it was like a treasure to those people. Particularly the aguardiente from San Fernando was appreciated above any other.[21]

An early ranching assignment (in 1833) was to oversee the slaughtering of cattle at the San José ranch, which belonged to the San Gabriel Mission. He reports that his contract with the friars there had no limit, i.e., he could slaughter as many cattle as he wanted, as long as he gave the mission half of the skins.

To do this work, he brought to the ranch 10 cowboys with their horses and 30 unmounted Indians. By then the friars knew that the Mexican government was about to secularize the missions, so they were eager to turn some of their cattle into "California banknotes" and to save what other assets they could from the impending destruction of their mission way of life.

Pico met a retired Mexican artillery officer named Juan Mariner (whose name was also written as "Mariné") who was an assistant to the friar in charge of Mission San Luis Rey, Father Antonio Peyri. Mariner told Pico that when he left his mission, Father Peyri had taken with him 32 barrels—ostensibly filled with olives, but in fact most of them were filled with bran (the hard outer layer of cereal grain) and with gold pieces (*onzas de oro*) and silver dollars. Mariner told Pico that he had packed the money with his own hands and that most of it was in gold.

Yet, together with *Californio* riches, there was also *Californio* poverty. At the presidio of San Diego, for example, Pico personally watched four common soldiers go to bed in a big tub made of skins—covering themselves with dry hay because they had absolutely nothing else to keep out the cold.[22]

A more positive account on *Californio* life comes from Rancho Cañada de Santa Ana, located in what is now Orange County, California. It was the property of Bernardo Yorba (1800–1858), son of the Spanish soldier José Antonio Yorba, who was one of the first Spanish soldiers to come to Alta California. Bernardo became one of the most successful ranchers there, with thousands of cattle and horses grazing on his land grants, which totaled more than 35,000 acres. He built a large adobe ranch house known as the Hacienda de Las Yorbas.

A descendant of Bernardo Yorba once described this ranch as a classic example of traditional *Californio* life at its very best, making the following points:

> By 1850 the Hacienda de Las Yorbas was the social and business center of the Santa Ana Valley. The master's house became a two story structure of about thirty rooms.... In all there were more than 50 rooms arranged about a court of patio in the rear of the main residence. More than one hundred lesser employees [i.e., these were unskilled Mexican workers; there were also skilled workers] were maintained on the ranch. The Indian peons lived in a little village of their own.... Ten steers a month were slaughtered to supply the hacienda.[23]

Big ranches such as this were economically independent, self-sustaining communities that needed very little from the outside world that the hide and tallow trade could not provide. They were also communities in which *Californio* men almost never had to work very hard. The family, household, religious and social obligations of *Californio* women, however, were virtually endless and left them very little time for themselves.

One bit of good news for them was that *Californio* women enjoyed much more legal protection for their own property than women did in the United States in general. Mexican law gave women the right to control their own property and wealth themselves. They could also litigate on questions related to their persons, their families, and their holdings. Daughters had the right to inherit property equally with male siblings. Women retained the right to whatever property of their own they had brought into the marriage. When they became widows, they inherited half of the property and wealth which had built up during their marriage.

Moreover, adult women could conduct their own legal affairs; draft their own wills without the consent of their husbands; serve as attorneys for elderly relatives; become the guardians of their children and grandchildren when their husbands died; and could adopt children without permission from the Mexican government.[24] Although *Californio* women were not confined to domestic activities and were never defined exclusively as wives and mothers, nevertheless some of them did devote themselves chiefly to home and family.[25] Señora Vallejo, the wife of General Vallejo, is a good example here. She described her own household staff in these words:

> Each child (of whom there were sixteen) has a personal attendant, while I have two for my own needs; four or five are occupied in grinding corn for tortillas, for so many visitors come here that three grinders do not suffice; six or seven serve in the kitchen, and five or six are always washing clothes for the children and other servants; and, finally, nearly a dozen are employed at spinning and weaving.[26]

The only major economic activity of the *Californios* before the Gold Rush was the hide and tallow trade. Writing in 1890, Prudencia Higuera, the daughter of a *Californio* rancher, remembered what happened in 1840 when an American ship sailed into San Pablo Bay, a tidal estuary that forms the northern extension of San Francisco Bay. Prudencia wrote:

> The next morning my father gave orders, and my brothers, with the peons [i.e., the Indian servants] went on horseback into the mountains and smaller valleys to round up all the best cattle. They drove them to the beach, killed them there, and salted the hides. They tried out [i.e., boiled] the tallow in some iron kettles....
> The captain soon came to our landing with a small boat and two sailors.... The captain looked over the hides, and then asked my father to get into the boat and go to the vessel.... [My father] came back the next day, bringing four boat-loads of cloth, axe, shoes, fish-lines, and many new things. There were two grindstones and some cheap jewelry. My brother had traded some deerskins for a gun and four tooth-brushes, the first ones I had ever seen.[27]

However, the most detailed and best written account of this trade comes from the American seaman and author Richard Henry Dana, Jr. (1815–1882), who worked hard along the Alta California coast from 1835 to 1836 gathering and curing bullock hides.

Dana had been a student at Harvard until prolonged trouble with his eyesight, which he suffered after a bout of measles, made it impossible for him to read a single page of print without experiencing great pain. Doctors could do nothing for him, so he had to drop out of Harvard. Taking a great risk in terms of his future life (he did not want to end up as a seaman), he resolved to go to sea "before the mast," that is, he would sign on a ship as a common sailor, rather than as an officer. His hope, which proved to be justified, was that a great deal of hard physical labor outdoors, well away from his books, would restore his vision. The end result of this adventure was his *Two Years Before the Mast* (1840), a lapidary study of the men, the ships, and the technology of the California hide trade.

Dana's descriptions of how he and his shipmates prepared hides for shipment give the reader an excellent insight into this very laborious business.

4. Ranchos

He explains that the morning after his arrival in San Diego, he began curing hides. He adds that for the reader to understand this process, he (Dana) must present the whole story of a hide from the time it is skinned off a bullock until it is put on board a Boston-bound ship. To make a long story short, here are the main steps Dana lists:

- After the hides are skinned from the cattle, holes are cut around them, near the edges, so they can be staked out in the hot sun to dry and will not shrink in the process.
- The hides are then soaked in the sea for 48 hours, after which they are taken out of the water, rolled up, and thrown into vats containing very strong brine. After 24 hours in them, they are carefully spread out on the ground and smoothed so that they will dry without any creases in them.
- Now the hardest part of the job begins. Dana and the other men have to inspect each hide very carefully and use their sharp sailor's knives to cut away any tiny bits of meat and fat—without cutting the hide itself. If this is not done properly, on a long voyage the hides will surely rot.
- Dana says that on his first day he was so slow and awkward he could clean only eight hides. After three weeks of constant labor, however, he was able to keep up with the other men and could clean 25 hides per day.
- After having been thoroughly cleaned and then beaten (to get the dust out of them), the hides were then put into a small storage house to await a ship that would take them to Boston.[28]

Another astute observer of the *Californio* scene was Thomas O. Larkin, the American Consul in Monterey. Although sometimes very critical of them, he came to enjoy very much living and working with the *Californios*. In 1856, for example, he wrote approvingly to an American businessman in Alta California about

> the times prior to July 1846 and all their honest pleasures [i.e., before the U.S.-Mexican War began], and the fleshpots of those days. Halcyon days they were. We shall not see their likes again.[29]

Larkin's point was well-taken. In 1845–1846, at the height of its pre–American prosperity Alta California exported 80,000 hides; 1,500,000 pounds of tallow; 10,000 *fanegas* of wheat; 1,000,000 feet of lumber, staves, and shingles; a thousand barrels of wine and brandy; beaver fur, sea otter pelts, and other skins valued at $20,000; $10,000 worth of soap; and 200 ounces of gold.[30]

Larkin also reported that, in effect, Alta California was ruled by 46 largely self-made *Californios*, most of them ranchers whose families had been the recipients of generous land grants.[31] As discussed earlier, their prosperity initially made possible a very colorful and, indeed, sometimes an extravagant life style, but in the long run the *diseños* on which they were based would prove to be their Achilles heel.

The fundamental reasons for their decline are very clear. First, as will be discussed later at more depth, in the wake of the U.S.-Mexican War the American victors demanded formal legal proof, e.g., accurate surveys, of land ownership. Since such surveys had never been required before and therefore had never been made, the *Californios* could not provide them to American lawyers. As a result, these ranchers were very likely to find themselves embroiled in long-running legal proceedings which they did not understand (very few of them spoke or read English well) and which almost none of them could afford.

Second, many ranchers continued and even increased the open-handed hospitality and generosity which had maintained their high social status and which had pleased them and their families personally. To do so, however, they had thoughtlessly signed mortgages or borrowed money at usurious rates of interest. The net result was that, as shall be seen, many of them would end up by losing all their land.

5

Presidios and Soldiers

Between 1789 and 1782 the Spanish built four small presidios, namely, at San Diego (1769), Monterey (1770), San Francisco (1776), and Santa Barbara (1782). The Spanish government divided Alta California into four military districts, each (in theory, at least) controlled and protected by a presidio. Later, after Mexico became independent, the Mexican government built a fifth and final presidio at Sonoma in 1810. It eventually became the headquarters of the Mexican Army in Alta California. The other presidios were abandoned and, in time, fell into ruins.

The presidios were built for four interlocking reasons:

1. To protect the friars, the mission staffs, and the *Californios* of the area by keeping the Mission Indians, i.e., those working for and living in the missions, under strict control.

2. To deter the "wild" Indians living in the regions beyond Spanish control from attacking the *Californios* and their ranchos.

3. To establish small towns (pueblos) of Spanish-speaking, Roman Catholic men and women whose descendants would hold the land for Spain in perpetuity.

4. To "show the flag" by making it clear to foreign countries (notably the United States, England, France, and Russia) that they could not hope to plant their own colonies in Alta California because it was already occupied and defended, first by Spain and then by Mexico.

Contemporary sources suggest that, in point of fact, the presidios always served a politically symbolic role rather than a serious military role. For example, writing in 1891 about his own experiences when he first came to Alta California in 1829, Alfred Robinson remembered that

> at the Presidio [of San Francisco], the place was almost entirely abandoned, as was the case at the Presidio in Monterey; and at the fort also, there not being half a

dozen soldiers there, with the *comandante*. It was no uncommon occurrence for a vessel to pass up through the Golden Gate at the hour of *siesta* in the afternoon, and reach her place of anchorage at Yerba Buena [a small island in San Francisco Bay], where she lay for two or three days, before it came to the knowledge of the post at the Presidio. Such was the state of affairs in California in this early period.[1]

Common to all four original presidios were their favorable locations as seaports. San Diego Bay, for example, had a narrow entrance that gave it some protection from ocean winds, but this bay was also relatively close to Mexico. Exaggerated reporting by the 17th century explorer Vizcaíno of the advantages of Monterey Bay resulted in its becoming the site of the capital of Alta California. San Francisco Bay was not only huge but settlement there established a Spanish presence along the northern coast of Alta California. Finally, the presidio on the Santa Barbara Channel was planned, among other things, as a jumping-off point for future Spanish expansion into the interior of Alta California.[2]

A presidio was essentially a square consisting of high walls with fortified projections, known as bastions, at its corners. Inside the walls were barracks, family quarters for the soldiers, an armory, a chapel, the commanding officer's headquarters, storerooms, guardhouse, and possibly a corral. Around the perimeter of the presidio a dry moat 12 feet wide and 6 feet deep might be dug to slow down the advance of any attackers. In some cases there was an outer defensive wall as well. The basic design of the presidios harked back to the European castle—a structure that had been well-suited to medieval Europe but was quite useless on the Alta California frontier.[3]

With his usual felicity of expression, Dana gives the reader a good introduction to Monterey itself and to the functions of the presidio there. He wrote:

> The pretty lawn on which [Monterey] stands, as green as sun and rain could make it; the pine woods on the south; the small river on the north side; the houses, with their white plastered sides and red-tiled roofs, dotted about on the green; the low, white presidio, with its soiled, tri-colored flag flying, and the discordant din of drums and trumpets for the noon parade; all brought up the scene we had witnessed here with so much pleasure nearly a year before.... It seemed almost like coming home.[4]

Dana also wrote:

> Monterey, as far as my observation goes, is decidedly the pleasantest and most civilized-looking place in California. In the centre of it is an open square, surrounded by four lines of one-story plastered buildings, with half a dozen cannon in its center, some mounted, some not. This is the "Presidio," or fort.
>
> Every town has a presidio in its centre; or rather, every presidio has a town built around it; for the forts were first built by the Mexican [actually, by the Spanish] government, and then the people built near them for protection. The presidio is entirely open and unfortified.

5. Presidios and Soldiers

There were several officers with long titles, and about eighty soldiers, but they were poorly paid, fed, clothed and disciplined. The governor-general, or, as he is commonly called, the "general," lives here; which makes it the seat of government. He is appointed by the central government at Mexico, and is the chief civil and military officer.

In addition to him, each town has a commandant, who is the chief military officer, and has charge of the fort, and of all transactions with foreigners and foreign vessels; and two or three alcaldes and corregidores [magistrates], elected by the inhabitants, who are the civil officers.[5]

On a day-to-day basis, the most important *Californio* soldier was the company sergeant, who had to make life-or-death decisions for the troops under his command and who had to account to his unit's officers for these decisions. Perhaps the best of these men was José Francisco Ortega, chief scout on Gaspar de Portolá's land expedition to Alta California in 1769. Ortega was probably the first European to see San Francisco Bay and, after years of distinguished military service, he would also become the patriarch of an important *Californio* family.

Writing in 1772 to Antonio María de Bucareli y Ursúa, the Viceroy of New Spain, Father Junípero Serra had this to say about Ortega:

> The Governor [Pedro Fages] employed him [in Alta California] in carrying provisions from Sinaloa, in going to and from San Diego, and in discovering and pointing out the proper sites for the five missions that are to be found in the stretch in between. During these explorations, while he was climbing mountains and crossing valleys, over and above what he had principally in mind, he discovered a way from Velicatá to San Diego which will save a distance of some 50 leagues [about 130 miles]; and this he will soon shorten still more, I can assure you...
>
> Now, as regards his fitness for the position [Serra wanted Ortega to be promoted to lieutenant], I can say that, as far as I have seen, in command of soldiers he is firm without rigidity and has prudence and common sense. I believe they will love him without ceasing to fear him; they will fear him sufficiently without ceasing to love him.[6]

Thanks to his own zeal and abilities and to Serra's very strong recommendation, Ortega was promoted to lieutenant and became Commandant of the presidio at San Diego in 1773, holding this post until 1781. He was the first Commandant of the presidio of Santa Barbara from 1782 to 1784; from 1787 to 1791 he was Commandant of the presidio of Monterey; and in 1792 he became Commandant of the presidio in Loreto.

Ortega retired as brevet captain with 40 years of service in 1795. (A brevet was a warrant authorizing a commissioned officer to hold a higher rank temporarily, but without receiving the pay of that rank except when actually serving in that role.) He then moved to the land grant he had been given the year before and which he had named Rancho Nuestra

Señora del Refugio (the Ranch of Our Lady of Refuge) near Santa Barbara. In 1798, however, he died at the age of 65 after a fall from his horse and was buried at Mission Santa Barbara.[7]

Ortega was clearly an outstanding soldier. However, most of the Americans and other foreigners who had personal experiences with *Californio* military personnel were not favorably impressed by them. Dana's comments about enlisted men, i.e., the 80 soldiers of Monterey mentioned above, are typical. Many of these men were unpaid convicts who had literally been rounded up from Mexico's prisons. Bancroft had very negative things to say about their officers. He tells the reader:

> In the latter part of 1845, the monthly pay-roll of officers, a few retired soldiers, and one widow, amounted to $2,059. There were officers enough for a force of 3,000 men, all drawing pay with more or less regularity. A number of these officers were useless, and many of them rendered no service. The rank and pay were given to them as a reward of partisanship. When the Americans invaded California, most of these fellows proved themselves utterly incapable.[8]

In the same passage quoted, Bancroft describes the behavior of José Castro, the general in charge of many of the *Californio* forces during the U.S-Mexican War. In his account, which has been shortened and summarized here, Bancroft begins by explaining that in July 1846 about 400 or 500 mounted *Californios* assembled in Los Angeles. They had eaten nothing for several days, except for some old oxen and whatever pears and apples they could steal from the nearby orchards. With one single exception, the officers were just as hungry as their men. The exception was José Castro, the well-fed commanding officer.

In the Soledad valley, Castro had received from the Guadalupe rancho a large supply of cooked provisions, for example, chickens and pastry. He kept all of this food to himself for own use and ate alone, under a tree, with his back turned toward his hungry companions. When he had finally satisfied his appetite, he wrapped up the remaining food and left it in a bundle on the ground, covered by his saddle.

At about midnight, however, his lieutenant, José Antonio Chavez, crawled to the spot and brought the remaining food back to his friends. He and they promptly finished it off. Chavez then took the chicken bones back to Castro's saddle and put them under it, together with some horse dung, Finally, on his way back to his friends, he found a bottle with brandy in it and promptly confiscated it for his and their enjoyment.

The next morning, when Castro discovered the trick played on him, he glared around with a fierce scowl and, using the vilest language, threatened to punish those who had done this to him. However, no one paid

5. Presidios and Soldiers

him the slightest attention. The outcome, however, was that, in the future, whenever new supplies were received, Castro would make his own orderly, Felipe Espinosa Barajas, personally accountable for them.[9]

Alta California itself was never a popular post for military men, being "back of beyond." Very few volunteered for duty there: in 1810, for example, the total force of the presidios was 412 officers and men, and in 1835 even fewer—only 307 officers and men.[10]

Not all these men lived in a presidio at the same time: some carried military mails to and from Loreto; others were assigned to scouting expeditions; still others were standing guard-duty in various places. The total population for all four presidios was approximately 1,200 people—an estimate that does not include their associated Indian workers or servants.

Most significantly, however, by 1815 each presidio had also become the nucleus of a little town (pueblo) that included both civilians and retired soldiers.[11] What would eventually become the most famous of these had been founded in 1781, with the sonorous name of El Pueblo de Nuestra Señora la Reina de los Ángeles de Porciúncula (the Town of Our Lady Queen of the Angeles of Porciúncula).[12] Los Angeles began with only 44 men, women, and children, known as *pobladores* ("original settlers"), but it would gradually become the principal urban center of southern Alta California, where economic and social life revolved around raising cattle on vast ranchos.

6

Pueblos and Their Inhabitants

To help reduce the heavy reliance of the Spanish army in Alta California on the missions and on the infrequent supply ships coming from San Blas, the Spanish government set up three pueblos in Alta California, located at Los Angeles, San Jose, and the Villa de Branciforte. A very brief word about each of them will be useful here because much less has been written about the pueblos than about the missions.

The basic job of the pueblos was to grow food for the officers and men of the presidios and for the surrounding communities. The ranchos themselves could produce large quantities of cowhides and tallow but, as a general rule, they did not grow much food beyond what they needed for their own use or could easily sell to local consumers. It is clear that the pueblos succeeded at their task.[1] San José, for example, began to generate large surpluses of grain not long after it was founded. Governor Filipe de Neve reported in 1781 that the presidios of Monterey and San Francisco were being "completely fed by the town of San José"[2]; during the rest of the 18th century, San José continued to supply large quantities of beans, wheat, and corn. Los Angeles, for its part, produced impressive amounts of corn. The net result was that, after 1790, supply ships were no longer needed to carry flour, corn, or beans from San Blas to Alta California.

At the end of 1830, the *Californio* Juan Bandini, who has already been mentioned, was working in the customs service in San Diego when he wrote "A Statistical Description of Alta California." This is a very useful document because it contains brief but accurate contemporary descriptions of the three pueblos. Bandini makes numerous points, which have been paraphrased below while trying to retain some of the cadences of the original translation.

Los Angeles (founded in 1781)

Alta California has three pueblos. The main one is Nuestra Señora de Los Angeles, which is located eight miles from Mission San Gabriel and is about 20 miles from San Pedro Bay. About 1500 souls live there. The church itself is a very good one, which is now in charge of a retired Franciscan missionary.

It has an *ayuntamiento* [i.e., a municipal corporation in charge of administering a town], composed of an *alcalde*, three *regidores* [members of the municipal corporation], and a *síndico* [a mission representative]. Thanks to its favorable location on a broad plain with full-flowing rivers, it will be able to support a large population and extensive agricultural production. This pueblo also produces between 5,000 to 6,000 hides a year, plus a large amount of tallow.

San José (founded in 1777)

The second pueblo is known as San José de Guadalupe. It is about 2.6 miles from Mission Santa Clara and 52 miles from the *presidio* of San Francisco. It has a beautiful river that empties into San Francisco Bay. Its church, which is only a shapeless hut, is directed by the missionary Father from Santa Clara. Its population is about 600 souls, whose principal occupations are cultivating wheat, corn, and other vegetables, as well as cattle and raising horses. In addition, the inhabitants hunt a large deer, known as the tule elk, which is abundant in that area.

Many ranches there can produce more than 152 pounds of tallow each year. This pueblo lies within the southern outskirts of San Francisco Bay and, if it becomes more fully developed, the population of the whole region will grow. Its vast plains can provide anything a farmer might need.

Villa de Branciforte (founded in 1797)

The third *pueblo* is the Villa de Branciforte, which is located two miles from Mission Santa Clara, about a mile and a half from the northern shore of Monterey Bay, and about 46 miles from the Monterey *presidio*. About 200 souls have settled there and are engaged in farming but Branciforte's production has been insignificant.

To add to what Bandini said, it can be noted here that, from its very early days, Branciforte always had serious problems and never managed to prosper in any way. Its inhabitants, many of whom were ex-convicts, were criticized as being lazy and much given to crime. By 1831, about 200 people, i.e., merchants, explorers, and retired soldiers, were still living there. (The town would be incorporated into the city of Santa Cruz in 1905.)

Later Developments

By about 1827, Los Angeles was the biggest pueblo and was clearly on its way up. It became a rival of Monterey for the prize of being the capital of Alta California, was the focal point of conspiracies to overthrow Mexican rule, and emerged as a key center in the turbulent politics of the region. A clear sign of the very unsettled political conditions was that after 1845 both the governor and the capital were located in Los Angeles, whereas the military commander and the Custom House were both located in Monterey. Thus, as the historian Neal Harlow remarked, "most of the country's antagonisms were neatly lined upon two irreconcilable sides."[3]

A French diplomat, Duflot de Mofras, who was inspecting California for his government, had this to say about Los Angeles in 1841:

> The pueblo of Los Angeles is extremely rich, for the spoils from the [secularization] of the neighboring missions have fallen into the hands of the local inhabitants; and within an area of 15 to 20 square leagues [66,420 to 88,560 acres], local residents have over 80,000 cattle, 25,000 horses, and 10,000 sheep. Vineyards yield 600 barrels of wine, and an equal amount of brandy; grains, however, contribute less than 3,000 *fanegas* [bushels].
>
> The light harvest arises from the lazy habits of the settlers, who are disinclined to work. All labor in El Pueblo is done by the Indians recruited from a small ranchería [an Indian settlement] on the banks of the outskirts of the village.... El Pueblo has in addition sixty *huertas*, or gardens, planted out to vines that cover an area roughly estimated at 100 *hectares* [247 acres]. Some soap, too, is manufactured locally, and a tannery is in operation. All commerce is carried out by foreigners....[4]

The next year, a British visitor, Sir George Simpson, who will be discussed later, saw Los Angeles in a much less favorable light. He wrote in 1842 that this pueblo was considered to be the noted abode of the lowest drunkards, gamblers, and thieves of Alta California. Nevertheless, he added, it had the good fortune to be situated in one of the loveliest and most fertile districts of California.[5]

In 1844 about 2,500 people were said to be living in Los Angeles, i.e., 627 men, 500 women, 720 children, 650 "domesticated" Indians, and 53

6. Pueblos and Their Inhabitants 49

foreigners.⁶ A ranching center that profited greatly from the gold miners' hunger for beef, Los Angeles was now hailed as "the queen of the cow counties." It also had access to the wider world, thanks to ocean shipping via the port at San Pedro. The city's long term economic prospects were thus quite favorable.

Lieutenant George Douglas Brewerton wrote this description of Los Angeles in 1848:

> The Pueblo de Los Angeles has a population of several hundred souls; and boasts a church, a padre, and three or four American shops; the streets are narrow, and the houses generally not over one story high, built of adobes, the roofs flat and covered with a composition of gravel mixed with a sort of mineral pitch, which the inhabitants say they find upon the sea-shore.
>
> This mode of roofing gives a perfectly waterproof covering, but has the rather unpleasant disadvantage of melting in warm weather, and in running down, fringes the sides of the buildings with long *pitchicles* (if we may be allowed to coin a word), thus giving the houses an exceedingly grotesque appearance; when the heat is extreme, pools of pitch are formed on the ground.
>
> The adobe is a brick, made of clay, and baked in the sun. Walls built of this material, from the great thickness necessary to secure strength, are warmer in winter, and cooler in summer, and are therefore better adapted to the climate than either wood or ordinary brick. In most respects, the town differs but little from other Mexican villages.⁷

Writing in 1881 about life in Los Angeles some 30 years earlier, the former Los Angeles Ranger Horace Bell, who will also be discussed later, described its most substantial homes in these warm terms:

> All the old Spanish houses had one grand room or *sala*, flanked by two other rooms, which made up the front of the houses. [The *sala* was a large barn-like room used either for a formal ball known as a *baile* or for a much less exclusive dance known as a fandango.]
>
> Two large wings extending back, with rooms generally used as dormitories, and a great high wall in the rear, forming an interior court or square, with wide corridors or verandas on the three sides, both outside and inside generally paved with brick tiles, a good pine plank floor in the three front rooms, and if not in the near dormitories, they had brick tile floors, the same as the floors on the veranda; adobe walls, well whitewashed, with chair-boards around the *sala*, good and substantial doors and windows, with shutters generally painted green, as were also the cornice and columns supporting the verandas, the whole covered with a flat roof, and now you have a description of an old-style angel habitation. [In this last phrase, Bell is making a play on the informal name of Los Angeles as "the City of the Angels."] The ruins of many yet remind us of the good old times.⁸

7

A Pirate Attack on Monterey

Hipólito (or Hypolite) Bouchard (1780–1837) was a French sailor and pirate who fought for Argentina, Chile, and Peru, harassing Spanish ships and facilities wherever he found them. Historical accounts of his attack on the Alta California coast vary in small details (there is no universally-agreed version of it), but the main points are clear enough. It is useful to consider them here because they show how unready and how unwilling the *Californios* were to defend their homeland in the face of a foreign attack.[1]

Their efforts to repel Bouchard and his men were disorganized and ineffective at best: indeed, the artillery commander of Monterey's fort very nearly ordered heavy cannon to be fired at one of his own officers. The *Californio* soldier José María Amador saw Governor Pablo Vincente de Solá, the senior Spanish officer in Monterey, not long after the attack. Amador wrote later:

> The Governor had dark rings under his eyes that reached down to his sideburns; they were caused by the grief he felt in his soul as a result of Bouchard and his insurgents having forced him and all his men to flee Monterey. Mr. Solá deserves to be called somewhat of a coward.[2]

The story of the Bouchard attack, as best it can be pieced together today from published sources in English, is that on or about 20 November 1818, a watchman at Punta de Pinos, located at the tip of the southern end of Monterey Bay, sighted two unfamiliar ships and raised the alarm. These ships turned out to be Bouchard's shallow-draft 60-gun corvette *Santa Rosa*, and his deep-draft frigate *La Argentina*. The Spanish authorities in Alta California, however, were already aware of an impending pirate attack and were on the lookout because, the month before, the Spanish vessel *Clarion* had reported that two pirate ships were planning to assault their coast.

7. A Pirate Attack on Monterey

Although his victims considered Bouchard simply to be a pirate, he in fact held a "letter of marque" issued by the new state of the United Provinces of the River Plate, the ancestor of today's Argentina. This document was a government license authorizing a person, officially known as a privateer, to attack and capture enemy vessels. Cruising for "prizes," i.e., searching the sea for enemy ships to seize while armed with a letter of marque was considered to be an exciting, honorable, and very profitable calling—in contrast to unlicensed piracy, which was universally condemned. In his adopted country of Argentina, Bouchard is revered today as a patriot: a modern American warship, the destroyer USS *Borie*, was sold to Argentina in 1972 and was renamed by the Argentinians as the *Hipólito Bouchard*.

When he heard that a pirate attack was in the offing, Governor Solá, who resided in Monterey, had ordered that all valuables be taken out of the city, as well as two-thirds of the gunpowder stored in military outposts there, and had sent to an inland mission at Soledad some of the women, children, and men unable to fight. However, half of the few soldiers at Solá's disposal were not stationed in Monterey itself but were instead guarding the outlying missions within Monterey's jurisdiction. Solá had only a minuscule force on hand, consisting of two officers, 19 cavalry soldiers, and one artillery lieutenant who himself had only four untrained militiamen ready to fire Monterey's cannons.

Moreover, the able-bodied male civilians of Monterey simply refused to fight either for or against Bouchard (he had wanted to "liberate" the city from Spanish rule), but preferred instead to avoid trouble entirely simply by staying in their own homes. The courageous General Mariano Guadalupe Vallejo, who was only an 11-year old boy then and who was not involved in the incident, later discussed this timid *Californio* response to the threat of violence that might have involved their own families. He explained it by writing that "in the breast of the old time Californians love of family was stronger than selfish and vile interest" and that (regarding the Californios' passivity in the face of Bouchard's attack) "had they been Yankees it is likely they would have acted differently," i.e., Vallejo believed that the Yankees would have fought the pirates.[3]

Monterey's original gun emplacement, known as *El Castillo* ("The Castle"), was armed with 10 brass 12-pound cannons (i.e., cannons that fired a cannonball weighing 12 pounds) and had an adequate supply of cannonballs. Nevertheless, because the *Californios* only rarely maintained any of their military equipment, this gun emplacement was totally useless, being described in 1804 by an American seaman as "a miserable battery

... altogether inadequate to what it is intended for." To cope with its evident shortcomings, the Spanish had set up a new temporary gun battery along the beach just north of the Custom House, from which point it could fire on ships in Monterey's anchorage.

Bouchard was commanding *La Argentina*; his colleague, the Englishman Peter Corney, was the senior officer in charge of the *Santa Rosa*. Both ships sailed into Monterey Bay as darkness fell. Bouchard kept *La Argentina* in the middle of the bay to prevent it from running aground, while *La Rosa* was anchored so close to the shore that the cannons of *El Castillo* could not be depressed sufficiently to hit anything but the highest parts of her masts.

That night, Corney refused to tell the Spanish authorities who he was, even though he was within easy shouting distance of the shore. Instead, as soon as dawn broke, he opened fire on the biggest houses in and near Monterey's presidio, reasoning that these would be most likely to support any Spanish force sent out to oppose his attack.

Neither Bouchard nor Corney, however, knew about the temporary gun emplacement, which now opened fire on the *Santa Rosa*, effectively trapping it close to the shore. If the corvette moved away from the shore, it would have become subject to fire from the heavy cannons of *El Castillo*. As it was, after the *Santa Rosa* was hit three times near the waterline by cannonballs fired from the temporary gun emplacement and began to take on water, Corney had to order his crew to surrender. As soon as they did, the Spanish ceased firing.

But Corney had a trick up his sleeve. He ordered his men to shift the corvette's cannons to the undamaged side of the ship, a move that lifted the damaged side out of the water and thus stopped the leaking. Corney with his heavily-armed crew now took to the lifeboats, but instead of making directly for shore, as the Spanish expected they would do, they rowed out to *La Argentina*, which all this time had been hovering safely in the bay just out of cannon range.

Now brimming with pirates, after sailing about 2 ½ miles to the west *La Argentina* landed 400 men and two cannons near where the Monterey Bay Aquarium and Hopkins Marine Station stand today. They captured *El Castillo* and their presence forced Governor Solá to flee from Monterey. The *Californio* soldiers and their families who had been living in Monterey's presidio retreated to a ranch near Salinas. At the same time, the friars of Mission San Carlos in Carmel fled up the Carmel Valley to what is now Rancho San Carlos.

Bouchard's men entered the presidio unchallenged (it had been totally abandoned by the Californios); ransacked it; stole from the soldiers' homes anything that was portable and of any value; and set everything else on fire. They cleverly destroyed *El Castillo*'s cannons by loading them, burying them muzzle-down half way into the ground, and then firing them. Upon being ignited (i.e., when being fired), the gunpowder in the cannons immediately generated huge pressures, which could not be released because of the blocked barrels. The result was that the brass barrels burst asunder.

Faced with such a stunning military defeat, Governor Solá called for reinforcements from both the San Francisco and the Santa Barbara presidios, but long before they had any chance of arriving, Bouchard had repaired his damaged corvette and had put to sea again without further incident. He and his men then sacked and burned a ranch north of Santa Barbara and also burned part of Mission San Juan Capistrano. After that, they sailed south and never returned to Alta California.

Bouchard, however, did not inflict any permanent damage on the Monterey area. Dorotea Valdez, a servant who was living at the presidio with Governor Solá's family, later reported that

> the despicable pirates had sacked our dwellings and then burned everything they could lay their hands on. But our people bravely faced up to an evil that they could do nothing about. With the assistance of carpenters, blacksmiths, and many neophytes [Mission Indians], in less than four months our pueblo looked as good as it had before the pirate captain arrived.[4]

An unexpected bit of good news was that one of the members of Bouchard's crew was captured during the raid. He was an American carpenter and millwright named Joseph Chapman (1784–1849), who received amnesty and became a highly useful citizen. He built the first mill in California at Mission Santa Ines and another at Mission San Gabriel. For the latter, in San Pedro he also built a 60-ton schooner for use in the coastal trade. Chapman became a Catholic, married a *Californio*, became a naturalized Mexican citizen, received a land grant, and served as an interpreter for the *Californio* community.[5]

8

The Old Spanish Trail

Designated in 2002 as part of the National Historic Trails System, the Old Spanish Trail was the major overland connection between northern New Mexico and southern California from 1744 to about 1848.[1] It was famously described in 1954 by a husband-and-wife team of American scholars (LeRoy R. Hafen and Ann W. Hafen) as "the longest, crookedest, most arduous pack mule route in the history of America."[2] Thanks to their path-breaking work, it has achieved an identity separate from all the other "southern routes" to the Pacific Ocean.

Never a wagon road, never a fast route, and never safe for summer travel because of the heat and the lack of water, it was still useable by horses and mules much of the year.[3] Its principal virtue was that it lay considerably to the north of hostile Indian territory. This trail linked the northern New Mexico settlements near and in Santa Fe with those of Los Angeles and Southern California. Serapes and other woolen goods were transported on mules from New Mexico to Alta California, which had virtually no wool processing industry and very few weavers and therefore welcomed this trade. On the return leg of the trip, stolen or purchased horses and mules were driven from California back to New Mexico, where these animals were in short supply and the demand for them was high.

Not only traders but also mountain men (i.e., beaver trappers), prospectors, and immigrants used the trail. Writing in 1848, George Frederick Ruxton (1821–1848), a young English adventurer and writer who had lived with mountain men in the Rockies, had this to say about the mountain men who were driving a herd of stolen California horses and mules along a desert section of the Old Spanish Trail:

> Descending a broken ridge, they at once struck into a distinct and tolerably well-worn track, into which the *cavallada* [i.e., their horse and mule herd] turned as easily and as instinctively as if they had been accustomed to travel on beaten roads.

8. The Old Spanish Trail

Along this they travelled merrily—their delight being, however, alloyed by frequent indications that hunger and thirst had done their work on the caravans which had preceded them on the trail.

They happened to strike it in the centre of a long stretch of desert, extending sixty miles without either water or pasture. Many animals had perished here, leaving their bones to bleach upon the plain. The soil was sandy, but rocks and stones covered the surface, disabling the feet of many of the young horses and mules; several of which, at this early stage of the journey, were already abandoned ... many of the horses having been left on the road, the Diggers [a band of local Indians] found so plentiful a supply of meat as to render unnecessary any attack on the formidable mountaineers.[4]

Kidnapped Indian children were trafficked along the trail, too. They were traded to local families who lived near the trail for horses, goods, or cash. Many of these children, especially the girls, would be trained by their new owners to become household servants and would spend the rest of their lives in this calling. For this reason, Indian girls were more valuable than Indian boys. If the latter survived, they would have been trained as vaqueros.

Because of the intervening deserts, canyonlands, and hostile Indians, the Old Spanish Trail did not run directly, i.e., more or less east-west, between Santa Fe and Los Angeles. Instead, it traced a huge 1,200-mile-long parabola from Santa Fe northwest into central Utah, where its northernmost point was near Castle Dale, Utah (about 115 miles southeast of Salt Lake City), and then turned southwest toward Los Angeles.

This parabola was not its only geographic complexity. When the trail left Santa Fe, it split into three roughly parallel routes: the Armijo Route, the Main Route, and the North Route. There were numerous minor variations in all these routes as travelers, taking account of the weather and other factors, struggled to find the easiest path to their destination. Only one round trip a year was about all that was possible.

Spain had wanted to establish a viable overland link between its holdings in California and those in New Mexico. Parts of what would become the Old Spanish Trail were first explored when Father Francisco Garcés set out from the Yuma villages along the Gila River in southern Arizona to look for a path to the California missions, beginning in 1774. Indian guides from friendly Mohave Indian villages on the Colorado River led him along Indian trails to the Mohave River. He followed the Mohave for several days, finally reaching Mission San Gabriel via the San Bernardino-San Gabriel Ranges. Some of the Indian routes that Garcés followed through the Mohave Desert would later became part of the western portion of the Old Spanish Trail.

The transportation and exchange of goods between New Mexico and California was begun by the Mexican trader Antonio Armijo, who in 1829–1830 led the first commercial caravan, consisting of 60 men and 100 mules, from Abiquiu, New Mexico, to Los Angeles. Over the next 20 years, Mexican and American traders traveled variants of the route that Armijo pioneered, frequently trading with Indian tribes along the way. The complex network known today as the Old Spanish Trail thus evolved from a combination of Indian footpaths, early trade routes, and accessible pasture and water for pack trains and stock drives. However, after the Americans took control of the Southwest in 1848, other shorter and less arduous routes to California emerged, so the use of the Old Spanish Trail sharply declined.

The first party to travel the entire distance over substantially the route that became the Old Spanish Trail was a 20-man group led by William Wolfskill and George C. Yount in the winter of 1831–32. J.J. Warner, an early settler on the Pacific coast and a Southern California historian, wrote that in Wolfskill's party there were New Mexicans bringing *serapes* and *fresadas* (woolen blankets) with them to trade with the Indians in exchange for beaver skins. On their arrival in California, they also traded some of their blankets to the rancheros in exchange for mules.

These caravans, which were a step beyond Armijo's earlier commercial venture, reached California each year. They brought in the woolen fabrics of New Mexico, and carried back home not only mules but also silk and other Chinese products that had been carried to Alta California by American ships. After following the Green and Virgin River routes, the caravans went over the Cajon Pass and finally reached Los Angeles.

From there, they spread all across Alta California, from San Diego to San Jose, and across San Francisco Bay to Sonoma and San Rafael. Finally, after having sold all the goods they had brought and having stocked up on items and mules to take back home, they gathered in Los Angeles before their annual return trip.[5]

Historians have long joked that the Old Spanish Trail was neither "old" nor "Spanish." The first documented use of this name (described then as "the Spanish Trail") came only in the 1840s from the pen of John Charles Frémont, the famous explorer and American Army officer who played an important role in the U.S.-Mexican War. It was then picked up and used by others, principally Anglo-American travelers. In the 19th century, however, Mexican traders referred to the trail as the *"Camino de California,* while *Californios* themselves called it the *"Camino de Santa Fe."*

8. The Old Spanish Trail

In any case, by 1841 the caravan business had become well organized, was governed by custom and local law, and was subject to government regulation. For example, the regular trade caravan of 1841 from New Mexico was led by Francisco Estevan Virgil. Governor Manuel Armijo of New Mexico issued instructions at Santa Fe on 6 August 1841 that Virgil and his men should be given permission to travel to California, and provided him with a passport and a detailed list of instructions with regard to the conduct of the caravan. It set out from New Mexico on 6 September 1841 and reached Los Angeles in late October 1841.

A good description of this trade comes from the French diplomat Duflot de Mofras, who reported to his government in 1841 that caravans traveled from New Mexico to Los Angeles and back each year. They typically consisted of 200 mounted men, driving mules laden with woolen blankets and other fabrics. Each item was valued at the equivalent of 3 to 5 silver dollars; the exchange rate in California was two blankets for one horse or one mule.

Duflot de Mofras added that the caravans left Santa Fe in October, before the snow fell in the mountains; eventually reached the outlying ranches of California; and then continued on to Los Angeles. The trip, a long and a difficult one, could take as much as 2 1/2 months to complete. Returning caravans left California in April to be able to cross the rivers before the snows melted. Each trip involved about 200 New Mexicans and some 60 North Americans. Returning caravans drove about 2,000 California horses with them to sell in New Mexico.[6]

In 1847, Mormons who had settled in Utah began to drive their wagons along the western half of the Old Spanish Trail while travelling between Salt Lake City and Los Angeles. Their route replicated or paralleled the trail for most of the distance between the hamlet of Paragonah, Utah, on the one hand, and the upcoming town of San Bernardino, California, on the other. This route would become a life-line for new immigrants to the Great Basin.[7]

In April 1848, having sold most of their wares, New Mexican traders set out from Los Angeles on the Old Spanish Trail on their return journey to Santa Fe. They were followed in early May by Kit Carson (one of the most famous of all the American frontiersmen) leading a small party of men. Carson had been sent east from California to deliver important dispatches to Washington, D.C., and was accompanied by a young U.S. Army lieutenant, George Douglas Brewerton, who was an excellent writer.

In the desert beyond the Mohave River, the Carson party caught up with and passed the slower-moving New Mexican traders. Brewerton captured both the spirit of the trip and the essence of Carson himself in lucid descriptions. He wrote of the trip:

> Our general course was by the great Spanish trail, and we made as rapid traveling as possible, with the view of overtaking the large Mexican caravan which was slowly wending its way back to the capital of New Mexico. This caravan consisted of some two or three hundred Mexican traders who go once a year to the Californian coast with a supply of blankets and other articles of New Mexican manufacture; and having disposed of their goods, invest the proceeds in Californian mules and horses, which they drive back across the desert. These people often realize high profits, as the animals are purchased for a mere trifle on the coast, bring high prices in Santa Fe...
>
> We finally overtook and passed this party, after some eight days' travel in the Desert. Their appearance was grotesque in the extreme. Imagine upward of two hundred Mexicans dressed in every variety of costume, from the embroidered jacket of the wealthy Californian, with its silver bell-shaped buttons, to the scanty habiliments of the skin-clad Indians, and you may form some faint idea of their dress...
>
> The line of march of this strange cavalcade occupied an extent of more than a mile; I could not help thinking while observing their dress and arms and equipments, that a few resolute men might have captured their property, and driven the traders like a flock of sheep. Many of these people had no fire-arms, being only provided with the short bow and arrows usually carried by New Mexican herdsmen. Others were armed with old English muskets, condemned long ago as unserviceable.... Another description of weapons appeared to be highly prized among them—these were old, worn-out dragoon sabres, dull and rusty, at best a most useless arm in contending with an enemy who fights only from inaccessible rocks and precipices; but when carried under the leathers of the saddle, and tied with all the manifold straps and knots with which the Mexican secures them, perfectly useless even at close quarters. [These sabers were carried only as proof of their owners' gentlemanly status, never as practical weapons.][8]

He wrote of Carson:

> The Kit Carson of my *imagination* was over six feet high—a sort of modern Hercules in his build—with an enormous beard, and a voice like a roused lion.... The *real* Kit Carson I found to be a plain, simple, unostentatious man; rather below the medium height, with brown, curling hair, little or no beard, and a voice as soft and gentle as a woman's....[9]

After 1848–1849, the relatively good wagon roads resulting from the Mexican War expeditions and from the California Gold Rush ended the annual packhorse caravan traffic, which had been the distinctive feature of the Old Spanish Trail. Traffic in Indian children, however, continued unabated. Reporting on conditions as they existed in 1851, the American trader Daniel W. Jones described how the slavery business was conducted by New Mexican traders along the Old Spanish Trail.

Since this trade was illegal, written accounts were rarely kept and very little documentation on it has survived. What is clear is that traders would set out on their journey with only a few goods, which they would then barter on the way with the Navajos and Utes in exchange for old horses. Jones sketched out the trade in these terms:

- The old horses were bought from and traded to the poorest Indians for their children. The Indians often ate the horses. The trade went on in California and also extended into Baja California. Children bought on the "down trip" would be traded to Mexican-Californians for horses, other goods, or cash. Jones said that in many cases a small outfit at the start would return with large herds of California livestock.
- All the children bought on the return trip to New Mexico would be sold there. Boys were valued at about $100 each but because the girls were thought to make excellent household servants, they cost much more—i.e., from $150 to $200 apiece. This slave trade, said Jones, gave rise to local wars between the native tribes of this country, from Salt Lake down to southern Utah. He added the Mexicans, and some American frontiersmen, were as fully established and as systematic in the trade as were the slavers on the high seas.[10]

The last use of the Old Spanish Trail for legitimate purposes was in the 1850s, when selected portions of the trail's eastern end were mapped by U.S. Government topographic expeditions. The western portion of the trail, which came to be used chiefly by the Mormons heading for California, would become known as the Mormon Road.

To summarize now, it can be said that the Old Spanish Trail played an important role in opening up the West to American settlement and American sovereignty. It demonstrated that the little-known and therefore previously intimidating world of mountains, deserts, and Indian lands in the Southwest could, with good equipment and proper planning, be crossed safely and, later, developed successfully.

9

Californio Men and *Californio* Women

In 1794, the Spanish explorer and cartographer Miguel Costansó defined *Californio* men and women (by whom he meant only the European Spaniards, Creoles, and people of mixed blood) as the *gente de razón*, in order to differentiate them very clearly from the native Indians.[1] This term literally means "people of reason" but "rational people" is a better translation. It reflects an important social distinction which was widely prevalent in colonial Spanish America and which referred to people who were culturally Hispanicized. None of the local men and women *who were not culturally Hispanicized* could ever be considered to be *gente do razón*.

What, then, can be said about the *gente de razón* of Alta California? Perhaps the most important conclusion is that there seems to have been very little "objective reality" at play here. As the historian David J. Weber has pointed out, earlier generations of American and other writers tended to depict the *Californios* as hopelessly lazy, ignorant, pre-industrial, illiterate, conservative, militarily weak, and generally backward. In sharp contrast, however, by the late 19th century, American and other writers were now reimagining the *Californios* as being exceedingly attractive, unhurried, untroubled, and gracious.

This sea-change in literary output did not reflect any demonstrable change in the historical reality on the ground. What it did reflect was the fact that Helen Hunt Jackson and other writers successfully created a charming genre of sentimental historical fiction to offset what they denounced as the excessive commercialism, materialism, vulgarity, and rootlessness of modern life. In short, they sought to recreate, on paper, the pastoral values they imagined had been dominant when the *Californios* were in the saddle.[2]

9. Californio *Men and* Californio *Women*

That said, it is worth looking here at some contemporary sources. José Arnaz, for example, came to Alta California from Spain in 1840 as the supercargo of a Mexican trading vessel and worked in that capacity for about three years. He then retired and went into business for himself in Los Angeles. In 1878 he provided the historian Bancroft with 100 pages of his manuscript entitled *Recuerdos* (*Memories*), which contained much valuable information on the lives and customs of the traders and *rancheros* in the 1840s. Bancroft printed the following except from this manuscript:

> On arriving at a rancho, the traveller was received with joy, and the best things were prepared for him, with horses and servants on leaving. Even their beds [i.e., those owners' beds] were given up. When the missions flourished a man could travel from one end of California to the other, obtaining horses, servants, food, etc., without cost to him, and this hospitality was kept up, or nearly so, by rancheros after the decline of the missions.[3]

In addition to being so hospitable, *Californios* were also among the very best horsemen in the world. Mark Twain was very impressed. He wrote:

> I had never seen such wild, free, magnificent horsemanship outside of a circus as these picturesquely-clad Mexicans, Californians and Mexicanized Americans displayed in Carson streets [i.e., in what is now Carson City, Nevada] every day. How they rode!
> Leaning just gently forward of the perpendicular, easy and nonchalant, with broad slouch-hat brim blown square up front, and the long *riata* [lariat] swinging above the head, they swept through town like the wind! The next minute they were only a sailing puff of dust on the far desert. If they trotted, they sat gallantly and gracefully, and seemed part of the horse; did not go jiggering up and down after the silly Miss-Nancy fashion of the riding schools [i.e., they did not "post" in the saddle to ease the jolts of the trot].[4]

Dana, for his part, has this to say:

> The men in Monterey appeared to me to be always on horseback. Horses are as abundant here as dogs and chickens were in Juan Fernandez [an island group in the South Pacific Ocean, located about 416 miles off the coast of Chile]. There are no stables to keep them in, but they are allowed to run wild and graze wherever they please, being branded, and having long leather ropes, called "lassos," attached to their necks and dragging along behind them, by which they can easily be taken.
> The men usually catch one in the morning, throw a saddle and bridle upon him, and use him for the day, and let him go at night, catching another the next day. When they go on long journeys, they ride one horse down, and catch another, throw the saddle and bridle upon him, and after riding him down, take a third, and so on to the end of the journey. There are probably no better riders in the world.... They can hardly go from one house to another without getting on a horse, there being generally several standing tied to the door posts of the little cottages.

> When they wish to show their activity, they make no use of their stirrups in mounting, but striking the horse, spring into the saddle as he starts, and sticking their long spurs into him, go off on the full run. Their spurs are cruel things, having four or five rowels, each an inch in length, dull and rusty. The flanks of the horses are often sore from them, and I have seen men come in from chasing bullocks with their horses' hind legs and quarters covered with blood.[5]

Californio gentlemen scorned physical labor as being degrading. There were only two exceptions to this rule. The first was that a modest amount of military service was acceptable—but only as an officer, never as an enlisted man. The second was that leading or participating in cattle roundups was also seen in a favorable light. Both of these undertakings offered high status, but neither of them was physically or intellectually very demanding, or cut deeply into a gentleman's all-important social obligations.

Foreign observers, on the other hand, heaped warm praise on the *Californio* women for being much harder working than their menfolk; for their hospitality and charity; and often for their fine manners. Five of these ladies—namely, Eulalia Callis, Rosalía Vallejo, Apolinaria Lorenzana, María de las Angustias de la Guerra (de Ord), and María Amparo Ruiz de Burton—are described below. Together with Eulalia Pérez, who has already been discussed, these ladies offer the modern reader some valuable insights into the characters and concerns of *Californio* women.

Eulalia Callis (1759–?)

Doña Callis, a Spanish lady from a well-connected Catalan family, was married to Don Pedro Fages, who in 1782 was appointed governor of the Californias and was assigned to Monterey.[6] Although she did not want to leave the comfort and sophistication of upper class life in Mexico City, her husband's wishes, coupled with family and social pressures, finally left her no choice but to move to Monterey.

Doña Callis was a very strong-minded woman who was willing to defend what she considered to be her rights. She petitioned for divorce from Don Pedro, on the grounds that he had committed adultery with a young Yuma Indian woman who was part of the household. The facts of the matter were never in dispute. As she stated in her petition to the local friar,

> I found my husband physically on top of one of his servants, a young Yuma Indian girl. Well-founded suspicions and the girl's easily obtained confession put me in the position of being the sentinel who discovered the incident. Even though prudence

should have prevailed (this was my crime,) I was overcome by passion, which fueled the flames of my rage, which caused me to cry out publicly against this infamy.[7]

What Doña Callis is saying here is that, ideally, she should have followed the dictates of *Californio* culture and should never have voiced her anger so publicly and so loudly. As it was, however, she categorically refused to back down—to the extent that at mass at the presidio church, the priest (who was also the judge of her petition) "ended up by vilifying me and had the soldiers throw me out of the church. This is what he said: 'Detain that woman so I can put a gag over her mouth.'"[8]

Doña Callis was legally within her rights to petition for protection from her husband but, in colonial Spanish America, divorce did not exist. In theory, her choices were either dissolution of the marriage or an annulment, neither of which she could obtain. She did get some qualified support from Nicolás Soler, the assistant inspector of presidios, who was eager to have the matter resolved. He wrote both to Doña Callis and Don Pedro, but was reluctant to intervene more actively. The bishop who reviewed her case concluded that since her accusation against her husband was not supported by any other "substantial" corroboration, the ecclesiastical court could not approve a divorce.[9]

To make a longer story very short, when she realized that neither church, state, nor her own circle of friends were willing or able to help her, she withdrew her petition, resumed married life with her husband, and eventually returned to Mexico City with him, where he died three years later.

Rosalía Vallejo Leese (1811–1889)

Rosalía Vallejo Leese, the sister of General Mariano Guadalupe Vallejo, had married the American entrepreneur and rancher Jacob P. Leese against her brother's wishes. She was interviewed in Monterey on 27 June 1874 by Henry Cerruti, one of Bancroft's writers.

Rosalía knew her own mind and was not at all shy about voicing strong opinions. When Cerruti asked her what she thought of the American occupation of Alta California, she told him that she disliked all the Americans. She complained bitterly that her husband had squandered her dowry and then deserted her, leaving her to bring up four young daughters and two sons by herself. Thanks to the decisions of the California courts and due to squatters, she had also lost the greater part of her landed property. Moreover, she had been badly treated by the men of the

Bear Flag Revolt (a short-lived revolt by local Americans in 1846), who had imprisoned two of her brothers and her husband and had plundered their provisions.

She told Cerruti that at about 5:30 in the morning on 14 June 1846, an old Mexican gentleman named Don Pepe de la Rosa told her that a group of 72 ragged desperados had surrounded General Vallejo's house in Sonoma. (In Spanish and Mexican California, the honorary title of "Don" was used to refer to any gentleman.) Many of these desperados were sailors from whaling ships who had jumped ship. They arrested General Vallejo, Captain Salvador Vallejo, and Colonel Victor Prudón. When she heard this alarming news, she quickly got dressed and rushed out to the street to see if there was any truth to what the old man had said.

She found out that it was true. A large group of rough-looking men were holding General Vallejo prisoner. Some of the men were wearing caps made from the skins of coyotes or wolves. Others were wearing slouch hats full of holes or straw hats as black as charcoal. Most of these marauders had on buckskin pants, but some were wearing blue pants that reached only to the knee. [Only seamen wore such pants.] Several of the men were not wearing shirts, and only 15 or 20 of them were wearing shoes.

The insurgents took their captives, including Rosalía's husband Jacob Leese, to Sacramento. The marauders who stayed behind in Sonoma then raised a piece of linen cloth on the flagpole located in the corner of the plaza near the old mission church. The cloth was about the size of a large towel, and they had painted a red bear and one star on it. (Other onlookers, both Mexicans and Americans, agreed that the red bear looked more like a red pig.)

Rosalía went on to denounce John C. Frémont as the man who had planned what she called "this all-out robbery of California." She said that during the whole time that Frémont and his "ring of thieves" were in Sonoma, robberies were very common. Women did not dare go out for a walk unless they were escorted by their husbands or their brothers.

One of Rosalía's servants was a young Indian girl about 17 years old. Rosalía told Cerruti that Frémont had repeatedly ordered her to send the Indian girl to the officers' barracks, but that she (Rosalía) had always been able, by resorting to trickery, to keep the girl away from the officers. At the end of the interview, Rosalía told Cerruti that the Americans had made her so furious that even though 28 years had gone by since then, she still refused to have anything to do with them and would never try to learn English.[10]

Apolinaria Lorenzana (1793–1884)

Interviewed in Santa Barbara on 14 March 1878 by Thomas Savage, this lady began life as a foundling delivered to the Real Casa de Expósitos (the Royal House for Abandoned Children) in Mexico City sometime in 1793. She lived there for seven years and was given an introduction to reading, arithmetic, grammar, sewing, embroidery, how to make artificial flowers, geography, music, and the catechism. In 1799, Apolinaria and some other children were removed from the Casa and were placed in the Real Hospicio de Pobres (the Royal Hospice for the Poor) in Mexico City.

From there, they traveled to San Blas and boarded the frigate *Concepción*, bound for Monterey, California. She was definitely a self-starter, telling Savage that when she was very young she was taught how to read and that later, in California, she taught herself how to write by copying the letters of the alphabet on empty cigarette papers or blank pieces of paper that had been thrown away.

Apolinaria was placed with various military families, where she taught other girls how to write, and passed on to them the skills she had learned at the Casa. She then went to San Diego, where she was placed with a newly married couple, Sergeant Mariano Mercado and his wife Josefa Sal, daughter of a prominent Spanish officer. Apolinaria served as a teacher at Sal's school and also took on greater and greater responsibilities at the mission there.

She managed many of its temporal affairs, acquired ranches, and hired people to manage them so that she herself could continue to work at the mission. She became known throughout Southern California as *La Beata*, "the pious woman." A very self-sufficient woman, she owned three ranchos at the same time (two were given to her by the Mexican government; the third she bought herself.)

She never married and she devoted her entire life to the service of others. She told Savage:

> I have no idea how many godchildren I have, nor do I know the number of girls for whom I have been godmother at their confirmation.... I had the satisfaction of being loved by young and old, and rich and poor. Maybe it was because I was good-natured and would do whatever I could to help people.[11]

However, the Californios' defeat in the U.S.-Mexican War changed her life very much for the worse. Many of the missions fell into ruins, the friars were expelled or died, and by the 1870s she was living in the Santa Barbara area, supported only by the charity of her friends.

María de las Angustias de la Guerra (de Ord), 1815–1890

Interviewed in Santa Barbara by Thomas Savage on 1 April 1878, this lady is of special significance here, not only because of her high social status but also because of her insightful critiques of patriarchy, politics, and the role of women in *Californio* life. She was also quite familiar with mission finances because her father was the banker for all the missions in Alta California. Savage wrote she was well known locally as an intelligent and well-informed lady familiar with the details of life in Alta California before the transfer of power to the United States.[12]

Angustias de la Guerra was present when the American fleet, led by Commodore John B. Sloat, raised the American flag at Monterey on 7 July 1846. It is therefore worth quoting her here at some length. She told Savage:

> The taking of California was not at all to the liking of the Californios, and least of all the women. But I must confess, California was on the road to utter ruin. On the one hand, the Indians were out of control, committing robberies and other crimes at the ranchos. Little or nothing was done to curb their pillaging.
>
> On the other hand, there was discord between the people of the north and the south. In addition, both north and south were against the Mexicans from the mainland. But the worst cancer of all was the widespread thievery. There was such squandering of government resources that the funds in the treasury office had bottomed out.
>
> Commander General Castro kept a roster of officers that was large enough to staff an army of three thousand men. Somehow they all received a salary. These officers had no other use for the money than to grease the palms of their supporters who would help them achieve their personal goals. Few of these officers served their country when the time came to defend it against the foreign invasion. The majority of them did about as much work as a figurehead on a ship.[13]

She was a fine observer of cultural differences. She recounts that at one point, when a Spaniard named Don Gregorio Ajuria was in her living room, he had something in his pocket that appeared to be bothering him. He put his hand into his pocket and pulled out two pieces of gold, which he gave to her young daughter to play with.

Shortly thereafter, she went into the dining room and watched an American friend weigh gold dust on a small scale. Every time he emptied the scale, he would carefully wipe it clean to be sure that none of the gold dust would be left behind. Later, she told some of her friends of the interesting contrast she had seen: on the one hand, a Spaniard giving gold away because it bothered him; on the other, an American cleaning the plate on his scale with the same care that a priest cleans his paten.[14]

María Amparo Ruiz de Burton, 1832–1895

The first female Mexican-American author to write in English, Ruiz de Burton published two books: *Who Would Have Thought It?* (1872), *The Squatter and the Don* (1885), and one play: *Don Quixote de la Mancha: A Comedy in Five Acts: Taken From Cervantes' Novel of That Name* (1876). Her work, which is a precursor of Chicano literature, shows that although the defeated Mexican population had been granted American citizenship by the 1848 Treaty of Guadalupe Hidalgo ending the U.S.-Mexican War (American citizenship had been automatically conferred on all former citizens of Mexico who remained in California one year after the signing of this treaty), in practice this group remained a subjugated national minority for many more decades.

Coming as she did from an upper class Catholic Mexican background, and marrying Henry S. Burton, the upper class Protestant American Army officer who was in charge of the American forces that occupied Baja California during the U.S.-Mexican War, Ruiz de Burton was a lady singularly well-placed to comment on religion, ethnicity, power, gender, and social class in mid-to-late 19th century America.[15] Her writings openly criticized American greed and racism, and depicted the *Californios* as a "white" population who had been violently dispossessed of their bucolic way of life by American aggression.

The Squatter and the Don is Ruiz de Burton's most famous work. It is a novel aimed at social reform rather than being merely a romantic novel by a woman writer. She published it in 1885 under the ironic pen name "C. Loyal," i.e., "Loyal Citizen," a reference in English to the conventional way of closing official letters in 19th century Mexico. The book, covering the years 1872 to 1885, examines, among other contemporary developments, the Land Act (also known as the Land Law) of 1851, which required *Californio* land owners to prove that they did have legal title to their land. *The Squatter and the Don* shows how so many *Californio* families lost their land due to litigation and to squatters.

To the observations and judgments of these ladies, one may usefully add the memories of Carlos Híjar, then an eight-year-old boy who came to Alta California in 1834 as part of the Híjar-Padrés colony. He gives such revealing details of *Californio* life—noticing what adults might fail to notice, and seeing everything with new, young eyes—that it is worth citing him here at some length, using his own words. He begins thus:

> When I touched the port of San Diego [i.e., when I arrived at San Diego] in 1834, I was very surprised to see the [male] residents with hair as long as that of women,

and made into a braid which fell over their shoulders or was put up carefully into the crown of their hats. These hats were rather coarse, with the brims very broad and the crown seven or eight inches tall, so that they looked like a pyramid truncated by a horizontal plane. Around this they always tied a band in the form of a ribbon or a silk handkerchief, either black or colored. They always wore the hat tipped forward so that it covered most of the forehead. They were very fond of riding.

The women wore tunics of calico, generally blue, always long in spite of the age of the individual. On their heads they wore a kerchief of black silk doubled into various folds and bound around the head in the manner of a turban. The footwear was of chamois, with a more or less high heel and with the tip of the shoe turned upward...

The largest part of the tasks was entrusted to the women. They busied themselves with their domestic duties, cut the wood necessary for the meal, sowed in the gardens the seeds indispensable to the household, using the hoe, pick, shovel, etc. and went to the water-holes to wash under an arbor which they themselves made. The men, on the other hand, spent their lives on horseback, riding through the fields, lassoing or killing cattle. Then they would take a piece of meat home and in doing so they were well satisfied, and the women were very happy and grateful...

The daily meal consisted of beef, parboiled, roasted, or fried, and beans; the bread was tortillas, which were absolutely essential to them. The most appetizing dish for any Californio was made by killing the cow when it was about to give birth, taking the calf from the womb and giving it to the women for them to prepare in any way they like. Whatever it might be, it would be a succulent mouthful...

To conclude our remarks on the Californios, we shall say a few words about their character. This, just as their customs [were], was generally very simple. The women always spent their lives in their domestic duties and in the tasks already mentioned, and the men always went through the country mounted on their horses, running, lassoing and killing deer and cattle. Their gatherings were very intimate and simple, and their treatment of each other was very affectionate and simple.... They all called each other cousins even though no bond of relationship united them. All the aforesaid, however, does not belie the fact that there were some individuals who abused such simplicity and candor, committing misdeeds which history must have by now assigned to them in its pages....[16]

The *Californios* excelled in some activities, but formal education was never one of them. In this oral culture, academic learning was not valued highly, either by *Californio* men or by *Californio* women. In fact, there was absolutely no organized system of schools in Alta California before the American conquest in 1848. Teaching, when it occurred at all, was conducted in an ad hoc manner by a few foreign merchants, who taught some of the sons of their *Californio* business partners how to read, write, and calculate, and by a few friars, who taught some of the brightest Indian boys how to read words and music so they could actively participate in the religious services at the missions. What little academic learning the *Californio* girls managed to pick up came entirely from their mothers or from their literate female relatives.

9. Californio *Men and* Californio *Women* 69

Writing in 1891, the American businessman Alfred Robinson summed up the long-term consequences of the *gente de razón* way of life in these words:

> The early Californians, having lived a life of indolence, without any aspirations for wealth beyond the immediate requirements of the day, naturally fell behind their more energetic successors [i.e., the Americans], and became impoverished and gradually dispossessed of their fortunes, as they idly stood by, on-lookers upon the bustle and enterprise of the new world before them, with its go-aheadativeness, and push-on, keep-moving celerity.[17]

However, what can be termed the typical, contemporary American view of the *Californio* story as expressed by Alfred Robinson is not complete without including a *Californio's* nostalgically-driven depiction of life before the American conquest. This point of view is best represented by Guadalupe Vallejo, the nephew of Mariano Guadalupe Vallejo, who wrote in 1890:

> It seems to me that there was never a more peaceful or happy people on the face of the earth than the Spanish, Mexican, and Indian population of Alta California before the American conquest. We were the pioneers of the Pacific coast, building towns and Missions while General Washington was carrying on the war of the Revolution, and we often talk together of the days when a few hundred large Spanish ranches and Mission tracts occupied the whole country from the Pacific to the San Joaquin. No class of people is more loyal than the Spanish Californians, but we shall always be especially proud of the traditions and memories of the long pastoral age before 1840...
> Family life among the old Spanish pioneers was an affair of dignity and ceremony, but it did not lack in affection. Children were brought up with great respect for their elders. It was the privilege of any elderly person to correct young people by words, or even by whipping them, and it was never told that anyone thus chastised made a complaint. Each of the old families taught their children the history of the family, and reverence toward religion. A few books, some in manuscript, were treasured in the household, but children were not allowed to read novels until they were grown. They saw little of other children, except their near relatives, but they had many enjoyments unknown to children now, and they grew up with remarkable strength and healthfulness.
> In these days of trade, bustle, and confusion, when many thousands of people live in the Californian valleys, which formerly were occupied only by a few Spanish families, the quiet and happy domestic life of the past seems like a dream. We, who loved it, often speak of those days, and especially of the duties of the large Spanish households, where so many dependents were to be cared for, and everything was done in a simple and primitive way.[18]

Another highly romanticized view of Mexican California comes from the author Helen Hunt Jackson, whose 1884 novel *Ramona* has already been mentioned. Although this novel focuses chiefly on the racial discrimination and hardships suffered by Ramona, a mixed-race Scots-Indian orphan girl, it also has many laudatory things to say about *gente de razón* life. Consider, for example, Jackson's description of the fictional home of Señora Moreno, the sister of Ramona's deceased foster mother—a home modeled in part on Rancho Camulos, which is located in the Santa Clara River Valley of Southern California and which is discussed in Appendix 2.

Jackson wrote:

> The Senora Moreno's house was one of the best specimens to be found in California of the representative house of the half barbaric, half elegant, wholly generous and free-handed life led there by Mexican men and women of some degree.... It was a picturesque life, with more of sentiment and gayety in it, more also that was truly dramatic, more romance, than will ever be seen again on those sunny shores...
>
> When the house was first built, General Moreno owned all the land within a radius of forty miles—forty miles westward, down the valley to the sea; forty miles eastward, into the San Fernando Mountains; and good forty miles more or less along the coast. The boundaries were not very strictly defined; there was no occasion, in those happy days, to reckon land by inches...
>
> The arched veranda along the front was a delightsome place. It must have been eighty feet long, at least, for the doors of five large rooms opened on it.... Here the Senora kept her flowers; great red water-jars, hand-made by the Indians of San Luis Obispo Mission, stood in close rows against the walls, and in them were always growing fine geraniums, carnations, and yellow-flowered musk.[19]

Their esthetic qualities may have delighted novelists, but on other fronts the *gente de razón* were much less admirable. Fundamentally, their lavish way of life was built on the forced labor of large numbers of subjugated Indians. Their lack of formal education resulted in widespread illiteracy and contributed to political and economic stagnation among the *Californios* themselves. Their inability and unwillingness to defend their homeland became one of the underlying reasons for Mexico's crushing defeat in the U.S.-Mexican War of 1846–1848. This latter point merits a brief discussion here.

Mexico's senior politicians and military leaders may have been corrupt and incompetent but they were not stupid.[20] They understood very clearly that any surrender of Mexican territory to the United States—that is, before Mexico was physically defeated on the field of battle by the Americans—would be a political death sentence for them. Thus in order to hang on to power themselves and continue to enjoy the rewards of office, they believed they had no choice but to keep Mexico intact as long as possible. They realized that their country was facing grave dangers from an expansionistic United States, but they did nothing at all to deal with this self-evident and growing threat.

Andrés Castillero was an able Mexican army officer initially serving on the frontier in Baja California.[21] He was sent to Alta California to prepare for the arrival of a military force which the Mexican government had planned to dispatch there to prevent California from being conquered by the Americans, as Texas had been.

In a candid letter he wrote to the minister of war in Mexico City in October 1837, Castillero frankly assessed the profound weaknesses of both Californias and strongly urged his government to strengthen the Mexican military presence there.[22] However, a change of the Mexican government at the end of 1845 abruptly ended this idea, so the planned force was never sent to Alta California.

Although Castillero himself went back to Alta California in 1845 to try, unsuccessfully, to strengthen its defenses against a possible American invasion, there is no evidence that any *gente de razón* leader or group ever came forward to support him in lobbying for an effective defense system. The net result was that as U.S. Consul Thomas O. Larkin so felicitously put it in 1845 on the eve of the U.S.-Mexican War, "the pear [i.e., California itself] is near ripe for falling."[23]

If the *Californios* as whole had any shortcoming, it was what the long-term American resident Eugene (or, more often, Don Eugenio) Rafael Plummer (1853-c. 1943) described, drawing on his own experiences for over 30 years as an official English-Spanish interpreter in the courts of Los Angeles, as "that old mañana habit."

Don Eugenio, the son of a Canadian couple, had grown up in Mexico and became a fixture in the legal and social scene of Los Angeles up until his death in about 1943. He explained that this regrettable habit consisted of the "failure to do certain fairly simple things within a specified time." Plummer used as an example the failure of the owners of the big Dominquez Ranch in the western part of the San Fernando Valley to take the elementary legal steps they needed to take in order to keep their ranch. Simply because they did not take these steps, they lost the ranch.[24]

Plummer also gives a much gentler and more soothing account of the mañana habit. On the street, he meets Juanito, a friend of his, who is scheduled to make a speech at a local fiesta. Plummer is responsible for helping to arrange the fiesta and he wants to make sure that Juanito is in fact ready to give his speech. Plummer therefore asks him about what he plans to say. Before answering, however, Juanito first wants to tell Plummer a long humorous story about a bear hunt, and then a second long humorous story about a shepherd.

Juanito, however, is laughing so hard at his own sense of humor that before he can begin the first story he is unable to tell it or move on to the second story. The result is that, in the end, he cannot tell Plummer either story. Plummer therefore says, very kindly and gently to him, "Perhaps *mañana*, perhaps *mañana*." Still shaking with laughter and with tears running down his face because of these untold but to him hilarious stories, Juanito replies: "As you like, Don Plummer. As you like."[25]

10

Foreigners in Alta California

Encounters that foreigners in Alta California had, first with the Spaniards and later with the *Californios*, can give the modern reader some valuable insights into the daily lives of these foreigners. Many of these encounters are mentioned elsewhere in this book but others can profitably be cited here. It must be noted, however, that some of these comments are patronizing or prejudicial. Nevertheless, since they do form part of California's historical record, they must not be ignored here.

A brief review of some of these encounters begins in 1799 with the founding of the Russian-American Company and the decisive role played in the sea otter trade by Alexander Baranov, its first manager.[1] Energetic, well-educated, well-traveled, and good writers, Russian officials were eager to learn as much as they could about Alta California because they needed to know a good deal about it in order to trade effectively. They were quick to praise the warmth and generosity of the Spaniards and the *Californios*, but were also willing to point out what they saw as the defects of these traditional seigneurial societies.

There were of course some differences between the Russians and the *Californios* but these did not cause major problems. Indeed, the two sides had much in common. Both were European invaders of California; colonizers of this remote part of the New World; patriots; Christians; and men familiar with governing diverse populations. Not surprisingly, they got along reasonably well on both business and on social levels over their 40 years of contact.[2]

Cultural issues aside, what is very clear is that the soft, warm, luxurious fur of the sea otter was in great demand in Russia and even more so in China, where the mandarins would pay very high prices for fine pelts. Baranov had become alarmed by the dwindling sea otter catch in Alaskan waters and for this reason in 1803 he dispatched an exploratory sea otter-hunting expedition to the California coast under the leadership of the American sea captain Joseph O'Cain.

Sailing as far south as Baja California, O'Cain found that there were many sea otters in these warmer southern waters. The quality of their fur was not as good as that of the Alaskan otters but there were enough of them along the California coast to promise good profits for the Russian-American Company. This fact, coupled with the urgent need for the Russians to find a way to feed their starving colonists in Alaska, is what motivated a high-ranking Russian official—the imperial chamberlain Nikolay Petrovich Rezanov (1764–1807)—to attempt to establish Russian trade relations by means of barter, first with the Spaniards and then with the Mexicans of Alta California.

Rezanov bought the ship *Juno* from Americans in Alaska and then sailed for San Francisco Bay early in 1806 to buy grain there from the missions and, if possible, to persuade the Spanish to agree to a trade relationship with Russia. He was well-aware that all the ports of California were technically closed to any trade with foreigners, so he was not surprised when he was ordered to anchor his ship not far from San Francisco's presidio. The commandant of this fort, Don José Argüello, was away on a trip but Rezanov was greeted by his son, Don Luis Antonio Argüello, and by several friars.

All these men were favorably impressed by Rezanov's official credentials, by his fine manners, by his well-armed and well-equipped ship, and by the prospect of a mutually-advantageous trade with Russia. Soon Rezanov was being warmly received at the presidio by the whole Argüello clan, including the commandant's pretty 15-year-old daughter, Doña Concepcíon Argüello. Such social exchanges would set the standard for many of the later contacts between the Spanish and Mexican rulers of California, on the one hand, and the Russians, on the other. Personal relations had to be balanced against the political and commercial realities, but this was not too difficult to accomplish: the parties involved understood that they would all benefit from the development of a Russia-California trade.

During the weeks that followed, Rezanov successfully bartered Russian utensils and tools for California wheat. When the commandant finally returned to the presidio, Rezanov was able to get his support for permission for Russia to trade with Spanish California. This idea was forwarded to Madrid for approval. In the meantime, however, Rezanov had fallen in love with Doña Concepción and had proposed marriage to her.

The language barrier between them was eased by the fact that Georg Heinrich van Langsdorff, the *Juno*'s doctor, was able to converse in Latin with the presidio's Franciscan friar, Father Uria. As a man of the world, Rezanov realized that, true love aside, a marital bond would certainly increase the prospects for a mutually beneficial trade relationship between the Russians and the *Californios*. Indeed, the doctor's journal candidly acknowledges this fact.

Rezanov's proposal was accepted by his lady-love on the eve of his departure. (The modern historian Rosaura Sánchez has observed that the combined appeal of social mobility, escape from a dreary existence, and the illusion of a fairy-tale romance must all have played a role in the fifteen-year-old's decision to accept this proposal by the much-older Rezanov.[3])

Upon returning to Sitka with a very welcome shipload of wheat and with the good news about a possible Russian-Spanish trade agreement with Alta California, he urged Baranov to make full use the then-uninhabited Alta California coastline near what is now Fort Ross, about 65 miles north of San Francisco, where a Russian trading post would be founded in 1812.

Rezanov then headed for St. Petersburg to report to the Tsar and to the Russian-America Company's headquarters. He tried to ride across Siberia to reach St. Petersburg but caught pneumonia three times; each time, he failed to recover fully before riding on. During his third relapse, he toppled off his horse and died in Siberia on 8 March 1807 near Krasnoyarsk.

Doña Concepción never received this terrible news and waited patiently for him for five years, until at last she learned from a visiting Russian officer that Rezanov was long dead. The officer gave her the locket which she had given Rezanov before he left on his journey, telling her that Rezanov's last words had been of her. She subsequently devoted her life to caring for others, by joining the Dominican sisterhood in Benicia, California and serving in it until her own death in 1857.

Although the Spanish government in California officially forbade its citizens from trading with foreigners, lively contraband exchanges began with Rezanov's visit and continued apace. The *Californios* supplied the Russians with wheat, fruit trees, cattle, and horses. Because the *Californios* manufactured very few products themselves, they were quite eager to obtain Russian-made metal and wooden goods, e.g., plows, axes, nails, wheels, metal cookware, and longboats (ships' boats).

When Mexico became independent of Spain in 1821, foreign trade was no longer against the law: *Californios* could now trade not only with the Russians in Fort Ross but also with any American or European ships calling at ports along the California coast. A wide range of manufactured items was involved in this commerce, e.g., small ships, barrels, tar, bricks, leather, boots, wool, flour, furniture, candles, and soap.

For local color, it is worth quoting here Dana's account of the Russians at San Francisco in 1835–1836 (punctuation as in the original):

> Here [San Francisco], at anchor, and the only vessel, was a brig [a square-rigged vessel with two masts] under Russian colors, from Asitka [i.e., Sitka], which had come down to winter, and to take in a supply of tallow and grain, great quantities of which are raised in the missions at the head of the bay. The second day after our arrival, we went aboard the brig...
>
> Although it was quite comfortable weather, and we had nothing on but straw hats, shirts, and duck trowsers, and were barefooted, [the Russians] had, every man of them, double-soled boots, coming up to the knees and well greased [i.e., waterproofed with beef fat applied by hand in a melted or soft state]; thick woolen trowsers, frocks, waistcoats, pea-jackets, woolen caps, and everything in true Nova Zembla rig [Nova Zembla is a barren archipelago in the Arctic Ocean]; and on the warmest days they made no change...
>
> They lived upon grease; eat it, drink it, slept in the midst of it, and their clothes were covered with it. To a Russian, grease is the greatest luxury.... It seems as if it were this saturation which makes them stand cold and rain so well.[4]

Although the *Californios* and the Russian-American Company wanted to expand their bilateral trade and to win official sanction for it, Tsar Nicholas I personally vetoed this idea. An arch-conservative, he refused to grant diplomatic recognition to the new Mexican Republic because he equated it with "revolution"—not only in Mexico itself but also, by extension, perhaps even in autocratic Russia.

In 1815, Semyon Yakovlevich Unkovsky, a Russian lieutenant, sailed around the world with the twin goals of delivering supplies to Russian America and opening Russian trade with Alta California. The New Archangel (i.e., Sitka)-to-San Francisco leg of his voyage took place from 25 July to 18 August 1815. Here are some of the points he made about the port of San Francisco:

> The locale of the port of San Francisco can be called unique in the world. The climate is fine and the soil is fertile, although still little cultivated. This territory gives promise of a large population in the future; at the present time under Spanish ownership this beautiful land is in almost a semi-wild state. The population of the Spanish colony is negligible, with one mission [Mission San Francisco de Asís, established in 1776] of two Franciscan friars; this small colony is completely under the influence of the savage Californians [i.e., the Indians]...
>
> Our sojourn at the port of San Francisco was most pleasant. The hospitality of the commandant, Don [Luis] Argüello and the two monks, Father Ramón and Father Juan, afforded us much and varied pleasure. For visiting the vicinity some excellent riding horses of the Andalusian breed with escorts were offered, and during the time that we were freed from our work we did not fail to take advantage of this offer...

10. Foreigners in Alta California

The [Russian-American Company] brig *Chirikov* raised anchor the day after our arrival and sailed back to Sitka with a supply of wheat [2,749 bushels] and salt.[5]

Achille Schabelski was the Russian interpreter aboard the Russian frigate *Apollon* when it visited California in 1822–1823. He was not favorably impressed by the Spaniards of Alta California, writing as follows:

> The Presidio is a large square structure of adobe bricks divided into several chambers and having more the appearance of a stable than of a European fort.
>
> It's difficult to fully present the miserable state in which the Spaniards in California live. An observer among them believes himself transported into the 16th century. The construction of the dwellings, their dress and that of their wives, the weapons, the furniture, and their opinions and prejudices make them appear to be contemporaries of Cortez or Pizarro. [Hernán Cortez, 1485–1547, won Mexico for Spain; Francisco Pizarro, 1478–1541, conquered the Inca Empire for Spain.] Possessing a land which enjoys a delightful temperature and extreme fertility, they make not the least effort to profit by their wonderful situation.
>
> The forts, built both at San Francisco and at Monterey, fallen into disrepair, are supplied with cannons on decrepit, old gun carriages which break at the first discharge of the cannon. I noticed in San Francisco such a one which dated from the year 1740. In visiting Monterey, I found only one soldier, asleep.[6]

The Russian writer Dmitry Zavalishin had this to say about the *Californios* in 1824:

> [In 1824] ... there was a complete lack of practical knowledge on the part of the *Californios*. Having heretofore been provided with everything [i.e., both by nature and by Spain before Mexico became independent in 1821], they did not think to engage themselves in anything except service [here Zavalishin is referring to serving as ranch hands], and in order to avoid boredom they occupied themselves with card playing and cockfighting in their free time...
>
> In the use of labor-saving devices the local Californios had not yet even surpassed the simple mill hand stone, and the women prepared flour by grinding the kernels on a slab with a pestle, just as paints are pulverized...
>
> The Californios were quite unable to derive household benefits from the most lavish gifts of nature. Despite the unusual abundance of cattle, fowl, and game, they were quite unable to prepare meat in salted, smoked, or dried-broth form as a domestic reserve or for sale to visiting ships. All the preparation of meat consisted of cutting it into thin slices, heavily rubbing both sides of the slices with a mixture of salt and ground cayenne pepper, and drying it in the sun.[7]

Kirill Khlebnikov, who for 15 years was the Russian Company's Russian-American agent in Alta California, came to know the province very well, visiting it 13 times and became able to communicate well in Spanish. Some of his observations, dating from about 1828, are as follows:

> The inhabitants of Spanish extraction who settled in Upper California long ago, as well as the soldiers and civilians who were transferred [there] later from various Mexican provinces, number no more than 2,000 males and up to 4 1/2 thousand souls of both sexes in 4 presidios and 3 villages and towns...

The Californian women are surprisingly fecund; nearly every couple has no fewer than 10 children, and many have from 15 to 18...

The Californios are generally indolent, and lacking in foresight, and their simple manner attests to their childlike state. Now the Mexican leadership is trying to introduce European customs, beginning with dress, dances, and food...

Californios are excellent horse riders. They begin to ride from childhood and with age they become skilled horsemen. They throw lassos unerringly over the horns of bulls and heads of horses when they have to catch them. They ride to hunt bears with lassos; after throwing one lasso over a bear's head and two over its legs, they lead it for a great distance. Often two men without any weapons and [with] only lassos set out on this dangerous pursuit...

The men do almost nothing, and if they can get the Indians from the missions for work, then they just walk about with their arms folded, having shown the Indians what to do. There is not one workman [i.e., not one craftsman] among them. Since the opening of free trade [beginning with the independence of Mexico in 1821] some inhabitants have begun to till the soil and sow wheat and become used to hard work, but they relinquish their idleness very, very reluctantly...

Californios always carry a large knife, which is wrapped up in something and placed behind their suede leggings; they use it at table. In arguments, they sometimes become heated to the point of craziness; sometimes, being unable to prove anything or to justify himself, one of them will instantly grasp his knife and without thinking stab his opponent...

When two or three persons [i.e., Californios] are invited to dinner, they are sure to bring ten or more friends with them without considering whether or not there is room on the ship for receiving them...

The slovenliness of the inhabitants is visible when approaching a settlement; everywhere around the houses are scattered the heads, horns, and hoofs of bulls, which usually every Saturday are driven to their yards and slaughtered, the meat and hides removed and the heads, hoofs, and innards discarded. Also, they never sweep away the refuse, not having the requisite place for it, and they spread it everywhere. After this [neglect] one can imagine what sort of air prevails over these settlements...

Most of these observations apply to the longtime residents, who are steeped in the old ways. The young people, especially those coming from Mexico (where education has been introduced) are very civil and affable and would perhaps be hospitable if only they were acquainted with housekeeping and thrift...

Given the present indifference of the inhabitants and the negligence of the missionaries, few of the country's products are exported. The main exports are uncured cattle hides, tallow, wheat, and a small number of [sea] otters...

California abounds with a variety of products, and with proper organization it could export rather a lot of cattle hides, horns, tallow, lard, wheat, flour, frijoles, peas, barley, corn, dried fruit, salted olives, olive oil, cheese, butter, salt, flax, hemp, cotton, sheep's wool, suede, ham, salted beef, soap, sea otter skins, spirits, and wine...

Money [for Alta California] is rarely provided by Mexico, and revenue is insufficient, so the government is in arrears to all of its employees. Under the Spanish government before the outbreak of the revolution in Mexico no funds were sent for about 12 years, and the lower officials received nothing (save provisions as part of their salaries), and [later] they were deprived of all their possessions, for the republican government did not assume any responsibility for these payments....[8]

10. Foreigners in Alta California

Non-Russian foreign comments are worth noting here, too. For example, Sir George Simpson's book, *An Overland Journey Around the World* (1847), chronicles his visit to Alta California in 1841–1842. Simpson had risen quickly through the ranks of the Hudson's Bay Company and before his 40th birthday was the governor of the company's extensive holdings in Canada. During his round-the-world travels, he made a lengthy detour to California to decide whether the Hudson Bay Company should invest there. He wanted to purchase Fort Ross but a Swiss immigrant named John Sutter, who was the proprietor of a 48,800-acre fortified trading post at the confluence of the Sacramento and American rivers, bought it first.

Lightly edited, here are some of Simpson's remarks about the *Californios* of San Francisco:

> The Californians of San Francisco number between 2,000 and 2,500, about 700 belonging to the village or *pueblo* of San José de Guadalupe and the remainder occupying about 30 farms of various sizes...
>
> On the score of industry, these good folks, as also their brethren of the other ports, are perhaps the least promising colonists of a new country in the world, being in this respect decidedly inferior to what the savages [the Indians] had become under the training of the priests, so that the spoliation [i.e., the secularization] of the missions, excepting that it has opened the province to general enterprise, has directly tended to nip civilization in the bud.
>
> ... the population of California ... has been drawn from the most indolent variety of an indolent species, being composed of superannuated troopers and retired office-holders and their descendants.
>
> [The *Californios*] were not likely to toil much more than what the cheap bounty of nature afforded them—horses to ride and beef to eat, with hides and tallow to exchange for such other supplies as they wanted. In a word, they displayed more than the proverbial indolence of a pastoral people, for they did not even devote their idle hours to the tending of their herds.
>
> As one might have expected, the children improved on the example of their parents through the influence of a systematic education—an education which gave them the *lasso* as a toy in infancy and the horse as a companion in boyhood, which, in short, trained them from the cradle to be mounted bullock-hunters, and nothing else; and if anything could aggravate their laziness, it was the circumstance that many of them dropped, as it were, into ready-made competency [i.e., ready-made prosperity] by sharing in the lands and cattle of the plundered missions.
>
> The only trouble which the Californians really take with their cattle is to brand them, when young, with their respective marks, and even this single task savors more of festivity than of labor.[9]

When Simpson wrote the above, there were probably about 800 Americans residing in Alta California, and perhaps about 500 other foreigners of various nationalities.[10] Most of them were living in the Sacramento Valley or near San Francisco Bay. Unlike the *Californios*, who much preferred the freedom, excitement, and "nobility" of ranching, almost all of these foreigners devoted themselves, if they worked at all, entirely to business.

As the American historian Justin Harvey Smith, a specialist on the U.S.-Mexican War, would put it in 1919,

> Some of the Americans took the trouble to go through the process of acquiring [Mexican] citizenship, and so could become the legal owners of land; but far the greater number were mere squatters, or else hung about the ranches of other Americans, working a little, hunting or trapping more, but mainly waiting for something to turn up.
> They were in general a rough-looking set: ... while some had excellent brains and hearts of gold, the scale ran down to a very low point. Little work and less law was the motto of not a few ... probably almost all agreed in despising the inefficiency of the native [i.e., the *Californio*], his passion for dress and dancing, his guitar, his bland smile, and his dainty politeness.[11]

In contrast to such rowdy Americans, Russian officials were far more polished. Alexander Markov, for example, worked as a supercargo (cargo expert) for the Russian-American Company and published some perceptive comments on his 1845 stay in Alta California. At that time, most Russian accounts of this region were drafted in a heavy, impersonal, bureaucratic manner. Markov, however, wrote what was essentially a chatty travel account and presented his views in a light, humorous way.

For example, when his ship was about 80 miles off the California coast, the navigator reported to the captain that a sailor had just died on board. Markov tells the reader:

> [The sailors] put the body in sailcloth, tied two cannon balls to its feet and pushed it overboard.
> "Well, mate, you were just sick of hardtack [i.e., ship's biscuit]," said one sailor, perched on the railing of the ship so as to receive the body; "Good lord, how he has put on weight; it'll be four puds [a pud was an old Russian unit of weight equal to 36.11 pounds]. Well, say farewell to his world. Ooh, how smartly he plunged to visit Leptune [i.e., Neptune], it seems he smelled the vodka." [here the sailor is referring to a legend that vodka spouted from Neptune's trident.][12]

In a more serious vein, however, Markov explained that the often foggy and always rock-bound approach to the port of San Francisco demanded seamanship of the highest caliber. He wrote that, to starboard, he and his mates could see the Farallon rocks, even though they were from time to time shrouded in fog, and he managed to take a bearing of the port of San Francisco itself. The Russians then set more sail and, after more than six hours of hard work, knew they were now near the shore because they could hear the waves breaking on it. Because of the fog, however, they still could not see the shore itself.

10. Foreigners in Alta California

Their position now seemed to be perilous, but the captain knew what he was doing and got the ship safely through the Golden Gate and into San Francisco Bay. The fog was at last behind them, and they could see many other ships anchored off the Presidio. As they dropped anchor, someone aboard an American brig shouted cheerfully to them, "Well done, Russians!"[13]

Here now is part of Markov's account of the subsequent meeting he and his ship's captain had with William A. Richardson, an Englishman who had initially deserted from a whaling ship in San Francisco and who was now the captain of that port:

> When we entered, [Richardson] arose smartly, bowed toward us, and asked us in English to seat ourselves near the divan, and he himself went into the opposite room.... After a minute he returned with a book in English in his hands and began to read the [Mexican] regulation on the right to trade within the limits of San Francisco.
>
> We ourselves knew very well that a ship did not have the right to enter San Francisco Bay without first having stopped in Monterey and obtained permission for the right to trade from [Alta] California's governor, who resided there permanently. But we did not want to go to Monterey by ship, because San Francisco lay closer to our course; moreover, it was surrounded by the settlements where we had to buy wheat, frijoles, peas corn, meat, tallow, *manteca* [lard], etc. for the island of Sitka. Furthermore, it was possible to reach Monterey from San Francisco by ship in one day, but for the trip back to San Francisco from Monterey one had to spend three weeks or more on account of the usual contrary current and constantly adverse NW winds.
>
> Thus, in order not to go to Monterey, we resorted to [a] stratagem: we deliberately lowered the main topgallant mast, as if it had been broken by a storm, and we told the captain of the port that without repairing the mast we could not go to Monterey and intended to reside here...
>
> Within 2 days we received permission from the governor of [Alta] California, Don [José] Castro, to buy in cash but not to sell or barter any of our goods without paying a special duty.[14]

11

Governing the *Californios*

For 79 years, i.e., from 1769, when Spain first began its occupation of California, until 1848, when Mexico was forced to cede Alta California to the United States under the terms of the Treaty of Guadalupe Hidalgo, most of this vast region was governed only very lightly, first by Spaniards and later by Mexicans. *How well* it was governed is a very different matter.

Richard Griswold del Castillo, for example, notes that the *Californios* rebelled against Mexican governors mainly because they wanted local rule and influence. Mexico itself experienced many rebellions against its central governments. These rebellions stemmed from a lack of agreement over legitimacy: Spanish authority was not completely rejected by many Mexicans, especially by devout Catholics. Moreover, Mexican governors tried to implement the ideals and laws of the new republic, but these were not always acceptable to some of the most powerful men in the land.[1]

In any case, the bottom line was that political life was unstable and even kaleidoscopic: all told, there were 10 Spanish governors and 14 Mexican governors.[2] Jockeying for political power became a full time job and sometimes led to revolutions and counter-revolutions. These eventually became the quickest and surest way to win and hold on to power.

Spanish Governors

From Spain's point of view, Alta California was only an extremely isolated frontier province and with so few cultural resources to offer that Spanish officers and soldiers alike tried hard to avoid being posted there. Over time, however, the Spanish did a remarkable job of turning a wilderness initially peopled only by numerous but autonomous Indian tribelets

11. Governing the Californios

into a more organized landscape lightly dotted with presidios, missions, pueblos, and ranchos.[3]

Before Mexico won its independence from Spain in 1821, the *Californios* had virtually no say in the selection of the men who governed them. The best description of these men was *gobernante*, which meant the official who was actually in direct control of a given region, regardless of his official title.[4] These generally able officials were always senior Spanish military officers and were very likely to be *peninsulars* as well—that is, full-blooded Spaniards who had been born in Spain—because nearly all political positions in the Spanish Indies were reserved for the members of this ruling class.

The 10 Spanish governors (Pedro Fages and José Joaquin de Arrillaga both served twice but are counted here only once each), with their dates of office and a few brief comments on them, are as follows:

1. *Gaspar de Portolá (1768–1770)*

    Gaspar de Portolá had been a soldier in the Spanish army in Italy and Portugal before being appointed governor of Las Californias from 1768 to 1770. A good organizer and a good explorer, as noted earlier, he pioneered the Spanish settlement of California.

2. *Pedro Fages (1770–1774 and 1782–1791)*

    After Portolá left California in 1770, Fages was in charge of the Presidio of Monterey. Later that same year, he led an expedition from Monterey to explore the eastern side of San Francisco Bay. In 1772 he explored even further east, becoming the first European to see the Sacramento-San Joaquin River Delta, the Central Valley, and the distant Sierra Nevada mountains. Fages had a nickname—*el oso*, "the bear"–which he earned while hunting bears near San Luis Obispo. He quarreled with Father Junípero Serra and was replaced by Fernando Rivera y Moncada in 1774.

3. *Fernando Rivera y Moncada (1774–1777)*

    Rivera, too, soon found himself in conflict with Serra when he (Rivera) opposed the settlement of Yerba Buena (present day San Francisco). After the Indians sacked Mission San Diego in 1775, it was Rivera's job to repress their revolt. In so doing, however, he entered the chapel with a drawn sword and forcibly removed an Indian member of the mission—in direct defiance of missionary orders. For this violation of ecclesiastical asylum, he was excommunicated by the Franciscans. His last assignment was as military commander in Loreto. He was killed during an Indian uprising on the lower Colorado River in 1781.

4. Filipe de Neve (1777–1782)

Neve was a founder of the city of Los Angeles and also helped to establish missions at Santa Barbara and San José. Like his predecessors, he also quarreled with Serra. Their disputes arose over the pros and cons of the eventual secularization of the missions and the distribution then of mission lands to the Indians and to the Spanish soldiers posted at the missions.

5. José Antonio Roméu (1791–1792)

Roméu was a career officer who steadily advanced in rank, but he appears to have had little if any direct contact with California. His military record shows that his most challenging assignment was to lead a Colorado River campaign against the rebellious Yuma Indians.

6. José Joaquín de Arrillaga (1792–1794 and 1800–1814)

Bancroft portrays Arrillaga as a competent official who obeyed orders so well and so tactfully that he made no enemies, but who lacked originality and "enthusiastic confidence in the future of the province."[5] In 1806, Arrillaga traded goods with the Russian-American Company manager Nikolai Rezanov, who had come down to Fort Ross, California from Sitka, Alaska.

7. Diego de Borica (1794–1800)

Working with Father Fermin Lasuén, Borica decided that five more missions were needed in 1795 along El Camino Real, the major travel artery of Alta California. For this reason, Borica sent out expeditions from four different missions to find suitable places for new settlements that would not be more than one day's travel apart. The reason for this requirement was that longer trips would require military escorts. The first new missionary site, selected in 1796, was Mission San José.

8. Pedro de Alberni (1747–1802)

Alberni was a career soldier who did exceptionally well when assigned as commander of the Spanish fort at Nootka Sound in British Columbia, Canada. Despite the hardships of this remote post, he erected buildings with boards made by the local Indians, dug wells, and established an efficient bakery for his men. Equally successful in later assignments, e.g., as overall commander of the four military garrisons Spain had in California (at Monterey, Santa Barbara, San Diego, and San Francisco), he was appointed Interim Governor of California in 1800 and served in that capacity until a new governor was assigned.

9. *José Darío Argüello (1814–1815)*
Under orders from Governor Filipe de Neve, Argüello led the first 10 Los Angeles *pobladores* ("original setters") and their livestock overland to found the Pueblo de Los Angeles on 4 September 1781. He later commanded the presidios of San Francisco and Monterey. In 1795 he was given a land grant, the Rancho de las Pulgas (Ranch of the Fleas), which, at 35,260 acres, was the largest land grant on the San Francisco Peninsula. Located in what is now San Mateo County, it encompassed the present communities of San Mateo, Belmont, San Carlos, Redwood City, Atherton, and Menlo Park.

10. *Pablo Vincente Solá (1815–1822)*
Solá was the last colonial governor. He presided over the transfer to Mexican rule which was accomplished without any disruption.

Mexican Governors

When discussing the political instability of *Californio* culture, Leonard Pitt wrote that

> its stock-in-trade was intrigue, not debate; rebellion, not compromise; élite leadership, not mass support; and, of course, the flaming *pronunciamiento* [i.e., a declaration of insurrection]. When everything else failed, men reached for their guns.... Because the Californians mixed serious ideological goals with naïve methods, their politics assumed a tragicomic air.... Governor Carlos Carrillo knew that his family laughingly compared him to Sancho Panza.[6]

Major factors in the chronic instability of the Mexican government, and some key reasons why the Mexican northern borderlands were rarely governed effectively include the following[7]:

- Mexico's republican regime was very shaky from the beginning, with continuing political struggles between centralists and federalists.
- The far northern frontier towns and provinces were always a low priority, first for Spain and then for Mexico. They received few resources because they were so far from the center of power and because communication was so slow.
- *Californios* themselves fundamentally disagreed about the proper role the Mexican government should play in their own lives. Some wanted much more autonomy and therefore less government; others called for a much stronger government

presence. The outcome of this stalemate was drift, indecision, and civil rivalry.
- When the Mexican governors tried to implement the new ideals and laws of an independent Mexico, rich and politically- influential Mexicans objected to them and found ways around them. The best example here is the secularization of the missions. The ostensible goal of this policy was to give freedom and land to the long-suffering Mission Indians themselves but, in practice, *Californio* families managed to use the policy to enrich themselves and their own families. From the Mexican government's point of view that was, of course, the unstated but real purpose of secularization.

As the first step in understanding the confusing political landscape of Upper California, it is best to begin with geography. The first seat of government during the Spanish occupation of California, which began in 1769, was Loreto. Both Baja and Alta California were jointly administered from there as a single entity known as *Las Californias*, which existed from 1768 to 1804. Its military commander was stationed in Monterey. In 1804, however, *Las Californias* was split into two provinces: Alta ("upper") California, and Baja ("lower") California.

As Alta California became more important than Baja California, however, the capital was relocated from Loreto to Monterey in 1777. Baja California was thereafter ruled by a lieutenant governor based in Loreto. Monterey would remain the capital of Alta California until 1849, when the seat of government was successively moved to San Jose, Vallejo, Benicia and, finally, in 1854, to Sacramento.

Military governors ruled from Monterey until 1777, while civil governors administered both Alta and Baja California from Monterey after 1777. In a revolution in 1821, Mexican patriots pushed the Spanish from power; after 1822, California was administered from Monterey as a province of Mexico.

The revolution ushered in a long period of unrest. Although California was far away from the main whirlpool of political struggles and thus escaped the bloodshed that characterized other parts of Mexico for many years, its already-frayed ties with Mexico unraveled even further. California governors also had to deal with conspiratorial maneuvering by their enemies. Mexico City was so far away and it lacked both the will and the means to help the *Californios*. As a result, many of them deeply resented Mexican rule. Well-stoked with self-confidence and regional pride, they would increasingly favor quasi-independence, full independence, or even foreign rule by some foreign power, e.g., by England or the United States.

The *Californios* endured a series of Mexican-appointed governors, all of whom either died in office or were forced out of office. These men were generally mediocre, autocratic, and far more interested in their own and their families' well-being than in that of their constituents. Native *Californio* governors, however, were not much better. They were usually ambitious, self-appointed men who held office *pro tempore* until Mexico City learned of the old governor's death or overthrow and finally got around to replacing him, either by appointing a new governor or merely by confirming the acting governor in office. This was a very slow process at best.

Californios had such negative experiences with their own governors that many of them strongly resented Mexico City's role in their internal affairs. They believed that they themselves were best able to manage their own unique way of life. When being interviewed by Thomas Savage, José María Amador was quite outspoken on the many failings of the *Californio* governors. Amador believed that they had ruined the economy, while at the same time enriching themselves and their cronies.

In addition, he blamed them for displaying very poor leadership in defending California from the American invaders during the U.S-Mexican War. In his judgment, what led to the relative ease with which the Americans took over California was that both Governor Pío Pico and General José Castro quickly fled to Mexico, leaving the *Californios* leaderless. When Pico and Castro disappeared, Amador said, all military resistance against the invaders came to an end.[8]

For better or worse, the 14 Mexican governors of Alta California, together with their dates in office and a few comments on them, are as follows:

1. *Pablo Vincente Solá, a holdover from the Spanish regime (1815–1822)*

The Viceroyalty of New Spain came to an end after Spain's defeat in the Mexican War of Independence in 1821. Solá, a serious, formal man, was a strict disciplinarian and would reprimand both officers and men publicly if he noticed that anything was out of order. His only major failure was that under his leadership Monterey was so poorly defended that it was sacked by a pirate attack in 1818.

Solá made seven large land grants to *Californios*. These included the 14,403-acre Rancho Rincón de San Pascual ("rincón" means "nook" or "corner" in Spanish), which is now the site of Pasadena, South Pasadena, portions of San Marino, and other smaller communities.

2. *Luis Antonio Argüello, acting governor (1822–1825)*

Argüello was the first native *Californio* to serve as governor of Alta California. He and his second wife inherited the enormous Rancho de la Pulgas. It embraced present-day San Mateo, Belmont, San Carlos, Redwood City, Atherton, and Menlo Park.

Argüello was a courageous man who could not easily be intimidated or bullied. Antonio María Osio (1800–1878), a respected *Californio*, recounts how, despite being in great pain because of a dislocated foot, Argüello made a formal call on Solá, then the new governor. During the meeting, Argüello had to support himself physically by using his sheathed sword as a cane. When Solá criticized him violently and unjustly over a minor issue, Argüello slightly moved the tip of his sword against the floor. Solá, quick to notice this, asked him why he had done so. Argüello replied that he wanted to be ready to defend himself in case Solá tried to beat him with his own cane, which Solá then held in his own hands. The end result was that Solá backed down; the two men were on good working terms thereafter.[9]

3. *José María de Echeandía, twice governor (1825–1831, and again—in the south only—from 1832 to 1833)*

Echeandía implemented the Mexican government's policy of secularizing the missions and distributing their lands to influential *Californios*. The former soldier José María Amador did not give Echeandía a good report card, writing that

> the troops were so abandoned by Echeandía that they lacked almost all the things necessary for survival; even basic provisions were lacking on several occasions. Consequently, there arose a marked discontent that finally exploded among the troops of Monterey in 1828. The troops picked up their weapons and abandoned the presidio and their officers, and they started wandering about in the countryside, each one of them trying to find a way to survive...
>
> At the end of 1829, the troops of Monterey rebelled again due to the same cause: the general state of abandonment they were in. The artillery detachment and the leather jacket soldiers [enlisted men] took their officers captive and put them in the jail.[10]

Echeandía so disliked the chilly, foggy climate of Northern California that he moved his headquarters to San Diego. Some of his contemporaries regarded him as a capricious despot who would carry out any whim of his own without regard for the results; others felt that he simply lacked energy; still others said that he was popular but overindulgent, careless, and a man of undecided character.[11] He continued living in California after the American takeover in 1847 until his death in 1871.

4. *Manuel Victoria, an abbreviated tour of duty (1831–1832)*

A revolt against his governorship resulted in a short (12 month) tenure in office. His removal and exile were due to his nullifying the order of his predecessor to secularize the missions and to distribute their holdings as land grants. Victoria defeated some rebel *Californios* in December 1831 at Cahuenga, near Los Angeles, but he was so badly wounded there that he had flee to Mexico. He never returned to Alta California.

5. *Agustin Vincente Zamorano, in the north only (1832–1833)*

After Governor Manuel Victoria was removed, Zamorano led a rebellion in Northern California, putting himself at the end of a small group of rebels in Monterey. He then served as provisional governor at Monterey, while José María de Echeandía (see above) was provisional governor at the Pueblo de Los Angeles in the south.

6. *José Figueroa, dividing up mission lands (1833–1835)*

In 1833 the Mexican Congress passed "An Act for the Secularization of the Missions of California." Figueroa supervised the process of secularization and the concomitant expulsion of Spanish Franciscan missionaries. He also issued 47 land grants to *Californios* and opposed the Híjar-Padrés colonization effort of 1834. Figueroa's two years in power are remembered as a time of tranquility in an often-turbulent land.[12]

7. *José Castro, acting governor (1835–1836)*

Together with Juan Bautista Alvarado, José Castro argued that the governors of Alta California should be born there and he called for a semi-independent status for this region. Courage in combat, however, was not his strong point. During one low-level skirmish in Alta California, for example, Pío Pico reports that Castro, then a general, was hiding behind a small hill near the only cannon. Pico says that Castro

> was wrapped in a serape [thus concealing his uniform], and instead of his [military] hat, he had another made of straw such as is made by the Indians. Indignant at his behavior, I [Pico] told him, "You are not a General, nor are you anything you are just a vaquero." He replied that I should not worry and I responded this was the time to exhibit his uniform and not be masquerading.[13]

Castro was a chief participant in the overthrow of Governor Gutiérrez in 1836, becoming the commanding general and the acting governor. During the U.S.-Mexican War, he led *Californio* forces against the Americans; when defeated, he fled to Sinaloa, Mexico, but returned to California in 1848. In 1856 he was appointed governor and military commander of Baja California but in 1860 he was assassinated by a Mexican bandit.

Bancroft sums him up as follows:

> Indeed, his record as a public man in Upper California was, on the whole, not a bad one. He had much energy, was popular with most classes, was true to his friends, and as a public officer fairly honest. He must have had some good qualities, yet it is clear that he had some very bad ones. He was addicted to many vices, and when drunk, especially in his later years was rough to the verge of brutality; yet a kind-hearted man when sober.[14]

8. *Nicolás Gutiérrez, twice acting governor (both times in 1836)*
Gutiérrez was ousted in 1836 by a revolt led by Juan Bautista Alverado, who was helped by a group of American settlers led by Isaac Graham. The sole "battle" of this revolt consisted of the insurgents firing a single artillery round at the governor's residence. This was enough, however, to cause Gutiérrez and his men to surrender. They were detained at Cabo San Lucas, at the tip of the Baja California peninsula, on an English brig before being sent to Mexico. Bancroft states that Gutiérrez was "an easy going, faithful officer of ordinary abilities and not very strict morals."[15]

9. *Mariano Chico, governor for three months (1836)*
Chico served one of the shortest terms as governor—only from April to July 1836. He was very unpopular and, apparently, not very brave. Moreover, at one point he appeared in the place of honor at a public function—accompanied by his mistress, whom he tried to pass off as his niece, and who was at that time under arrest for adultery.[16] Fearing that a revolt was brewing, he returned to Mexico, ostensibly to get more troops, but was reprimanded for leaving his post and did not return to California.

10. *Juan Bautista Alvarado, twice governor (1836–1837 and again in 1838–1842)*
At age 27, Alvarado was appointed governor but the city council of Los Angeles protested. This led to a brief civil war, at end of which Alvarado was recognized as governor. During the secularization of the missions and subsequent parceling out their land to *Californios*, Alvarado took no land for himself, though he did legitimately trade in ranch properties.

Alvarado married Doña Martina Castro on 24 August 1839 in Santa Clara, but did not attend his own wedding, arranging instead for his half-brother, José Antonio Estrada, to stand in for him. The explanation Alvarado put forward to explain this unusual "wedding by proxy" was that a French admiral aboard the French frigate *Artemisa* had just arrived in Monterey and wanted to meet with him.[17] In fact, however, Alvarado was drunk at the time and was unable to function. After the wedding, he lived with his bride in Monterey but continued to visit his mistress, Raymunda, who lived nearby. One of his daughters said that Raymunda had refused to marry him because of his excessive drinking.

In January 1842, fearing that the United States planned to attack Mexico, Mexican president López de Santa Anna sent Brigadier General Manuel Micheltorena (see below) to California with 300 unruly convict-troops. Before Micheltorena reached Monterey, however, American Commodore Thomas ap Catesby Jones ("ap" means "son of" in Welsh) mistakenly thought that war had broken out between the United States and Mexico and sailed into Monterey Bay to demand the surrender of the presidio there. Faced with overwhelming American naval power, Alvarado had no choice but to surrender.

After the Bear Flag Revolt and the outbreak of war in 1846, Pío Pico (see below) and José Castro would flee to Mexico; Alvarado would be captured. After his release, he spent the rest of the war on his estate in Monterey. He was offered the governorship but declined it.

11. *Carlos Antonio Carrillo, an ineffective leader (1837–1838)*

Carrillo, who had been a soldier, politician, and rancher, was appointed governor in 1837. He made Los Angeles his capital but during his two years there he could function only ineffectively because Alvarado (see above) refused to give up his own consuming interest in the governorship. His jurisdiction was never recognized in Northern California.

Carrillo was personally popular, and his failure as governor is said to have been due chiefly to his own lack of assertiveness vis-à-vis Alvarado.[18] Pío Pico gives this glimpse of him:

> Carlos Antonio Carrillo was a man of great height and bulk—of handsome appearance and [a] truly fine looking man; bushy beard and with very curly, black hair; fair, rosy complexion and large black eyes. He was in the habit of always keeping his head covered with a black handkerchief, tied with a knot in front and his hat way back on his head. He was a man of strong and capricious temperament. Some days he conducted himself as if he were a lunatic. When he was a soldier, or, better said, when he was a corporal and a sergeant, he was exceedingly despotic—with those under his command.[19]

12. *Manuel Micheltorena (1842–1845)*

Micheltorena was instrumental in the secularization of mission lands. However, with his loyalties rooted in the politics of Mexico City, he encountered criticism, opposition, and, eventually, open warfare from the *Californios*. They were infuriated by his motley "army" of undisciplined soldiers, which they derisively referred to as *cholos*—a pejorative term which could mean either "mixed-race children of Indian-Negro parents" or "thieves and pickpockets rounded up from the jails."

José María Amador, a former presidio soldier himself, said that Micheltorena's battalion

> was composed mainly of heartless people, men taken out of the prisons and from the presidio of Chapala [a fort in central Mexico], and with a great number of officers who should have decorated the chains [of a prison] ... many of them were as bad or worse than the most wicked soldiers under their command.[20]

Not surprisingly, in 1845 these despised men were unable to win a skirmish with the troops of Juan Bautista Alvarado, so Micheltorena had to leave for Mexico. Amador reports, however, that "up until the last moment [of his departure], deference was paid to him according to his rank."[21]

13. *Pío Pico, an able leader (1845–1846)*

Pico has been discussed earlier in this book but a bit more can be added here. He was one of most able *Californios* and, as mentioned earlier, has left to posterity a *Narración Historica* (Historical Narrative) which gives good details about the political processes of the time. One of Pico's later biographers (Martin Cole, former Curator of the Pío Pico State Historical Monument in California) had this to say about him in 1973—and, by extension, about most other *Californio* politicians as well:

> In his early manhood, Pío Pico was first and foremost a revolutionist. It is necessary to understand that revolutions and counter-revolutions in the Mexican period were the accepted manner for political advancement. Governorships during those years of unrest sometimes changed hands several times a year, and a governor might be in and out and then back in office in a short space of time. One persistent protagonist was Pío Pico.[22]

After serving as governor for 20 days as in 1832, Pico served in this role twice more—1845–1846 and again in 1853. When American troops occupied Los Angeles and San Diego in 1846 during the U.S-Mexican War, however, Pico fled to Sonora. His ostensible purpose was to persuade the Mexican Congress to send troops to defend Alta California. There was absolutely no chance the Congress could or would do this, however, so his real purpose was to avoid being captured by the Americans. He did not return to Los Angeles until after the end of the war, at which point he only reluctantly accepted Mexico's defeat.

In his *Narración Historica*, Pico made a special point of denying the widespread rumor that he had pocketed the money generated by the secularization of the missions. He strongly rebutted this charge, writing that it was not true that

> in the last days of my command in California I had sold the missions, receiving twenty thousand dollars or more for them, which I had taken with me when I left the country...

11. *Governing the* Californios

Some [i.e., some of the *Californios* who bought the missions] gave money or goods to Comandante-General Castro, but at no time did they give the amount that appears on the bill of sale. I can swear to the fact that not one single dollar came to my hands from the sale of the missions.

When I left the country the government owed me all my salaries as governor.... Although I did not have thousands of dollars on hand, I never lacked for money. My reputation and credit were good and on my word alone I could obtain anything I wished. That is why when the time came that I was to leave the country, I did not have to rely on public funds to cover the expense of my trip.[23]

14. *José María Flores, last governor before Mexico's surrender to the United States (1846–1847)*

After American forces had briefly occupied Los Angeles in August and September 1846, Flores called the Departmental Assembly of California back into session and reorganized the remaining California government. On 1 November 1846 he became the temporary governor and *comandante general*. Flores retained power during a short-lived local revolt, but after skirmishes with the militarily-superior Americans, he decided to flee California for the safety of Sonora. This he did on the night of 11 January 1847 after turning over his command to Andrés Pico (Pío Pico's brother), who would then negotiate with the Americans the Treaty of Cahuenga which ended the fighting in Alta California.

12

Californios in the U.S.-Mexican War of 1846–1848

If there was one underlying cause for this war, it was that a very weak, disorganized Mexico was physically too close to a very strong, unified, expansionist United States. As General Porfirio Díaz, president of Mexico from 1877 to 1911, would later put it (in Spanish) with a memorable turn of phrase: "Poor Mexico! So far from God, and so close to the United States."

From the American point of view there were two reasons for this controversial war, one ideological and the other practical. The ideological reason arose from the concept of Manifest Destiny. This was the belief that the American people were somehow "destined"—divinely or otherwise—to expand all the way from the Atlantic to the Pacific. The practical reason was that American control of California itself was held to be the vital keystone in the arch of Manifest Destiny.

From the Mexican point of view, the highly aggressive Americans had attacked Mexico unjustly and without any provocation. Mexico's acute sense of honor therefore ruled out the possibility of any surrender of its "national heritage," i.e., of Mexican territory, to the United States. The upshot was that Mexico felt that it had no choice but to go to war against the United States, even though some Mexican army officers did realize that, given the many weaknesses of Mexico and the many strengths of the United States, Mexico was virtually certain to be defeated in such a conflict.[1]

The results of the war are still very evident today. Having lost the war, Mexico was forced to surrender to the United States more than half a million square miles of its territory, i.e., the lands that now constitute California, Utah, Nevada, and parts of Arizona, New Mexico, Wyoming, and Colorado. The war also left a lasting—and continuing—residue of bitterness in the minds of many Mexicans, who believed that their honor had been trampled underfoot by their aggressive, more powerful, self-centered, and racist northern neighbor.

The "conquest of California" (Americans were using this phrase as early as 1847) differed fundamentally in scale and in character from combat in other theaters of the war. It took place on a more intimate and geographically more constricted stage. It did not have as many dramatic death-or-glory scenes, consisting instead only of a series of infrequent, small-scale, low-level incidents. As a result, there were very few American or Mexican casualties during the California campaigns: many towns in the Californias immediately surrendered without a single shot being fired by either side.

The modest amount of fighting that did occur involved only small groups of *Californios* who were opposed to the American invasion of California, and equally small groups of American soldiers, Marines, militiamen, and sailors who supported it. There was in fact only one "real" fight during the California campaigns in which the *Californios* themselves played an active and victorious role—the battle of San Pascual on 6–7 December 1846.

As will be seen in the following pages, this fight was where *Californio* lancers led by Captain Andrés Pico defeated American soldiers of General Stephen Watts Kearny. Lancers were the elite arm of the Mexican cavalry and were expert with their long lances, which in their previous jobs as *vaqueros* they had routinely used to slaughter large numbers of cattle. In combat, lances were fitted with a small piece of red cloth near their tips: this fluttered in the wind of the charge and was thought to frighten the enemy's horses.

Never having seen lancers in action, however, and having a low opinion of Mexicans in general, the Americans entirely failed to understand that lances were in fact a formidable close range weapon in the hands of experts. It was solely thanks to their lances that the *Californios* won this battle, which was both the bloodiest battle of the war and the high-water mark of *Californio* resistance to the American invaders.

Trying now to penetrate the fog which has long shrouded some details of this battle, it is clear that on 5 December 1846 Pico was camped at the Indian settlement (*rancheria*) of San Pascual in the San Pasqual Valley, which is located near San Diego. Although there is conflicting testimony on this point, Pico did not know that Kearny and 100 American soldiers were nearby. Kearny and his men were conducting a forced march of about 1,700 miles (this was said to have been the longest march in American military history) from Fort Leavenworth, Kansas to Alta California to take part in the war there.[2]

According to the *Californio* Antonio María Osio, an Indian rushed into Pico's camp at about 1:00 a.m. on 6 December 1846 and told him that the Americans were close at hand and were planning to attack the *Californios* at daybreak. Osio says that Pico questioned the Indian but refused to believe his story. The Indian left, only to come back half an hour later with news that the Americans were now getting closer. Upon hearing this, Pico ordered his troops to mount up and to prepare for battle. He would later tell a Mexican colleague that he had not wanted to fight then and there, but had been forced to do so by circumstances which made it impossible for him to do anything else.

The Americans had broken camp in the early hours of 6 December and were near San Pascual about daybreak. Reaching the top of a slight rise, they could see the *rancheria* of San Pascual spread out before them and could see that the *Californios* were already drawn up, ready and waiting to receive their charge. The Americans did indeed charge but because Captain Johnston and his 12 dragoons (light cavalrymen) were so eager and so well-mounted, they surged far ahead of the main body of American troops. The disastrous result was that by the time they reached the waiting *Californios*, they were quite alone.

Quick to take advantage of this mistake, the *Californios* stood fast, fired a volley, and then attacked the Americans with their lances. At the volley, Captain Johnston immediately fell dead with a bullet through his head; several other Americans were wounded. A furious hand-to-hand struggle then ensued, which ended only when the main body of Americans reached the scene of battle. Pico's men then turned and fled, hotly pursued by the Americans.

The Americans were mounted on a wide variety of horses and mules, some of them well-rested and fast but most of them tired and slow. The result was that the American line of pursuit was strung out for more than one mile. Osio says that Pico feigned a retreat to lure the Americans further on. What is certain is that after retreating some distance, Pico then suddenly wheeled his column and rushed back to attack the Americans. Osio describes this action as follows:

- When Pico made his decision to attack the Americans and so informed his men, they were not at all discouraged by the facts that Kearny's troops were better trained than they were and that the odds were therefore in his favor.

12. Californios *in the U.S.-Mexican War*

- When Pico saw that the Americans were now close to his lancers, he rode quickly away, pretending to be retreating. His plan was to lure Kearny's soldiers to a specific place where his lancers could attack them without any obstacles getting in their way. Pico therefore let the Americans ride into the place he had chosen and then shouted to his own troops: "Halt. Face the enemy. Charge!"
- Positioning himself at the head of his small force, Pico was relying on the impact on the Americans that his charging horses would have and on the skills of his lancers. As the first man to charge, he collided with the captain of Kearny's force, who fired at him with a pistol but missed. Pico then thrust his sword through the captain's body and killed him.[3]

The conflict was brief but hard-fought. It had been raining on and off for several days. As a result, the gunpowder in the muskets of the Americans was so damp that often they would not fire. However, since pistols were carried in holsters which could be closed or worn under a coat, their gunpowder was more likely to stay dry and the pistol was likely to fire.

Felicita, a San Pascual Indian woman who was present at the battle, vividly recalled this scene:

> The Americans did not shoot their guns many times; perhaps the rain had made the powder wet. They struck with [the butts of] their guns and used the sword, until the Mexicans used their long lances and the *riatas* [lariats]. The mules that the Americans rode were frightened and ran all through the willows by the river. After them rode the Mexicans on their swift horses, striking with the lance and *lassoing* with the *riata*; it was a very terrible time.[4]

With their muskets useless, the Americans had no choice but to swing them like clubs. Their own sabers were no match for the long lances of the *Californios*. José F. Palomares, one of Pico's men at the battle, described it in these words:

> With our lances and swords we attacked the enemy forces, who could not make good use of either their firearms or their swords…. We did not fire a single shot, the combat was more favorable to us with our sidearms (swords). Quickly the battle became so bloody that we became intermingled one with the other and barely were able to distinguish one from the other by voice and by the dim light which began to break.[5]

Hand-to-hand fighting raged for several minutes, until the rest of Kearny's force arrived with two howitzers. The *Californios* fled again—but this time it was not a ruse. The exact number of casualties on both sides is still uncertain, but good guesses are that 19 Americans were killed and 15 were wounded. Two of the American wounded died later. Both Kearny and Marine Corps Lieutenant Archibald Gillespie, his deputy, were badly wounded. *Californio* losses, on the other hand, were very light: no men were killed, 11 were wounded and one was captured.

Early in the morning of 7 December, the Americans began to travel toward San Diego. En route, however, they were attacked by *Californio* cavalrymen who had occupied a nearby hill, but a small group of American soldiers drove them off. No Americans were killed in this skirmish but several were badly wounded. The Americans were exhausted, however, and decided to camp on the hill and await reinforcements from San Diego.

Navy Lieutenant E.F. Beale, Kit Carson (who was then serving as Kearny's guide to California), and a local Indian volunteered to creep after dark through the *Californio* lines and seek help from American forces in San Diego. At great personal risk and after great suffering (e.g., walking for miles, barefoot, over cactus-studded land), they managed to accomplish this successfully. They learned, however, that Commodore Stockton already knew about Kearny's plight and had already sent a relief expedition toward San Pasqual.

The upshot was that Kearny and his surviving men finally arrived safely at San Diego on 12 December. Kearny later admitted that it was only the arrival of the rescue party from San Diego that had saved the Americans from complete disaster. Stockton and other naval officers considered the battle to have been a clear defeat for the U.S. Army. The *Californios*, for their part, saw the battle as a significant victory for their own side, and happily spread news of it around the region.[6]

13

Land Titles

Because land in Alta California had originally been very plentiful and very easy to acquire, *Californios* never had to resort to forging papers or lying to get land titles. Bureaucratically, the process was a slow but very simple one, and rancheros carried out the few legal steps needed "in simplicity and in good faith," as one of them later put it.[1]

However, as mentioned in the Introduction to this book, after the end of the U.S.-Mexican War in 1848 the U.S. Congress passed a law that called into question the validity of the land titles on which *Californio* ranches, and thus *Californio* prosperity, were ultimately based. Most of the Mexican land claims were formerly mission land and lay within about 30 miles of the California coast between Sonoma and San Diego, but a few were in the Central Valley. It is important to examine the land title issue in some detail, drawing heavily on W.W. [William Wilcox] Robinson's definitive study, *Land in California*, which was published by the University of California Press in 1948.[2]

Before discussing the chain of title for Rancho San Pascual in what is now Pasadena; the U.S. Land Commission's work; and, finally, the fraudulent Limantour Claim, some technical definitions are needed here:

- A chain of title is the sequence of ownership of a given piece of land, as confirmed by the public records of property transfers.
- A perfect title is a title deed for real estate that does not have any liens attached to it. Perfect titles are also sometimes referred to as good titles. Most properties are sold with perfect or good titles. Perfecting a title is the process of clearing all prior claims on a title to allow for its sale or assignment. Perfect titles stand in contrast to "quiet titles" or "cloud on titles," which are by definition imperfect titles."[3]

- Public and privately owned lands in California have traditionally been grouped according to title. For the purposes of this book, the most important lands, and the only ones which will be reviewed here, are the rancho and pueblo lands whose titles were granted by or were derived from Spanish or Mexican authority before the American period in California's history, and which later received United States confirmation. These lands included some of the very best pasture and agricultural properties in the state.[4]
- Ranchos made up the bulk of private land holdings in California in 1846. They generally extended along the coast, from Sonoma to south of San Diego. There were also some private land holdings in parts of the Central Valley but few, if any, in other parts of the state.

Chain of Title for Rancho San Pascual[5]

The historical background of Rancho San Pascual is only one of the many interesting stories of the 500 and more ranchos in California. A step-by-step discussion of it, drawn from W.W. Robinson's study, gives a good insight into traditional chain of title procedures there.

With the Spanish occupation of Alta California in 1769, the absolute title to the San Pascual area, as well as to all other parts of the region, was vested, under the provisions of the Laws of the Indies, in the King of Spain. The Indians were recognized as the technical owners of the territory they needed to sustain themselves but, in practice, the "civilizing process" they were subjected to by force greatly reduced any theoretical land needs they may have had.

The lands of San Pascual, together with their Indian inhabitants, fell under the jurisdiction of the San Gabriel Mission. The secularization of the missions resulted in secular administrator Colonel Nicholás Gutiérrez being placed in charge at San Gabriel in 1834.

Juan Mariner, who has already been mentioned in this book (he married Eulalia Pérez), was a 63-year-old Spanish ex-artilleryman who had retired from the army in 1821 with the rank of lieutenant. He lived at Mission San Gabriel and was a close friend of Father José Bernardo Sánchez, the head of the mission. Mariner's story begins with a petition to the government dated July 15, 1833. This was the first step required of a prospective ranch owner under Mexico's rules and regulations for colonization.

13. Land Titles

The law also required Governor Figueroa to investigate the merits of Mariner's petition. The governor found that there was no obstacle to granting this property to him. Further background checks with the town hall of Los Angeles and with the *alcalde* there did not reveal any problems, either. With the petition and these favorable reports in front of him, Governor Figueroa declared, on 6 May 1834, that Don Juan Mariner was to be the owner of this property, which was officially known as Rancho Rincon de San Pascual. The formal grant of title was dated 18 February 1835, and the Territorial Deputation, California's Assembly, approved the transfer of land to Mariner on 29 Aug 1835.

Mariner had still to be officially given possession of the property, but this matter was a local affair to be taken care of by the mayor of Los Angeles and assistants. It was a job for chain-bearers and amateur surveyors proceeding on horseback around the boundaries of the rancho, using a cord 100 varas [about 92 yards] long, to each end of which was fastened a wooden stake, and placing proper land marks as they went.

Juan Mariner died in 1838, three years after receiving the formal grant of title for the rancho. His widow kept the house and garden there; his son Fruto sold his own interest in the rancho to José Pérez, Eulalia's cousin, on 1 April 1839. But Mariner, it seems, had really been no ranchero at all. He had failed—and his heirs had failed—to use and cultivate the property, as required by law. As a result, on 10 April 1840 José Pérez and his friend Enrique Sepúlveda claimed that in legal terms the land had been abandoned for the past four years. Accordingly, on 24 Sept 1840, Governor Alvarado made a provisional grant of the rancho to Pérez and Sepúlveda. The new owners took possession, with their horses and cattle; each built a small house near the Arroyo Seco.

Pérez died in 1841 and Sepúlveda in 1843. The next owner was Manuel Garfias, a young officer in the Mexican army; on 28 Nov 1843 he received the formal grant from Governor Micheltorena and took possession.

The transition to American rule in 1848 was an easy one, since local government was unaffected for the time being, and the local officials continued in office. When the three members of the Board of United States Land Commissioners arrived in Los Angeles in August 1852, they were greeted most warmly, especially by those who expected to file land claims. Manuel Garfias gave a grand ball in their honor at his adobe home in Los Angeles. When Garfias filed his claim to San Pascual on Sept. 16, 1852, he accompanied it with a wealth of evidence and with depositions by prominent landholders in Southern California.

The claim was approved April 25, 1854. Confirmation by the district court came on March 6, 1856. The survey, when completed, included 13,693.93 acres in the rancho. On April 3, 1863, the United States patent was issued. Abraham Lincoln's signature appeared in this document, which was recorded in the County Recorder's office in Los Angeles. (The Recorder's Office was part of the system of American county and town governments organized by the California legislature in 1850, as provided for by the constitution of California adopted in 1849.)

Garfias built an adobe house on the property. Judge Benjamin S. Eaton, coming to San Pascual Rancho in 1858, visited the "Garfias hacienda," which was a well-built and, at $5,000, a very expensive home. San Pascual was not the best of the cattle ranges, however. When dry years came, the fortunes of Manual Garfias suffered. His mortgages, which had been negotiated at the usual ruinous rates of interest, forced him to sell his property. In January 1859, Garfias therefore deeded the ranch to Benjamin D. Wilson. Finally, in 1875, the ranch became the site of the nascent city of Pasadena.

The walls of the Garfias adobe were pulled down during the Southern California building boom of the 1880s to make way for a subdivision. The ancient oak tree, known as the Cathedral Oak, which it faced was still growing near the edge of the arroyo as late as 1948.

The U.S. Land Commission and Its Work[6]

In 1851, California Senator William M. Gwin put forward in Congress a bill which became on 3 March 1851 "An Act to Ascertain and Settle Private Land Claims in the State of California." Although the Treaty of Guadalupe Hidalgo had, in Articles VIII and IX, specifically promised full and complete protection of all the property rights of Mexicans, the Senate removed that protection when ratifying the treaty. As a result, the above Act, which gave birth to the Board of California Land Commission, put the burden of proof squarely—and, in the opinion of the *Californios*, most unfairly—upon every *Californio* who claimed to own land. The Act provided that

> each and every person claiming lands in California by virtue of any right or title derived from the Spanish or Mexican government, shall present the same to the said commissioners [there were three of them] when sitting as a board, together with such documentary evidence and testimony of witnesses as the said claimant relies upon to support such claims.[7]

13. Land Titles

It must be admitted here the question of land titles in California was never an easy one. When the American legal expert William Carey Jones was sent there to study this complicated issue, he began in the former capital of Monterey, where he found that the records of land titles were imperfect and in a state of confusion. For example, records prior to 1839 seemed to be missing, and no record book had been started for 1846. What most impressed Jones, however, was the huge size of some of the land grants which had been allowed under Mexican law. These could be as big as 11 square leagues of land, i.e., nearly 500,000 acres.[8] He realized that it would not be easy, or perhaps even possible, to persuade Congress to transfer such big grants to private owners.

California Secretary of State Halleck issued a report which was delivered to Governor Mason on 1 March 1849 and which identified and highlighted many title defects and title problems. For example, Halleck believed that Pío Pico had antedated some grants made after the United States had taken possession of California on 7 July 1846. There were also possible frauds and irregularities in the sale of pueblo lands.

In the end, Gwin's views prevailed and were reflected in the Act. His views were very similar to those of American voters, who very much wanted California's bounty to be available to all land-hungry and democratically-inclined Americans. The voters were not favorably impressed by the gigantic size of some of the *Californios'* holdings, which they knew the *Californios* had acquired simply as gifts from their government.

The Commission began its work in San Francisco in January 1852; studied cases involving titles to about 12,000,000 acres of land; and continued in existence until March 1856. During these years, affected *Californios* made great efforts to prove that they did in fact own the lands they were still living on. They searched for the original grants from Mexican governors; called on relatives and friends to testify on their behalf; hired American lawyers (not all of whom were honest men); traveled widely at their own expense, and had copies made of archived files relating to their ranchos. Many *Californios*, who as a group were poorly educated, did not speak or read English, and knew nothing about the complexities of American law, often had to borrow money at very high interest rates, e.g., 10 percent per month, mortgage their lands, or sell their livestock in order to pay their lawyers and their state taxes. In many cases, these moves would lead to their own financial ruin.

In his book *Spanish and Mexican Private Land Grants* (1923), William G. Morrow found that of the 813 cases considered (this figure was later revised to 809 cases), 604 were finally confirmed, 190 were finally rejected, and 19 were withdrawn. Many of these cases were appealed, so the final decisions were made by higher legal bodies, i.e., by the District Court, the Circuit Court, the Circuit Court of Appeals, and the United States Supreme Court.[9] At the end of this long process, a total of 582 land claims were finally patented, i.e., officially approved.[10]

The human cost of this process, however, was very high. The average length of time that a *Californio* had to wait for his patent, i.e., official approval of his claim, was 17 years, assuming that it was indeed finally granted. Lengthy delays were due to protracted litigation, appeals by government lawyers, and the difficulties of getting approved surveys. Another bit of very bad news was that while this slow process was grinding on, rancho lands could not be sold because they did not have perfect titles.

Moreover, properties were soon overrun by well-armed squatters who held only "shotgun titles" to the land. W.W. Robinson put it very well:

> Even before California became a part of the Union—September 9, 1850—the wagons of the immigrants were moving in and coming to stop in the good valley lands of the rancheros. Squatters began early to organize armed bands to get what they wanted. Some were interested in ranches. Some began staking out, or helping themselves to, lots on the outskirts of growing towns like San Francisco and Sacramento...
>
> [Newcomers to California] found on their arrival that all the best land in California, or at least the most usable, was included in enormous grants made by the Mexican regime. To many of these "North American adventurers," as native Californians like to refer to them, the great landowners were merely monopolists who ... were obstructing the path or progress of civilization. After all, California had been captured, as well as bought, from Mexico...
>
> When they found the best land claimed under Mexican titles or held by speculators who had bought them up, clashes were inevitable. Hardly any part of inhabited California was free from violence.[11]

The bottom line was that most *Californios* were either bankrupted in the process of seeking clear titles or were forced to give up and sell out at very low prices. W.W. Robinson's summation of this whole process was a fair one. He wrote: "It was a ruinous period for Spanish Californians. Apparently the Treaty of Guadalupe Hidalgo was not taken literally by the United States."[12]

In 1871, the celebrated American journalist, philosopher, and political economist Henry George (1839–1897) arrived at these findings:

> If the history of Mexican grants of California is ever written, it will be a history of greed, of perjury, of corruption, of spoliation and high-handed robbery, for which it will be difficult to find a parallel...
>
> It would have been better, far better if the American government had agreed to permit these grant holders [i.e., the *Californios*] to retain a certain amount of land

around their improvements, and compounded for the rest the grants called for, by payment of a certain sum per acre, turning it into the public domain.[13]

Bancroft, for his part, denounced the whole land claims process in general but vitriolic terms in 1882. He wrote:

> It was to the Californians owning lands under genuine and valid titles, seven eighths of the claimants ... that great wrong was done. They were virtually robbed by the government that was bound to protect them. As a rule, they lost nearly all their possessions in the struggle before the successive tribunals to escape from real and imaginary dangers of total loss. The lawyers took immense fees in land and cattle, often for slight services or none at all. It was in no sense the protection promised by the treaty to finally confirm a title after a struggle of eight to twenty-five years when half or all of the estate had passed from the possession of the original claimant; it was simply confiscation, and that not in the real interests of the United States, or of American settlers, but only of speculating land sharpers.[14]

In summary, one can say that the land settlement process failed in three important ways. It bankrupted many of the *Californios* themselves. It encouraged American settlers to take the law into their own hands by squatting and by other questionable or clearly illegal actions. Finally, it rewarded the smooth-talking speculators, lawyers, and adventurers who exploited the naïve *Californios* and who profited from legal delays and confusion.[15]

The Limantour Claim

Joseph Yves Limantour (1812–1885) was a French seaman and trader who first came to California from Mexico in 1841 as the captain of a small ship carrying French goods. In San Francisco he met the French diplomat Duflot de Mofras, who has been mentioned earlier in this book, who advised him to invest in California land.[16] Over the next six years Limantour made several visits to San Francisco—not to invest in land, but to sell guns to the *Californios* and to encourage them to resist the influx of the Americans.

In 1847, the United States sloop-of-war *Warren*, under the command of Commodore Biddle, seized Limantour's ship in San Pedro. By then, however, Limantour had jettisoned his cargo of arms and ammunition, so Biddle had no legal grounds on which to hold him. Limantour fled to Mexico, where he spent the next five years living peacefully and uneventfully.

In 1852 he reappeared in San Francisco, now armed with documents allegedly signed by Governor Micheltorena, which asserted that Limantour was the owner of eight gigantic land claims in California. The two most remarkable claims covered, respectively, the city of San Francisco, and all the islands of San Francisco Bay and those up to 35 miles out to sea. It was estimated that Limantour's claim was worth more than the total value of all railroad fortunes of the world.

The good news was that like most other land swindles in early California, Limantour's case soon unraveled. A *Californio* named Augustus Jouan, whom Limantour had treated badly, revealed that Limantour had admitted privately that his grants were mere fabrications. Limantour had said that he had changed dates and figures. It became known, moreover, that a Frenchman named Jancomet had forged the grants nine years before they were said to have been signed by the Governor.

Limantour was therefore arrested and was indicted for forgery and perjury. The judge who presided at the cases involving Limantour's claims wrote that fraud and false testimony had been used so flagrantly in them that they were "without parallel in the judicial history of the country."[17] Limantour, however, was one step ahead of the law: he jumped bail and escaped.

14

Kaleidoscope of *Californio* Events

Brief multinational observations of life in Alta California, ranging from 1806 to 1888, are considered below. Some of these authors have already been or will be discussed in this book but they are all worth citing now because of their personal experiences and because of the local color they provide. Listed in chronological order they are as follows:

Georg von Langsdorff (1806)

A brilliant German-Russian naturalist, explorer, diplomat, and doctor, von Langsdorff had this to say about the *Californios* (spelling as in the original):

> The immense herds of cattle now seen here [in the Monterey area] are supposed to have sprung from five head brought to this *misión* in the year 1776. The *gobernador* [governor] of Monterey [José Joaquin de Arrillaga, governor of California in 1791–1794 and again from 1800 to 1806], and with whom we had become acquainted during our stay, informed me that the cattle had increased to such a degree in the years immediately proceeding—in the three northerly and contiguous *misiones* of San Francisco, Santa Clara, and Santa Cruz—that some months ago he had been compelled to send out a party of soldiers to kill not less than 20,000 [this figure is surely exaggerated], wherever they should meet them, as he began to be afraid that from the immense increase there might in a short time be a lack of sufficient pasture.[1]

Carlos Antonio Carrillo (1831)

Carrillo was Alta California's delegate to a national conference in Mexico City. As a territory in the Mexican republic, California was entitled to send one delegate from Baja California and one delegate from Alta California to this conference. At the conference, Carrillo argued that the last traces of the Spanish colonial system must be removed if Alta California was ever to advance and to prosper.

In his view, the traditional Spanish system gave far too much power to military commanders, thus making it impossible for the *Californios* to achieve their goal of full equality before the law. In his speech to the congress, which took no action on his call to reform the legal system, Carrillo said (the italics as in the original translation):

> White people [i.e., *Californios* and Caucasian foreigners living in Alta California] and free Indians [Indians who were not attached to a mission] ... are subjected to the military and political authority delegated by the Commander in Chief to his subordinate Captains and Commandants of the *presidios* to such an extent that even the constitutional *alcaldes* of the *presidio* settlement are completely under the authority of said Commandants. The *alcaldes* are thus prevented from exercising the authority vested in them by law...
>
> From this source has flowed the accumulation of evils inflicted upon the unhappy population, governed as they are at the discretion of Military Commanders great and small who hold in their hands all executive and judicial powers, the exercise of which no one is able to dispute....[2]

Antonio Coronel (1834)

Dancing was a great passion with the *Californios*. The best analysis of this very popular pastime was written by Antonio Coronel in 1834. It was later described by Bancroft in a long account which has been shortened and lightly edited here.

Bancroft wrote:

> For a ball, a large space in front of the house selected was roofed with boughs, three of its sides being covered with white cotton stuff adorned with ribbons and artificial flowers. The fourth side was left open and there horsemen collected in a group, a strong fence preventing the intrusion of the horses. Around the three enclosing sides were seats for women. The musicians, consisting of a violinist, a guitarist, and two or three singers, stationed themselves in a corner, where they were out of the way.
>
> The master of ceremonies led out the women when they danced singly, beginning at one end of the salon. Clapping his hands, he took steps to the music in front of her whom he desired to call out. She rising went to the center of the salon and, with both hands taking hold and extending her skirts, began to dance to the sound of the music. After taking a turn or two in the center of the salon, she retired and another took her place.
>
> While the women were dancing, the men on horseback kept up a continual movement and, sky-larking, coming and going, and disputing places, each endeavoring to

force his horse to the front. If the piece were to be danced by a couple, the horsemen who wished to take part dismounted, removed their spurs, and hung them on the saddle-bow; then, hat in hand, they entered the salon and [each] took out the female [he had] selected. The piece concluded, the women retired to their seats and the men remounted.³

Richard Henry Dana, Jr. (1840)

Dana may have suffered from the Protestant upper class social myopia which was not uncommon among the New England thinkers of his time, but his comments on daily life in Alta California always ring true. This is what he wrote about California revolutions:

> Revolutions are matters of constant occurrence in California. They are got up by men who are at the foot of the ladder and in desperate circumstances, just as a new political party is started by such men in our own country. The only object, of course, is the loaves and fishes [a Biblical reference meaning that such men go into politics purely out of self-interest], and instead of caucusing, paragraphing, libeling, feasting, promising, and lying as with us, they take up muskets and bayonets, and seizing upon the presidio and custom-house divide the spoils, and declare a new dynasty.⁴

Pío Pico (1846)

Twice governor of Alta California, Pío Pico, too, clearly understood the threats inherent in unbridled immigration into Alta California by well-organized, heavily-armed, land-hungry American settlers. This is what he told a Mexican military council in Monterey in 1846:

> We find ourselves suddenly threatened by hordes of Yankee emigrants, who have begun to flock into our country, and whose progress we cannot arrest. Already the wagons of that perfidious people scaled the almost inaccessible summits of the Sierra Nevada, crossed the entire continent, and penetrated the fruitful valley of the Sacramento. What that astonishing people will next undertake, I cannot say; but in whatever enterprise they embark they will be sure to prove successful. Already are these adventurous land voyagers spreading far and wide over a country which seems suited to their tastes. They are cultivating farms, establishing vineyards, building workshops, and doing a thousand other things which seem natural to them but which Californians neglect or despise.⁵

Alfred Robinson (1846)

The American businessman Alfred Robinson, who came to Alta California in 1829 to work in the hide and tallow trade as an employee of the

Boston-based firm of Bryant, Sturgis and Company, was one of the most experienced foreign observers of the *Californio* way of life. When he first visited San Diego early in his career, he found that it was booming. However, moving the monopoly of the Custom House to Monterey; the development of Los Angeles as a major cattle-raising, cattle-exporting place; and the Indian uprisings of the 1830s and later all combined to help end the ascendancy of San Diego in *Californio* life.[6]

Concerning Indian uprisings, it must be explained here that after the secularization of the missions in the early 1830s, the Indians were free at last and were no longer subject to control by the small number of *Californio* soldiers based at presidios or missions. Since some of the Indians had been embittered by the harsh treatment they had received at the missions and since there was no police force of any kind in Alta California, Indian hostilities quickly increased throughout the San Diego area.

Indeed, throughout 1836 and 1837, Indian attacks reached new heights and several times forced the evacuation of ranches, even threatening San Diego itself. Indian violence continued through 1840.[7] For this reason, when Alfred Robinson revisited San Diego again in 1840, he found it to be in a very sorry state indeed. He wrote in 1846:

> At this period of events, I embarked on board the ship Alert, and again visited San Diego. Here everything was prostrated—the presidio ruined, the mission depopulated, the town almost deserted and its few inhabitants miserably poor. It had changed! From being once the life of and the most important place in California, it was now become the gloomiest and most desolate. With great difficulty I succeeded in procuring horses to return north, by land, and in doing which the person with whom I contracted compelled me to pay an enormous compensation.[8]

Rev. Walter Colton (1850)

Colton was a chaplain for the U.S. Navy and was also the *alcalde* of Monterey and the author of two books about California. He served as *alcalde* from 1846 to 1848, a challenging job that required him to be, at the same time, judge, sheriff, and governor over much of Northern California. Acclaimed as a fair judge, he also left his mark by fining every gambler $20 to help cover the cost of building California's first schoolhouse. His book, *Three Years in California* (1850), contains many dramatic examples of *Californio* life—for example, a grizzly bear hunt conducted by *vaqueros* armed only with lassos and by male and female riders carrying single-shot pistols.

Colton wrote:

> Bruin [a German nickname meaning "brown bear") was wounded, but resolute and undaunted; the fire rolled from his red eyes like a flash of lightning out of forked cloud.... The pistols were reloaded, and the señoritas and caballeros [a *caballero* was a prosperous and expensively equipped horseman] all dashed up for another shower of fire and lead. As the smoke cleared, bruin was found with the lasso slack, a sure evidence that the horse who managed it knew his antagonist was dead.[9]

Antonio María Osio (1851)

Osio worked for the Mexican customs service in San Francisco and was also a historian. In his *History of Alta California* (1851), he argued that although the *Californios* had tried hard to develop Alta California, first Spain and then Mexico had never given them the support necessary to make this possible. He wrote that the mission system was never as effective as its proponents had claimed it to be. Finally, he also discussed the successes and failures of all the governors of Alta California between 1825 and 1846.

His book is valuable not only as local history but also because of the conversational tone he consciously adopts with the reader. Osio often addresses the reader directly, using such friendly and encouraging phrases as "Take note," "Look," and "Imagine."[10]

He is also a good storyteller: witness his account of how in 1818 a five-ton barge, rowed by *Californio* soldiers with no boating experience and towing an awkward raft, was carried out to sea beyond the Golden Gate. This situation arose because Don Luis Argüello, captain of the San Francisco presidio, had decided to renovate some of the dilapidated wooden buildings there.

Since there were not enough trees near the presidio itself, he sent his men to Corte Madera, located north of the Golden Gate in what is now Marin County, to get the wood needed. He had a barge built there and also a big raft. He knew nothing about boats himself but from an old Indian named Marin he learned about the strong tides in these waters and the need to time any crossing of San Francisco Bay very carefully. Armed with this timely knowledge and aided by a great deal of good luck, he was able to function successfully as captain of the barge.

Osio recounts the following incident:

> The first time that Señor Argüello entrusted command of the barge to the corporal of his company, who he thought had acquired the necessary skills, he had the pleasure of seeing the barge sail past Angel Island before losing sight of it. [The barge

was being rowed, not sailed, and was being carried by the outgoing tide. Angel Island is a small island in San Francisco Bay.] It soon arrived at its destination.

As he was towing the large raft on the return trip, the corporal congratulated himself on how quickly he had learned to navigate the vessel. As he was boasting to himself about his skill, he found himself even with Alcatraz [another island in the bay] near the Sausalito side. But he was unaware that the current was at its strongest. When he realized his error in having taken that route, he rowed as hard as he could toward the pier [near the presidio], but he could not get the raft across the strong current. Under these difficult circumstances, night fell on them.

When dawn broke they discovered that they had been carried outside the bay to the Farallon Islands about eight leagues [almost 21 miles] from the presidio. There they discussed whether they should abandon the raft and try to make it to Point Reyes [north of San Francisco], but when the regular southeast wind began to blow, they decided not to leave the raft behind. Instead they decided to head for the mouth of San Francisco Bay.

Because the raft was very large and heavy, they made little progress, and by night they had only reached Point Bonetes [now known as Point Bonita, i.e., the northwestern tip of the mouth of San Francisco Bay]. Since the previous trips had lasted only about five to eight hours, they had not bothered to bring food or water along, and were beginning to get hungry and thirsty. Fortunately, at dawn they found themselves in shoal water. The wind was favorable, so they were able to arrive with their cargo at about two in the afternoon.

This accident taught them a good, if harsh, lesson. On subsequent trips they would take care not to endanger their lives by testing their strength on the oars against the greater force of the current. Rather, they would need to wait and take advantage of its natural ebb and flow. Finally, they would need to provide themselves with sufficient food for three days.[11]

Henry Cerruti (1874)

A gifted but a very mercurial personality, Cerruti was one of Bancroft's most productive interviewers. Fifteen years after Cerruti's death (by suicide: he had borrowed money from his friends to speculate in mining stocks, which then tumbled in value), Bancroft remembered him, very fondly, with these words:

> Poor dear Cerruti! If I had him back with me alive, I would not give him up for all Nevada's mines. His ever welcome presence; his ever pleasing speech, racy in its harmless bluster; his ever charming ways, fascinating in their guileful simplicity, the far-reaching earth does not contain his like. Alas, Cerruti! With another I might say, [here Bancroft is evoking Shakespeare's *Henry IV*] I could not have lost a better man.[12]

When working for Bancroft, Cerruti's most stellar achievement was to persuade General Vallejo, who had been the wealthiest and most powerful *Californio* living north of Monterey, to donate his personal papers to Bancroft. Cerruti wrote:

14. Kaleidoscope of Californio Events

... the idea struck me that it would be a good thing all round if the General should donate his papers to Squire Bancroft. No sooner had that thought come into my mind that I got up from my chair and went into the room where General Vallejo was engaged in conversation with Mr. Savage [Thomas Savage, one of Bancroft's interviewers]. I listened a moment or two and then broached the subject which had induced me to intrude upon his privacy. I admit that at first I did not speak in a very intelligible manner, for I felt kind of ashamed because I knew that the General looked upon his ancient documents as old and trusty friends...

I remembered every conversation held between General Vallejo and me on the subject of the collection I was urging him to deliver into strange hands. But as I was aware that Mr. Bancroft would make good use of the papers, I picked up courage, mustered into service a few intelligible sentences, and succeeded in gaining my point. No sooner had I received the desired answer than I notified Mr. Oak [Henry Lebbeus Oak, another of Bancroft's assistants] of the fact, and he told it to Squire Bancroft, who forthwith proceeded to express his thanks to General Vallejo.[13]

José María Amador (1877)

A former presidio soldier who had risen to become a member of the *Californio* elite, Amador was interviewed by Thomas Savage in 1877. Amador told him:

> I remember that in 1821 the flag of [Mexican] independence was raised in California.... At that time, I was serving in the *soldado de cuera* ["leather jacket"] company of San Francisco when the order came from Monterey to implement the new order of things. Captain Argüello received the order and immediately carried it out.
>
> Captain Argüello was a man well liked by the troops for his kindnesses yet without weakening discipline. One of his idiosyncrasies was that if a soldier in formation lost his boot, a hat, or any other clothing item, it would remain on the ground until he [Argüello] picked it up. [He, then, would] put it back on the soldier with his own hands while saying the following words, "careless sack of *azumbre* [an *azumbre* was a container for liquids and held about two quarts]." This would be the only reprimand [he would give them].[14]

María Inocenta Pico (1878)

The last woman to be interviewed by Thomas Savage was María Inocenta Pico, widow of the soldier Don Miguel Avila. In 1839, Avila had been granted the San Miguelito rancho, located along the coast south of San Luis Obispo. Like many other *Californios*, he struggled to protect his lands from newly-arrived Americans. During her interview with Savage, she recounted to him how she may have saved her husband's life when he had been taken prisoner during an uprising against General Micheltorena and was in danger of being executed.

She told Savage that she quickly packed a wide variety of excellent provisions for the general and his officers—e.g., chickens, mutton, cakes, cheese enchiladas, good wine, and whiskey. She arranged everything in an elegant manner, with fine napkins, and sent it off on two mules that were fully loaded down. Separately, she also sent food for her husband.

Her rapid response may well have saved her husband's life. In any case, the general wrote her a letter, sending it back by the muleteer who had brought the provisions. The general assured her that her husband would not be harmed and would be freed at a town not far away. To be on the safe side, however, she continued to send more provisions to the general until her husband was set free. The general kept his word: her husband was set free unharmed. The general also returned all the horses his men had stolen from her ranch. They came back without their ears or their tails, but she said that "this did not matter to me at all," because her husband was in good health.[15]

In her interview, María Inocenta Pico also discussed education in Alta California. She told Savage that a great many girls did not finish their studies because their mothers took them out of school to marry them off. This was due to what she denounced as the bad custom of marrying off very young girls as soon as eligible men asked for their hands.[16]

Hubert Howe Bancroft (1888)

In his own time, Bancroft was the most influential foreign writer on the *Californios* and was one of the very few commentators who had anything substantive to say about education in Alta California. His views on the educational system (or, more accurately, on *the total lack of such a system*) are worth noting here.

In a chapter entitled "A Futile Fight with Ignorance" in his 808-page opus *California Pastoral* (1888), Bancroft makes the following points, which echo his cadences and words very closely but are not always given verbatim. He wrote:

> From the earliest settlement of California until it became part of the United States, it had no well-established system of schools. All of the instruction imparted to Californio children was due to the spasmodic and short-lived efforts of rulers [i.e., the governors of Alta California], who, on coming into office, deemed it their duty to initiate reform, and yet lacked the ability and power to overcome the obstacles which at every step confronted them.
>
> These obstacles were ever alike in kind, although varying in degree, and consisted in the chronic depletion of the public treasury, and an inveterate unwillingness on

the part of the people, which was theirs by right of inheritance from illiterate ancestors, to give their children an education better than that which had fallen to their own lot...

Almost without exception, the early settlers, drawn from the humbler ranks of Spanish colonial society, were unable either to read or to write. The alcalde of San Francisco could not sign his name to a document conveying the possession of land...

As little learning as the boys received [i.e., from barely-literate soldiers serving as part-time schoolmasters], far less was imparted to the girls. It was not necessary or desirable that a woman should know anything beyond household duties.... [However], in the towns, the daughters of some of the prominent families assembled at the house of the mother of one of them, who taught them to read and write, though to a lesser extent than boys...

In May 1834 Governor Figueroa reported to the central government in Mexico City that there were primary schools only at Monterey, Santa Barbara, and Los Angeles. However, these were taught by ill-qualified inexperienced men, and were attended by but few children...

In 1845 only eleven of twenty-five voters at San Diego were able to write. That same year the [American] alcalde Leese of Sonoma reported to the governor that while Sonoma had about 100 inhabitants, only two could write [it turned out, in fact, that only one man could write].[17]

Pioneer John Bidwell (1890)

In 1841 John Bidwell (1819–1900) led the first group of emigrants, now known as the Bidwell-Bartleson Party, overland to Alta California along the route that would eventually become the main California trail. As a successful pioneer, farmer, soldier, statesman, and philanthropist, his views on the *Californios* are well worth reading today. The following excerpt is from his December 1890 article in *The Century Magazine* (see Bibliography):

> The kindness and hospitality of the native Californians have not been overstated. Up to the time the Mexican régime ceased in California they had a custom of never charging for anything; that is to say, for entertainment, food, use of horses, etc. You were supposed, even if you visited a friend, to bring your blankets with you, and one would be very thoughtless if he traveled and did not take a knife with him to cut his meat. When you had eaten, the invariable custom was to rise, deliver to the woman or hostess the plate on which you had eaten the meat and beans—for this was all they had—say, "*Muchas gracias, Señora*" ["Many thanks, madame"]; and the hostess invariably replied "*Buen provecho*" ["May it do you much good"].
>
> When you wanted a horse to ride, you would take it to the next ranch—it might be twenty, thirty, or fifty miles—and turn it out there, and sometime or other in reclaiming his stock the owner would get it back. In this way you might travel from one end of California to the other.[18]

15

Mariano Guadalupe Vallejo

Vallejo has already been mentioned several times in this book but much more can usefully be said here about his career, his ranch (Rancho Petaluma), and his homestead (Lachryma Montis).

In *The Year of Decision: 1846*, published in 1943, Bernard DeVoto, winner of the Pulitzer Prize and National Book Award, praised Mariano Guadalupe Vallejo as "perhaps the most considerable citizen of California."[1] This is a sound and reasoned judgment. Although not without minor faults—e.g., a tendency to follow unwise investment advice, and a willingness to keep large numbers of Indians working on his lands under the most deplorable conditions, Vallejo remains one the most intelligent, most experienced, and most admirable of all the *Californio* men.

A political liberal at heart, he nevertheless carved out a personal fiefdom for himself in Sonoma and became the richest and most powerful man north of Monterey.[2] The town of Vallejo, California is named for him, and the nearby city of Benicia is named for his wife. Vallejo's life spanned the colonial, the Mexican, and the American eras in California but, like the lives of so many other prominent *Californios*, it ended sadly and in financial ruin.

Although Vallejo was arguably the most prominent *Californio* and was justly famous in his own time, few of his own writings are available today in published form and in English. He did write a long (895-page) manuscript in Spanish on the history of California, but this was destroyed in 1867 by a fire in his house. The Bancroft Library now has a five-volume manuscript by him in Spanish entitled *Recuerdos Historicos*, which he gave to Bancroft in 1875. An abstract in English explains that this is a "Historical and personal account of Alta California, including political history, 1769–1848; social life and customs of the Californios; biographical information on notable persons."

Although at some point this manuscript was translated into English by Earl E. Hewitt, it has never been published and for this reason it is not easily accessible. However, by piecing together accounts from a wide range of other primary and secondary sources, it is possible to reach an understanding of Vallejo's life and times.[3]

He was an extremely intelligent and extremely able man. Born into an upper class *Californio* family in Monterey, he was honed for leadership beginning at an early age. His mentor when he was young was Governor Pablo Vincente de Solá. Remarkably, thanks to their close relationship, in a culture whose strong point was the spoken word rather that the written word, Vallejo was encouraged by Solá to read government documents and newspapers from Mexico City and to peruse his personal library.

Vallejo later worked as a clerk for William Hartnell, an English merchant, who taught him English, French, and Latin. When news of Mexico's independence from Spain reached Monterey, Vallejo, who was then the personal secretary of the new governor of California, Luis Argüello, promptly joined the new Mexican army as a cadet. He was so able that soon he was appointed to the territorial legislature—a clear sign of the confidence that his colleagues had in him. In 1829, he also successfully led a unit of Mexican soldiers against a rebellious band of Indians.

His rise to power continued unabated as he became commander of the San Francisco presidio in 1833; supervised the secularization of Mission San Francisco Solano and the distribution of its roughly 1,000,000 acres; was granted Rancho Petaluma (near present-day Petaluma, California) by Governor José Figueroa in 1833, a holding that was eventually enlarged to embrace 66,000 acres and was probably the largest such complex in California; and, in 1835, was named director of colonization and *comandante* (commander) of the highest military division in Northern California. To counter a perceived but actually non-existent Russian threat from Fort Ross, Vallejo later began to build a presidio in Sonoma. He also had a fine two-story house built there (most of the buildings in California at that time had only one story).

Increasingly involved in domestic and regional politics, Vallejo came to believe that Mexico's best hope for any future economic, social, and cultural progress lay with the United States rather than with Mexico itself. Vallejo was very critical of the incompetent, corrupt Mexican government and consistently identified with the Mexican liberals who called for rule by law and who wanted an efficient government with constitutionally limited powers. He also wanted the government to be independent of the Catholic Church.[4]

Financially, Vallejo was securely placed. Bancroft reports that he owned about 33 leagues, equivalent to 146,000 acres, with 400 to 500 acres being under cultivation and the rest used for pasturage. He had 12,000 to 15,000 head of cattle; 7,000 to 8,000 horses, and 2,000 to 3,000 sheep. Bancroft adds Vallejo had 300 men working his lands, "with their usual proportion of females and children, all kept in a nearly naked state, poorly fed, and never paid."[5]

When Manuel Torres, a visitor from Peru, called at Vallejo's home, he was struck by the number of Indian servants employed there. He wrote:

> When visiting the Vallejo mansion, I commented to Doña Francisca [Benicia, i.e., Mrs. Vallejo] as to the extraordinary number of natives [Indians] employed in the courtyard. These, she explained, were the domestics needed to run her large household.
>
> Each of her children (there were eight of them at that time) had his own body servant. Then there were seven women to do the cooking and six to do the wash, while on festive occasions seven or eight were kept to grind corn for the tortillas. Another dozen were employed to do the spinning and weaving. In addition there were those who looked after the cleaning and those who tended the gardens and looked after the horses. Each servant specialized in doing one task and would be insulted to perform some other duty.[6]

Despite his own liberal political leanings, Vallejo could not ignore his duties as an army officer. For this reason, he pointedly warned the Ministry of War in Mexico City about the threat posed by the increasing flow of Americans into Alta California. In 1841 he wrote:

> The total population of California does not exceed six thousand souls [Vallejo's estimate does not include the Indians], and of these two-thirds must be counted as women and children, leaving scarcely two thousand men. But we cannot count on the fifteen thousand Indians in the towns and missions, because they inspire more fear than confidence. Thus we have this lamentable situation in a country worthy of a better fate. And if the invasion which is taking place from all sides is carried out, all I can assure you is that the Californians will die; I cannot dare to assure you that California can be saved. This people, loyal to their flag, will follow the same course and die.[7]

Vallejo, however, also understood the important fact that these energetic newcomers had many valuable skills of great potential value to California. As he would explain years later in his memoirs,

> The arrival of so many people from the outside world was highly satisfying to us *arribeños* [northern Californians] who were ... gratified to see numerous parties of industrious individuals come and settle among us permanently. Although they were not possessed of wealth, they could be a powerful stimulus to our agriculture which, unfortunately, was still in a state of inactivity, owing to a lack of strong and intelligent workers....[8]

Despite his pro–American inclinations, during the Bear Flag Revolt Vallejo was taken prisoner by the Americans and was held under miserable conditions at Sutter's Fort (located near the confluence of the American and Sacramento rivers in present-day Sacramento, California) for two months without any formal charges being filed against him. After being released from this captivity, he wrote to U.S. Consul Larkin from Sonoma:

> I left the Sacramento [i.e., Sutter's Fort], half dead and arrived here almost without life; but I am now much better.... The political change [i.e., the American conquest] has cost a great deal to my person and mind, and likewise to my property. I have lost more than a thousand live horned cattle, six hundred tame horses, and many other things of value which were taken from my house here and in Petaluma. My wheat crops are entirely lost ... and I assure you that 200 fanegas of sowing [approximately 350 acres, producing about 25,000 bushels of wheat] in good condition as mine was is a considerable loss. All is lost, and the only hope for making it up is to work again.[9]

Despite the harsh treatment he received in his captivity (he contracted malaria, which reduced his weight to only 98 pounds), he eventually decided to cast his lot with the American victors in hopes of improving post-war conditions for his fellow *Californios* and, in the process, for himself as well. He did receive some well-deserved recognition after the U.S.-Mexican War. He was elected state senator in 1849 and, the next year Rev. Walter Colton, a chaplain and former *alcalde* of Monterey, dedicated a well-written book, *Three Years in California*, to him, using these warm words:

> To Gen. Mariano Guadalupe Vallejo, one of California's most distinguished sons, in whom the interests of freedom, humanity, and education have found an able advocate and munificent benefactor, this volume is most respectfully dedicated by his friend, the author.[10]

Colton had very solid grounds on which to praise Vallejo as a "munificent benefactor." In 1850, while still a state senator, Vallejo tried to settle the state capital problem (there was considerable dispute about where the capital should be sited) by giving California 156 acres of land on the west end of Carquinez Strait. This is a narrow tidal strait in Northern California and is part of the tidal estuary of the Sacramento and San Joaquin rivers as they flow into San Francisco Bay.

Vallejo wanted to call this place "Eureka" but his friends convinced him that "Vallejo" would be a more fitting name. In addition to land, Vallejo also offered California $370,000 in cash, earmarked for the construction of public buildings (e.g., a university, governor's mansion, capital building, orphanage, and insane asylum). Moreover, guaranteeing this generous offer, Vallejo posted a bond for $500,000 and swore that he was not only good for this amount but also had real property worth $1,000,000 over and above all the liabilities and demands against him.[11]

In 1852, however, John McDougal had became California's second governor and had unexpectedly ordered that the state's offices be moved to Vallejo, which was then little more than a muddy construction site. Because they could not work there efficiently, the legislators voted to adjourn and to reconvene in Sacramento. By 1855 it had become the capital. Vallejo was released from his bond but had already spent $98,000 of his own money on his ill-fated capital project. That same year, the U.S. Government granted him only $48,700 of the $117,875 he had claimed but, fearing political defeat at the hands of increasingly militant squatters in the Sonoma area, Vallejo withdrew from state government and moved himself and his family to a new home near Sonoma. He poetically named it Lachryma Montis ("Tear of the Mountain"), after an ever-flowing spring on the land.

In the 1860s, Vallejo was earning about $96,000 each year from sales of hides and tallow. However, much of his wealth was tied up in ranch and agricultural land, which made him very vulnerable to legal decisions involving real estate. He was thus hit hard when in 1862 the U.S. Supreme Court overturned a lower court's confirmation of the grant for Vallejo's ranch in Soscol in the Napa Valley.

Governor Micheltorena had granted the Soscol property to Vallejo in 1844, who would later spend tens of thousands of dollars defending his claim on it, even though by then he had already sold more than half of the acreage involved. To lose his remaining title to this ranch was a great financial setback for Vallejo and a great personal disgrace for him: friends of his who had bought part of his property had believed that his title was entirely secure.

Thus Vallejo fell upon hard times. With almost all his land and cattle gone, he now derived his modest income only from the rental of small plots of land for truck gardening and from what a local water company would pay him for the sale of piped water from the spring at Lachryma Montis. At the end of his life in 1890, all that remained of his once far-flung holdings, which had stretched from Mendocino County on the north coast of California to the Carquinez Strait, were 228 acres surrounding the Lachryma Montis homestead, one cow, and two old horses.

Summarizing such an eventful life in a few words is not easy, but it can be said here that one of Vallejo's best qualities was his empathy with his fellow *Californios*. He understood in his final years that they were undergoing financial hardships even greater than his own. He could see with his own eyes the tribulations they were enduring, and he wrote about the sad conditions of "our Spanish-speaking people [who] are almost all of them uprooted from their own lands and it is unbelievable that the majority of the time they have nothing to eat—so great is their poverty."[12]

Finally, and stating his case very strongly here to achieve a poetic effect, he also wrote to his son Platon:

> If the Californians could all gather together to breathe a lament, it would reach Heaven as a moving sigh which would cause fear and consternation in the Universe. What misery! And it is much more intense than when everyone without exception lived in abundance. The country was the true Eden, the land of promise where hunger was never known, nor charity—if you can just utter such an expression since no one had to exercise it.[13]

Rancho Petaluma

"Rancho Petaluma Adobe" is now the official name of the historic ranch house built from adobe bricks for General Vallejo. This building is the biggest privately-owned adobe structure in California and is the best and largest example of Monterey Colonial architecture in the United States. Construction began in 1834 and was finished in 1857. Located on the eastern edge of Petaluma, California and now preserved as the Petaluma Adobe State Historic Park, it is listed on the U.S. National Register of Historic Places and is also a U.S. National Historic Landmark and California Historical Landmark #18.

The genesis of Rancho Petaluma was the Mexican government's 1834 order to Lieutenant Vallejo, then commandant of the presidio at San Francisco, to establish a town at Sonoma.[14] Toward this end, Governor José Figueroa granted Vallejo 44,000 acres there (later expanded to 66,000 acres) in order to increase the Mexican presence in the area and thus to forestall any intervention by the Russians, who had a settlement on the coast at Fort Ross. In 1836, construction began on the Petaluma Adobe, the main headquarters of the ranch. This two-story U-shaped structure was a massive undertaking for the time and place (at least 2,000 Indian workers provided most of the labor); even after 10 years, work was still being done on it.

A deep roofed veranda encircled both stories of the building and was instrumental in protecting the vulnerable adobe bricks from the weather. The National Park Service adds that

> across from the U-shaped building that stands today, another structure once existed, creating an interior courtyard surrounded in all four sides. During the heyday

of Rancho Petaluma, this rectangular complex would have been alive with the sounds of hooves and hundreds of workers, the smells of hide processing and boiling fat, the whisper of looms weaving necessary blankets for the cold season, and heat pouring from the blacksmith's anvil as he shaped and sharpened farm equipment. The Petaluma Abbey also housed storage space for grain and vegetable crops, as well as residential units on the second floor for both workers and guests of Vallejo.[15]

From 1834 to 1846, Rancho Petaluma was the most prosperous ranch in Northern California, selling its wares to merchant ships arriving on the California coast, or trading its raw materials for goods manufactured abroad. During Vallejo's arrest and imprisonment during the Bear Flag Revolt, however, the ranch was looted and most of the farm workers fled. Vallejo sold it in 1857 and it began to run downhill. The State of California bought it in 1951 and has since then made it a popular tourist attraction.

Vallejo himself lived on this ranch only at brief periods during certain times of the year, spending most of his time in the Sonoma area at his home at Lachryma Montis. He also had other ranches and held title to a total of about 175,000 acres. When he was not 'in residence" at Rancho Petaluma, he relied on his majordomo (foreman), Miguel Alvarado, to manage and oversee all the day-to-day activities at the ranch.

Lachryma Montis

When Vallejo and his family moved into his new home in Sonoma towards the end of 1852, he had already invested more than $150,000 in it.[16] This two-story, "Carpenter Gothic-Victorian"-style, wood frame house had been designed, prefabricated, and partially assembled on the east coast of the United States. It was then shipped around Cape Horn and erected at its present site in Sonoma. Timbers for the house were cut and numbered in Europe and were sent to California. Its bricks came around the Horn as ballast in sailing ships.

Vallejo and his wife lived in Lachryma Montis for more than 35 years but he had to deal with a series of economic setbacks and was eventually forced to sell most of his once-vast land holdings.

Although during the 1850s and 1860s Vallejo had become a pioneer in California's nascent wine industry, in the 1870s the vine louse Phylloxera devastated his vineyards and ended his hopes for commercial wine production. The only bit of good economic news was that he was able, using redwood pipes, to sell spring water to the city of Sonoma. This gave him a modest but regular income. In 1881 he also sold an easement to the Sonoma Valley Railroad, bisecting his property

In 1933 the Vallejo home and about 20 acres of the original land were acquired by the State of California to protect and preserve this historic site and Vallejo's own collection of historic artifacts and documents. The home was added to the National Register of Historic Places in 1972. It now is California Historical Landmark Number 4 and is part of the Sonoma State Historic Park.

16

The Eclipse of the Old *Californio* Order
From Rancho to Barrio

This is a complicated subject that defies any single or easy explanation. It involves not only the eclipse of the old order itself but also the *Californios'* subsequent submergence and survival in the barrios of California. For both these reasons, it is worth exploring here at some length, in a wide-ranging chapter that stretches from 1810 to 1890.

The earliest recorded use of the term "barrio," meaning a zone or a dependency of a city, dates from the 11th century and may have come from similar words in Latin, Catalonian, or Arabic.[1] "Barrio," however, was not used in California before the U.S.-Mexican War. After the American victory in the war in 1848, however, it gradually came to mean the neighborhood of a town or city where only impoverished Spanish-speaking people lived. In Los Angeles, for example, in the early 1870s Spanish-language editors had begun to write about the unique problems of the barrio there, which English-speakers knew as "Sonora Town" because so many Mexicans from Sonora lived in it.

The *Californios* experienced calamities at different times and in different places. As noted in the Introduction, in Northern California a great deal of land-grabbing and violence occurred as a flood of newcomers descended on the area during the 1848–1858 Gold Rush. This sounded the death knell of large-scale ranching there; in retrospect, it was also the first step in the gradual process of *Californio* families drifting into the barrios. At the same time, however, in the absence of such external forces, the traditional pastoral life of Southern California continued relatively unchanged until a much later period. Indeed, it was not until the 1870s that *Californios* in the southern part of the state were plunged into poverty, too.

16. The Eclipse of the Old Californio Order

The best general commentary on the eclipse of the old *Californio* order is probably Leonard Pitt's 1966 study, *The Decline of the Californios*. He reached these conclusions:

> Even with the aid of hindsight and detailed empirical research, the "final cause" of the Californio's pitiful collapse escapes the scholar. It remains a difficult exercise in historical causation to unravel the complex factors and extract the immediate from the remote causes, the human from the impersonal, the economic from the cultural or social; each contributed its own way.
>
> Clearly, the land problem stands at dead center of the matter, but even on this question there is still no consensus.... Perhaps the proper response is that, except for a few scheming Yankee speculators, the Land Law injured all parties irrespective of nationality...
>
> Culture conflict explains a great deal. Quite plainly, the Californian's economic naiveté and his penchant for conspicuous consumption led him to the brink of disaster....[2]

A modest but relevant example of culture conflict is the case of Mauricio Gonzales, the inheritor of Rancho San Miguelito de Trinidad. In 1841 or 1842, Lieutenant José Rafael Gonzales, a veteran of the Mexican war for independence from Spain, had successfully petitioned Governor Alvarado for a grant of 22,135 acres in what is now southern Monterey County between the San Antonio River and the Santa Lucia Mountains. Gonzales lived in Monterey and continued to do so after he was granted this ranch. He did well enough as a semi-absentee rancher so that in 1846 the American Consul, Thomas O. Larkin, could report that Gonzales had land, cattle, and social "influence" in the area.

When Gonzales's son Mauricio took over the ranch, Mauricio borrowed money against it and, one may guess, spent the proceeds in the lavish style beloved by the *Californio* gentry when they could afford to do so. The death blows to Mauricio's ambitions were the great droughts of 1863 and 1864, which killed more than 5,000 head of his cattle. When Mauricio was unable to meet his mortgage payments, the lender foreclosed in 1864 and this young man lost all his land. He then fell into poverty, to the extent that by 1877 he was reported to be "driving an express wagon" to make a living.[3]

It is not clear where Mauricio was living then, but Monterey seems a reasonable guess. It must be noted here that Monterey had an early social history quite different from that of any other city in California: Monterey was divided along class lines rather than ethnic lines. For example, wealthy Mexican and wealthy Caucasians lived together in similar neighborhoods and were friends. Poorer folks, of various ethnic backgrounds, lived in other areas and socialized together. Intermarriage within class lines was common, but intermarriage outside of these lines was extremely rare. The key point here, however, is that what Monterey, remarkably and unlike many other California cities, did *not* have was a barrio.[4]

The phrase "from rancho to barrio" implies both the physical displacement of the *Californios* and, more profoundly, the accompanying psychological fall from grace, i.e., the gradual loss of personal status, self-respect, and prestige that *Californios* must have experienced when they left their familiar ranchos. There was no vast tsunami of *Californios* moving directly from ranchos to barrios, but some population movement certainly did occur.

The net result was what the modern historian Albert Camarillo described as happening in Santa Barbara, though his words apply to many other towns and cities in California as well. He wrote:

> The loss of land, the decline of the pastoral economy, and the continuation of racial antagonism, together with the onset of political powerlessness, began to create a new reality in Santa Barbara. That new reality was perhaps best reflected in what can be called the *barrioization* of the Mexican population—the formation of residentially and socially segregated Chicano barrios or neighborhoods.[5]

One major reason for the population drift toward the barrios was economic instability. At first, many of the *Californio* ranchers had managed to cope with their mounting legal fees, taxes, and other debts simply by mortgaging, but not relinquishing, ownership of most of their land; later on, however, they had to abandon, once and for all, both their ancestral lands and any hope of financial recovery.

Writing in 1909, a contemporary specialist on this period, James M. Guinn (1834–1918), summed up the situation of the dispossessed Californios as follows:

> There are few more pathetic stories in the annals of our local history than the story of the decline and fall of the cattle barons of California; nor is there any episode in our history the causes of which are so imperfectly understood. By the cattle barons I mean the rancheros who, at the time of the conquest of California by the Americans, held possession in large tracts of nearly all the arable lands between San Francisco and San Diego...
>
> Their doom came quickly. Nearly all the great ranches were mortgaged. With no means to restock them, without income to pay interest or principal, the mortgagors foreclosed and took possession of the desolated cattle ranges. Within five years after the famine [i.e., the droughts of the mid- 1860s] nearly all the great ranchos had changed hands...
>
> ... it seems almost farcical that the cattle barons should have lost their possessions for the trifling amounts they owed. The possession of $20,000, at the critical moment when dispossession threatened him, would have saved from bankruptcy the

16. The Eclipse of the Old Californio Order

great cattle baron [José de la Guerra y Noriega, 1779–1858] who owned the ranches Simi, Los Posos, Conejo, San Julian and Espodo, aggregating over 200,000 acres—lost on an encumbrance of ten cents an acre. Many of the best ranches were mortgaged on the basis of twenty-five cents an acre. Figure interest at five per cent per month compounded monthly, the ruling rate in early days, and it is easy to see why a principality could be lost for what was a mere pittance at the beginning of the indebtedness.[6]

By the 1870s, due to a range of intractable problems, i.e., very high rates of interest for mortgages, expensive litigation regarding their land, state and local taxes, low beef prices caused by cheaper out-of-state competition, bad investments, prejudicial laws targeting Hispanics, alternating cycles of flood and drought, increased American immigration, and their own penchant for conspicuous consumption, many *Californio* ranchers, especially in Southern California, found themselves in deep economic trouble.

The psychological fall from grace mentioned earlier left them feeling dispossessed and marginalized. Pío Pico, the last governor of Mexican California, had been aghast at the growing number of American immigrants surging into Alta California and had asked rhetorically:

What are we to do then [i.e., to cope with this great influx]? Shall we remain supine, while these daring strangers are overrunning our fertile plains, and gradually outnumbering and displacing us? Shall these incursions go on unchecked, until we shall become strangers in our own land?[7]

During the decade of the 1870s, *Californios* could look back on their ancestral past with a bittersweet mixture of pride, nostalgia, and resentment.[8] Their immediate future, however, did not look very bright. Mariano Guadalupe Vallejo made an excellent point when he complained that "the Americans as soon as they saw they were a majority treated us not like brothers but like a conquered people."[9]

Indeed, in retrospect, by 1870 the process of proletarianization—that is to say, the emergence of a permanent Mexican working class consisting of unemployed or underemployed, displaced, and unskilled or semiskilled men and women, was already well underway in the barrios. It had begun in the 1860s and was nearly complete by 1880.[10]

Remarkably, however, not much is known today about what actually happened to most of the *Californios* who lost their ranches and jobs due to foreclosures or other problems: the secondary literature on their fate is scant.[11] At the end of the U.S.-Mexican War in 1848, there may have been about 10,000 *Californios* (estimates vary from 5,000 to 15,000).[12] Later on, as torrents of English-speaking Anglo-American and other migrants began to pour into California during and after the Gold Rush, the Spanish-speaking population of the state fell to 15 percent of the total by 1850 and to only four percent by 1870.[13] (Their descendants, however, have multiplied rapidly. It was estimated in 2004 that there were then between 320,000 and 500,000 descendants of *Californios*, and there must be many more today.[14])

Faced with declining prospects, some *Californios* decided that the best—or perhaps the only—way they could cope with this new reality was simply to continue to work and to live, now as employees, on the ranches that they no longer owned. Others, however, moved away to cultivate small plots of land close to nearby pueblos, or struggled to make ends meet as day laborers and as part-time workers in the cattle business. Still others abandoned the pastoral life entirely and went to look for work in the gold or silver mines.

Those who were more upwardly-mobile, who had some training, or who could develop the marketable skills needed to survive in urban areas, gravitated instead toward the rapidly-expanding barrios of Los Angeles, Santa Barbara, San Jose, and Sacramento. Only a small handful of the most famous "old" *Californio* families—most notably the descendants of José de la Guerra y Noriega, who had once owned over 250,000 acres of land stocked with 58,000 cattle and an equal number of horses and sheep in present-day Santa Barbara, Ventura, Marin, and Sacramento counties—managed to retain some of their wealth and social status through the late 19th century.[15] Even so, however, one of José's daughters (Doña Teresa de la Guerra de Hartnell) reported that by 1858 "the lawyers and the squatters had seized the greater part of her father's immense land holdings."[16]

José de la Guerra y Noriega himself was a career army officer who served on active duty for 52 years and who was popularly known as *El Capitán*. The modern scholars Ramón Gutiérrez and Richard Orsi have described him in these warm words:

> Revered and respected, a lord of land, labor, and cattle, he exercised wide authority while assuming responsibility for the well-being not only of family and friends but of the larger community as well.[17]

His family home in Santa Barbara was named Casa de la Guerra and is now listed in the U.S. Register of Historic Places. It was the center of social life in the city. Dana's ship happened to be in port at Santa Barbara when José's daughter, Anita de la Guerra, was married to the American businessman Alfred Robinson. Dana's account of this wedding is too long to

16. The Eclipse of the Old Californio Order

be quoted here in full, but the following extracts catch its local color and give the reader a good picture of upper class *Californio* life before its eclipse.

Dana wrote in 1840:

> Great preparations were making on shore for the marriage of our agent [Alfred Robinson], who was to marry Donna Annetea de G[uerra] de N[criega]..., youngest daughter of Don Antonio N[oriega], the grandee of the place and the head of the first family in California. Our steward was ashore for three days, making pastry and cake, and some of the best of our stores were sent off with him. On the day appointed for the wedding, we took the captain ashore in the gig [a small boat reserved for the captains use], and had orders to come for him at night, with leave to go up to the house and see the fandango...
>
> The bride's father's house was the principal one in the place, with a large court in front, in which a tent was built, capable of containing several hundred people. As we drew near, we heard the accustomed sound of violins and guitars and saw a great motion of the people within. Going in, we found nearly all the people of the town—men, women, and children—collected and crowded together, leaving barely room for the dancers; for on these occasions no invitations are given, but every one is expected to come, though there is always a private entertainment within the house for particular friends...
>
> A great deal was said about our friend Don Juan Bandini, and when he did appear, which was at the close of the evening, he certainly gave us the most graceful dancing that I had ever seen.... His slight and graceful figure was well calculated for dancing, and he moved about with the grace and daintiness of a young fawn.[18]

José de la Guerra y Noriega lived in Casa de la Guerra until his death in 1858; his descendants continued to live in this home until 1943. Although the combination of severe droughts and family disputes chipped away much of the family's ranchland and its fortune, when the first modern Old Spanish Days Fiesta was held in Santa Barbara in 1924, many parties and teas in honor of early *Californio* families were given at Casa de la Guerra.[19]

The average *Californio*, however, was much more likely to end up in a barrio rather than in a mansion. In the 19th century, despite its poverty, the barrio held out some important advantages. It was where Spanish-speaking newcomers could settle down peacefully and could find warm companionship, a familiar religion, low-level jobs, and cheap housing. In 1877, a visitor to Pueblo Viejo ("Old Town"), the impoverished barrio of Santa Barbara, had this to say about it:

> It looks as if Time had stood still. All at once goodbye to modern days.... Out of the past as through an unseen gateway, you travel into the midst of an array of dull drab-colored adobe houses, broken down and decaying adobe walls, windowless ruins, and dark foreign-looking faces.... It doesn't seem as if this could be part of the beautiful city of Santa Barbara.[20]

The Santa Barbara Historical Society Library has two revealing photos of the home of a Mexican working-class family in Pueblo Viejo, the first showing this home (the Jesus Valenzuela adobe) before, and the second during its decline in the 1880s. The "before" picture shows a modest but well-ordered homestead with two women, both reasonably well-dressed, busily working in the front yard at their household tasks. The "in decline" photo shows the same house but it is now in a semi-derelict state, with no work going on anywhere: one man is holding a young child, while another, shabbily-dressed, is simply looking at the camera.[21]

In much the same vein, an American reporter wrote of Pueblo Viejo in 1886:

> [This area] still retains almost unchanged the features and characteristics of Santa Barbara of forty or fifty years ago. There is to be seen in that quarter a labyrinth of by-ways and alleys, the existence of which most residents of Santa Barbara are unaware. And yet all of these buildings are the homes of the poorer class of Californians, and by strolling through this section many manners and customs peculiar to the early settlement of the place are to be observed.[22]

Most of the Mexicans living in Pueblo Viejo were poor but the saddest cases were those of the men who had formerly been rich, namely, some of the *Californio* rancheros, but who were now destitute. After they lost their land because they could not pay the mortgages, taxes, or legal fees, they also found that they lacked any of the skills needed to support themselves in non-ranching life. Thus they became objects of charity. Teodoro Arrellanes, for example, who was said to have been one of the richest ranchers in Southern California, died relatively poor in 1877—while living on a rancho free of charge and being supported there by the kindness of its owners.

In Northern California, all the old monolithic ranches had been dissected by fences in the early 1850s and had been broken up into farms. This region was now occupied only by squatters or low-income, small-scale owners. In Southern California, however, a few of the baronial southern ranches still managed to survive in relative peace and quiet. Indeed, in Southern California "life in the 'cow counties' in 1853 went on as calmly as it had two decades earlier."[23]

The traditional rancho culture stubbornly persisted there, even though the ranchos themselves had begun to slide downhill economically. Don Eugenio Plummer, who was introduced earlier in this book and who was one of the best-informed and most engaging "I-was-there" commentators on *Californio* life, was able, apparently without making any great effort, to name 68 families or branches of families who still mingled at

16. The Eclipse of the Old Californio Order

"fiestas large and small all over the county [of Los Angeles] and up Ventura and Santa Barbara way" and who danced in all their traditional *Californio* finery.[24] Remarkably, even at this time, when all urban talk centered on the arrival of the railroad, the rancheros still clung stubbornly to their ancestral *Californio* ways. Plummer himself, for example, eschewed any means of pleasure-driving on Sunday that was faster than the traditional wooden-wheeled cart.[25]

A love of partying and of personal display reflects a fundamental fact of life about *Californio* culture: high social status encouraged lavish hospitality, generosity, and expensive clothing. A gentleman's preferred way of life had revolved around supervising (from horseback, of course) the rounding up and slaughtering of large numbers of cattle, during which his teams of Mexican and Indian vaqueros did all the hard and dangerous work. This style of life had great attractions. It was never intellectually challenging; in fact, it did not require any book-learning whatsoever. It was *macho*, colorful, exciting, and conferred high social status. The cattle-slaughtering process known as the *nuqueo* (see Appendix 3) is a classic case in point.

The idyllic *Californio* way of life was possible only because the climate was usually mild; excellent cattle-raising land was freely available; and there were always "tame" Indians right at hand, more or less free of charge, to do all the heavy or dangerous work. When these easy conditions began to change after the U.S.-Mexican War, however, the average *Californio* gentleman found himself quite unprepared to cope with a new reality dominated by aggressive, highly competitive, legal-minded foreigners who were the shock troops of pitiless market forces.[26]

Many specific factors contributed to the eclipse of the old order but several of them stand out prominently here. The profound uncertainty (only in American eyes, to be sure) over the status of *Californio* land titles would not only run up ruinous legal costs for the *Californio* ranchers but would also strengthen the American conviction that ownership by one individual or one family of such immense ranches obtained as grants, free of charge, was basically unfair.

American politicians, for their part, believed that hard-working Jeffersonian "yeoman farmer" settlers could get along quite well with much smaller plots of land. For example, the Donation Land Claim Act of 1850 was approved by Congress to promote homestead settlements in the Oregon Territory in the Pacific Northwest, i.e., in the present-day states of Oregon, Washington, Idaho, and part of Wyoming. This Act therefore granted 320 acres free of charge to any unmarried white male citizen 18 or older and 640 acres to every married couple arriving in the Oregon Territory before the end of December 1850. Later on, in 1862, Congress passed the first Homestead Act. Largely designed to encourage settlement in the Great Plains states, it applied to Oregon as well but it granted a settler only 160 acres.

Moreover (and again from the American point of view) *Californio* land titles on properties both large and small were often unclear, overlapping, and of dubious validity. A small number of interrelated and socially well-connected *Californios* owned much of the best land. In 1849, for example, it was estimated that 200 *Californio* families owned 14 million acres, in parcels ranging in size from 1 to 11 leagues (there were nearly 4,500 acres in a league).[27]

Since the histories of the land grants were already well-known to the *Californios* themselves, they never saw any need to explain or justify them in print to the Americans. Even if they had wished to do so, however, most of the ranch owners themselves, let alone their employees, were illiterate. Moreover, very few of them spoke English well, if at all, and almost none of them had any understanding of American law or of rudimentary finance.

The result of this shortcoming was that the illiteracy and economic naiveté of many of the older patriarchal landowners made them easy targets for the smooth-talking strangers who came forward and presented themselves as reliable, experienced lawyers and financial advisors. Don Eugenio Plummer, for example, said that an Irish-Mexican confidence-man named Pancho Johnson, who was fluent both in English and in Spanish, had "swindled many an old Don" in Sonora Town.

Johnson was so good at his calling, in fact, that when Vincente Lugo, a prosperous *Californio* rancher, learned that Johnson had forged his (Lugo's) signature on a promissory note for $1,000 and had cashed the note and spent the proceeds, Lugo made no effort at all to recover his money. The reason was that Johnson had bragged to his friends that Lugo's signature on any bit of paper would be accepted everywhere as being as good as gold. Lugo valued his own reputation as a very generous *patron* (boss) so highly that not only did he not take any legal action against Johnson, but he also told him that if he ever needed money again he should come directly to Lugo's ranch and would be given it in cash.

Johnson eventually fled to Mexico, where he teamed up with "Six-Toed Pete" (whose real name was Pedro Bandillo) and tried to start a revolution there. Both men were driven out of that country, however, Bandillo later dying in Santa Monica and Pancho Johnson dying, according to Don Eugenio, "the devil knows where."[28]

16. The Eclipse of the Old Californio Order

Such charlatans often claimed that they could easily resolve all of a *Californio*'s land problems and could quickly lead him into lucrative investments. Since the big ranchero often desperately needed cash to pay his mounting legal fees and taxes—and also needed to have enough money left over so that he could continue to host fiestas and live in a grand manner—he would thoughtlessly sign mortgage documents that would eventually ruin him. Indeed, simply by foreclosing a mortgage, a moneylender could acquire land far more easily and more quickly than could a host of squatters and lawyers.[29]

American, Mexican, and other swindlers flourished in this shady environment. Professional squatters who had temporarily occupied *California* lands and who were nothing more than thugs were sometimes hired by American settlers' leagues to frighten and drive away any newly-arrived legitimate settlers who wanted to work these lands. If the thugs succeeded, land jobbers, i.e., men who traded in land, would then buy up and consolidate the now-vacant claims and sell them at a profit.

Other tactics included the use of "third-party" suits (these were legal actions launched in addition to those submitted by claimants) and many other forms of time-consuming, expensive legal harassments, e.g., reliance on writs, injunctions, and counterclaims in the courts.

As mentioned earlier, land ownership in the north of California had changed radically after the Gold Rush. By 1856, thanks to a combination of violence, legislation, lawsuits, financial manipulation, and outright purchase, local Americans now owned much of what had previously been *Californio* land. One of the most tragic stories involves the Berreyesa family of Rancho Milpitas near San Jose.

Squatters had begun to settle on the Berreyesas' land in 1852. Moreover, a senior member of the family had become insane due to his grief at the deaths of his nephews and brothers in the U.S.-Mexican War. A scoundrel named James Jakes took advantage of this man's insanity and managed to seize some of the family's property.

At the same time, the Berreyesa family was also having trouble substantiating its title to the New Almadén quicksilver mine in what is now Santa Clara County. ("Quicksilver," i.e., mercury, was used in producing gold.) One night masked riders seized a family member on a trumped-up charge of murder and hanged him from an oak tree near San Jose. Two other Berreyesa men were also lynched, one in 1854 and the other in 1857. Moreover, American lawyers representing the family in a case before the U.S. Supreme Court vanished, along with irreplaceable documents essential to the case.

These actions so enraged another senior family member that, irrationally, he himself burned other important documents. From there on the family's troubles mounted fast and faster, with the result that, in the end, the surviving 70 members of the family had no land at all left and no money. They therefore had to throw themselves on the mercy of the San Jose town government and beg to be given a small plot of land to use as a homesite. As Antonio Berreyesa lamented in 1877, of all the old *Californio* families, his was "the one which most justly complained of the bad faith of the adventurers and squatters and of the treachery of American lawyers."[30]

In this same era, prospects for the *Californios* were not very good in Southern California, either. Rancho Santiago de Santa Ana, for example, was a 63,414-acre land grant in what is now Orange County. In 1810 it had been given by Governor José Joaquín Arrillaga to José Antonio Yorba and his nephew Pablo Peralta. Extending some 22 miles eastward from the Santa Ana River to the Santa Ana Mountains, Rancho Santa Ana was at one time such a busy and well-populated place that 10 steers had to be butchered each month to feed the families, friends, hangers-on, and workers who congregated there every day.[31] Despite this prosperity, however, after the Yorba family sold the ranch to José Antonio Andrés Sepúlveda in 1854, he lost it later on when he went bankrupt trying to defend his land claims in court.

Loss of their land was not the only problem facing the *Californios*. The earlier California hide and tallow trade had ended with the U.S.-Mexican War; in its place there arose the far more lucrative beef trade. At the height of the Gold Rush, miners who yearned for beef drove the value of a longhorn from the previous $1 to $2 for its hide and fat alone (most of the meat was simply left to rot or was eaten by wild animals) to as much as $70 for its meat. Since the cost of producing a steer did not increase then, *Californio* ranchers, especially those in Southern California, were caught up in a sudden wave of prosperity.

They assumed that these flush times would last forever. In furtherance of this fantasy, they spent money like princes, signing up for new mortgages at usurious interest rates and hosting elaborate fiestas. In 1858, however, ranchers in other states started to ship herds of their own cattle to California, which began to undercut the artificially high prices there.

This economic downturn was exacerbated by kinship issues. The family ties that bound *Californio* ranchers together were silken but strong. If the phrase "the old boy network" applies very well to Britain before World War I, perhaps the phrase "old family network" can be coined here

16. The Eclipse of the Old Californio Order

to describe the Californios' intertwined and mutually-supporting family relationships. By invoking such ties, some of the big ranchers persuaded their relatives and friends to back their dubious mortgage loans. Pío Pico and his brother Andrés, for example, ensnared so many other backers in their own network of mortgage loans that when the Pico brothers failed to pay notes when they fell due, other ranchers with more robust finances were ruined.

Californio life initially revolved around the ranchos, but, later on, urban life would gradually surpass them. In 1854 there were about 5,000 people living in Los Angeles alone, i.e., some 1,500 to 2,000 resident Americans, a few hundred transients, and the rest from Mexico or from European countries. The first Spanish-language newspaper in California after the American occupation was *El Clamor Publico* ("Public Outcry"). Founded in Los Angeles in 1855 by Francisco P. Ramirez, a 19-year-old printer and editor, during its four-year life it was an important cultural force in the Spanish-speaking community and was an active defender of the interests of the Mexican people.[32]

On the one hand, Los Angeles had a few white-washed clapboard buildings that must have reminded staid visitors of New England. On the other hand, however, it was also eager to offer its more rowdy citizens a rollicking good time. For example, a former Chinese ghetto known as the *Calle de los Negros* (literally "Street of the Blacks" but translated by the Anglo-Americans of that time as "Nigger Alley") was a narrow, block-long slum packed solidly with gambling parlors, saloons, and brothels. It was never a safe passageway for the unarmed or the faint-hearted stranger.

Horace Bell (1830–1918) was a founding member of the Los Angeles Rangers, a militia company that pursued outlaws in the violent, lawless parts of Southern California. He was also a soldier, lawyer, journalist, newspaper publisher, and author of two books on the history of Southern California. Writing in 1881 about his early experiences as a young man in Los Angeles, Bell described the *Calle de los Negros* there in colorful terms. (His reference below to "seeing the elephant" was an American frontier expression meaning 'to witness something unique and truly marvelous.")

Bell wrote:

> From the great gambling house on the plaza we hied us to the classic precincts of the "Calle de los Negros," which was the most perfect and full grown pandemonium this writer, who had seen the "elephant" before, and has since been more than familiar with him under many phases, has ever beheld.
>
> There were four or five gambling places, and the crowd from the old Coronel building on the Los Angeles street corner to the plaza was so dense that we could barely squeeze through. Americans, Spaniards, Indians and foreigners, rushing and

crowding along from one gambling house to another, from table to table, all chinking the everlasting eight square $50 pieces up and down in their palms. [Here Bell is referring to the silver coins minted in the Spanish Empire after 1598 and variously known as pieces of eight, eight-real coins, or Spanish dollars.]

There were several bands of music of the primitive Mexican-Indian kind that sent forth the most discordant sound, by no means in harmony with the eternal jingle of gold...

Every few minutes a rush would be made, and may be a pistol shot would be heard, and when the confusion incident to the rush would have somewhat subsided and inquiry made, you would learn that it was only a knife fight between two Mexicans, or a gambler had caught somebody cheating and had perforated him with a bullet. Such things were a matter of course, and no complaint or arrests were ever made. An officer would not have had the temerity to attempt an arrest in "Negro Alley," at that time.[33]

Bell also has some enlightening comments about the most extravagant days of Los Angeles. He tells the reader:

Los Angeles, at the time of my arrival, was certainly a nice looking place.... The streets were thronged throughout the entire day with splendidly mounted and richly dressed *caballeros*, most of whom wore suits of clothes that cost all the way from $500 to $1,000, with saddle and horse trappings that cost even more.... Of one of the Logos [here Bell means the prominent Lugo family], I remember, it was said that his horse equipments [i.e., his saddle, bridle, reins, etc.] cost $2,000. Everybody in Los Angeles seemed rich, everybody *was* rich, and money was more plentiful at that time, than in any other place of like size, I venture to say, in the world.[34]

The cattle boom ended abruptly in the mid–1860s; at one point, the price of California cattle fell to 37 ½ cents a head in Santa Barbara.[35] The historic drought of 1862–1865 was a disaster of Biblical proportions for Southern California ranchers. Between January 1862 and March 1864, only four inches of rain fell in Southern California, and as many as 200,000 head of cattle died of starvation and thirst.

Bell later wrote this summary on the "ruin of the rancheros":

To close this pathetic chapter we will conclude by saying that the Californians struggled along under these mountains of usury [they had to borrow money at high interest rates in order to live and pay their debts] as long as their cattle resources held out. But in 1863–4 there came two successive years of drought. The cattle and horses died and the ranchos—the land—began going to pay interest. That was the beginning of the end.[36]

The drought itself had been preceded by unusually heavy rains that generated big floods. It was also accompanied by a smallpox epidemic that took its heaviest toll on the poorest Mexicans and on the local Indians, who either could not obtain or who refused to use vaccine.

To save at least some of his cattle, Juan Forster of Rancho Santa Margarita (modern-day Camp Pendleton) was forced to drive his herds into

16. The Eclipse of the Old Californio Order

the mountains, where there was still some grass and water. He reported that

> the climate was bone dry.... There was no moisture and our cattle died off in very great numbers.... Before the year 1864 had passed away, there was perfect devastation. Such a thing was never before known in California.... We poor Rancheros have had a damned bad string of luck these last two years and if it is going to continue I don't know what will become of us.[37]

The Great Drought virtually ruined Southern California's cattle industry, with herds declining by about 46 percent across the board. In Los Angeles County the loss was more than 70 percent. In 1862, Santa Barbara had 200,000 head of cattle; in 1865 only 5,000 were left. By 1870, about 13,000 head remained of the more than 100,000 cattle that had earlier roamed the hills of Southern California.[38] The one bit of good news was that a more diversified agricultural economy gradually developed in this region as ranchers learned to plant feed crops to reduce their reliance on natural forage. They also began to raise more sheep, which could eat a widely-available local weed and could endure drought much better than cattle.

For many *Californio* families in the "cow-country," prosperity was never assured. Horace Bell remembered that when he returned to Los Angeles in 1866 after the American Civil War,

> the region had become terribly poor and very much demoralized.... The wealth of the Californians was gone, the cattle had all died, the Spanish [i.e., Mexican] grandees who in '56 had adorned themselves in rich velvets, broadcloth and gold embroidery, were now in '66 wearing old soldiers' cast off clothes.[39]

Before the drought, almost all the ranches worth more than $10,000 had been owned by old *Californio* families; by 1870, however, these same families now held less than 25 percent of them. Thus what teams of lawyers, squatters, and moneylenders had managed to achieve in Northern California by chopping up baronial estates and selling the remnants to settlers, the drought alone had managed to do in Southern California.

Three examples from Los Angeles County can be put forward now to show the economic currents at play. The three *Californios* involved in these dramas were, respectively, Ygnacio del Valle, Vincente Lugo, and Julio Verduro.[40]

Ygnacio del Valle was the *alcalde* of the Pueblo de Los Angeles and a member of the California State Assembly. He and his family moved into Rancho Camulos (which, as mentioned earlier, is discussed in Appendix 2) in order to save money, but to do so he had to reduce the size of the ranch from 48,000 acres to a mere 1,500 acres or so. In addition, he had to mortgage it to a neighbor and moneylender named Newhall for $15,776.

Mr. Newhall seems to have been something of a saint because he never put any pressure at all on Ygnacio to repay him. As a result, the debt grew enormously every year, until Ygnacio finally died in 1880 at the age of 72 without ever having paid it off. Indeed, he had stipulated in his will that after his wife's death the ranch should be divided among his six children. There was apparently no mention in the will of the ever-mounting debt, and it appears that it was never repaid.

In fact, in the early 1880s, thanks largely to Mr. Newhall's forbearance the family was still living comfortably at the ranch, with the young and very able Reginaldo del Valle now presiding as its overseer. Reginaldo, an able politician, later became known as the "boss of the Spanish vote." Elected as a state senator in 1882, he would serve on numerous government boards and civic committees in California until his death in 1938.

Vincente Lugo's lands, however, went into a more precipitous decline. As a young man, he once had run 48,000 cattle on his father's vast holdings, and in 1850 he still owned an 8,856-acre ranch well-stocked with cattle. In the wake of the drought, however, he did not have one steer left to his name. Undeterred, he leased some of his land to an American sheep man and began pastoral life again with a modest assortment of cows and chickens. By saving his earnings, he was able to recover control of 800 acres around his old ranch house. He sold 400 of these acres in 1869 and 1870 at $8 to $10 per acre, and then gave 40 acres to his son Blas.

Finally, Julio Verdugo's story shows the danger of acting without thinking far enough ahead. In 1861 he mortgaged his 36,403-acre Rancho San Rafael (now the site of Glendale and part of Burbank, California) to upgrade his ranch house, buy provisions, and pay his taxes. Toward these ends, he signed a $3,445.37 loan at 3 percent monthly interest, payable quarterly. By 1870, however, this loan had ballooned into a debt of $58,750. It led to a foreclosure, a sheriff's sale, and Julio's personal financial ruin.[41]

His American lawyers bought the ranch for themselves, and the court ordered Julio to surrender to his American creditors another ranch that he owned (Rancho La Cañada). Julio then traded whatever land he had left for a neighboring ranch (the 6,600-acre Rancho Los Feliz) but he constantly had to sell off bits and pieces of it to his creditors and his lawyers. He was still not solvent, however, when Rancho Los Feliz was finally divided by a court in 1871. All he had left at the end of the trail was a gift of 200 acres—deeded to him by Alfred B. Chapman, an American buyer who took pity on him.

As the ranchos declined due to the drought and financial mismanagement, the *Californio* minor gentry, vaqueros, and common laborers

16. The Eclipse of the Old Californio Order

alike were forced to look for new kinds of work. In the countryside, there were often low-paid jobs open for farm workers, sheep-shearers, and miners. In the towns, *Californio* men could become broom makers, barbers, gamblers, butchers, or *zanjeros* (keepers of the irrigation ditches). *Californio* women from good families who had profited from childhood training in sewing could become seamstresses; others sought work as domestics or, very rarely, as prostitutes.

Even as the influence of the *Californios* themselves waned, a never-ending flow of immigrants from Mexico and other Spanish-speaking countries kept Spanish-Mexican traditions alive and well in California itself. Not all of these men and women fared well, however. The Panic of 1873 was a financial crisis that triggered a major depression in Europe and in North America. It lasted from 1873 to 1879 and produced devastating effects on the *Californios* in Southern California. Some of them had sold their ranch lands and town lots when prices were high but had later bought them back again at even higher prices—planning to hold them for only a short time and then resell them at a substantial profit. Alas, when the real estate bubble burst, they found themselves owning once-expensive properties that were now practically worthless.

Population growth, however, did create new jobs in Southern California. In 1875 the *Los Angeles Directory* listed what the residents of that city were doing. There were then 107 carpenters; 72 fruit dealers; 50 lawyers; 43 blacksmiths; 33 printers; 32 physicians and surgeons; 30 boot and shoe dealers and makers; 30 butchers; 28 teachers; 28 wagon and carriage dealers and makers; 27 saddle and harness makers; 23 upholsterers; 23 house and sign painters; 22 clergymen; 22 livery and feed stables; 2 real estate men, 19 clothing and dry goods dealers; 19 bakers; 18 hotels and lodging houses; 18 dealers in general merchandise; 14 jewelers; 13 editors and publishers; 11 restaurants; and 10 drug stores.[42]

Five years later, i.e., by 1880, Los Angeles had grown to a population of 33,000 people; the combined value of its real estate and personal property was $16,400,000. Other California cities lagged far behind. Their combined values were as follows then:

- Monterey: $7,100,000
- Santa Barbara: $5,300,000
- San Luis Obispo: $4,400,000
- San Diego: $3,500,000
- Ventura: $3,300,000
- San Bernardino: $2,500,000[43]

Regarding Los Angeles, it should be noted that by 1880 many of the Mexican-American families who owned real estate there were relatively new to the city. They were not in fact remnants of the conservative old *Californio* order but were instead part and parcel of a new and much broader Mexican-American speculative process of buying and reselling property within, say, a 10-year period in order to get a position on the property ladder.

Outside the cities and towns, dispossessed *Californios* had a good chance of finding jobs in the mines. As early as 1865, for example, in a *Harper's Magazine* article on the cinnabar (mercury) mines, a reporter found that "by far the larger portion of work-people in California are Mexicans."[44] Several hundred Mexican gold miners labored in Soledad Canyon in 1880. Until 1887, more than half of the world's mercury supply came from California, much of it produced by the New Almadén Quicksilver Mine near Santa Clara.

Having said this, it must be admitted that not all the Spanish-speaking inhabitants of California were law-abiding citizens. A life of crime did attract some young men. Many of these outlaws were Mexican or other recent immigrants, but a few were the descendants of respectable *Californio* families.

Regardless of their social backgrounds, however, they soon developed expertise in highway robbery, stagecoach holdups, and cattle rustling. One of the most infamous was Tiburcio Vásquez, a charming and very handsome cattle rustler, stagecoach robber, jailbird, murderer—and a great man with the ladies. When he was hanged in 1875 by Santa Clara Sheriff John H. Adams, the only word he spoke from the gallows was "Pronto" ["quickly"]. See Appendix 4, "An interview with the *Californio* bandit Tiburcio Vasquez," for his 15 May 1874 interview with the Los Angeles *Star*.

On a less dramatic but more positive note, in political terms one of the most successful *Californios* was Romualdo Pacheco, who rose to become governor of California. Born to a *Californio* army officer in Santa Barbara in 1831, he received an excellent education in the Sandwich Islands, i.e., Hawaii, and showed himself especially good with numbers. This ability got him a job as a supercargo on trading ships plying the California coast.

At the end of the U.S.-Mexican War, Romualdo took over the management of his mother's rancho in San Luis Obispo and in 1853, at the age of 22, won an assembly seat. He was a state senator as a Democrat in 1858 and as a Union Democrat in 1862. After serving in the Union Army in

16. The Eclipse of the Old Californio Order

1863 during the Civil War, he became a Republican and was elected state treasurer, serving for four years. He became lieutenant governor in 1871 and governor in 1875. After leaving office, he sold stocks in San Francisco. From 1878 to 1882 he served two terms in Washington, D.C., as Santa Clara's congressman, finally spending his retirement years in Mexico and Texas.[45]

The greatest single political problem that Spanish-speakers faced in Los Angeles in later years was their dwindling numbers. The catch-all phrase "Spanish-speakers" must be used here because no separate records were kept on the *Californios* per se. There were about 12,000 Spanish-speakers in Los Angeles in 1887, but they then comprised less than 10 percent of the total population. Moreover, many of them were newcomers to California who were not familiar with and were not involved in the complexities of *gringo* (American) politics. As the non–Spanish population of the city soared, however, Los Angeles would become a booming commercial center and the best-known city in the American West.

One of the most notable results of this growth in the Los Angeles area was the greatly-increased pace of the transformation of *Californio* ranchos into non–*Californio* farms and towns. In 1887, for example, brokers and buyers conducted between 30 and 70 real estate transactions every day. The net result was that former rancho lands flowed steadily away from the original *Californio* owners and into the hands of American financiers, speculators, railroad developers, town promoters, and irrigation companies. Indeed, more 100 new towns and thousands of orchards and farms were planned for southern California before the boom collapsed in 1888. This riches-to-rags process permanently disrupted the legal and daily life of most of the few remaining *Californio* rancheros.[46]

Three decades of commercial growth in the Los Angeles area during 1850–1880 did not make any earth-shaking changes in the occupational structure there. The simplistic notion that after the U.S.-Mexican War all the Mexican ranchers of the American Southwest were reduced to becoming simple day laborers is not supported by the information available on their occupations.

The historian Richard Griswold del Castillo, for example, placed Mexican-American occupations in Los Angeles into five different categories during 1850–1890. He ranked these in terms of their socio-economic status, noting how complex and how difficult he and other scholars have found this task to be, given the highly individualistic nature of the Mexican prestige system as it had evolved in the Southwest. His five categories were as follows[47]:

- The most prestigious occupational group was that of the rancheros. Regardless of how much land or money they actually had then, they were still respected by both the Anglo-American and the Spanish-speaking communities.
- Next in occupational rank were the professionals, e.g., the government officials, lawyers, doctors, teachers, friars, and nuns. They also had high status because of their education and because they did not work with their hands. Moreover, they also served as intermediaries with the broader Anglo-American community.
- After them came the commercial occupations, namely, the small merchants and craftsmen who owned their own businesses. However, because of the long-standing Hidalgo ("gentleman" in Spanish) tradition that did not value working with one's hands, there were not too many of these shop-owners and they did not have a high social standing.
- The two lowest-ranked groups were those of the skilled and the unskilled laborers. They were at the very bottom of the socio-economic pyramid because they lacked property, money, education, and influence.

By the 1880s, *Californios* were only a small percentage of the residents of California and posed no challenge to the prevailing Anglo-American supremacy in politics, business, and society. If the working-level occupational structure of Southern California did not change radically, however, the region as a whole certainly did. After 1885, in fact, the gradual evolution from its modest beginnings as a remote, impoverished Mexican cattle frontier to being a flourishing part of the United States was nearly complete.

This dramatic shift was brought about by many different but mutually-reinforcing factors in which the *Californios* themselves played only very modest supporting roles. Immigration into California increased. The remaining cattle ranches were split up into orchards, vineyards, and grain fields, now held by a much wider range of small-scale, non–*Californio* owners. The spread of irrigation systems and of more diversified farming was yet another nail in the coffin of the former *Californio* cattle kingdoms.

Moreover, at the same time, interest rates declined and money became more plentiful. Perhaps most importantly in the long run, new railroad construction shrank distances and broke down earlier walls of

16. The Eclipse of the Old Californio Order

economic and cultural isolation. When the Atchison, Topeka, and Santa Fe (ATSE) Railroad charted its own course across the United States in 1885, it decided to make Los Angeles its western terminus. This decision stimulated the region's rapid economic growth: indeed, the first trainload of oranges was shipped in 1886. The next year the price of an ATSE ticket from Kansas City, Missouri to Los Angeles fell to a promotional low of only $1.00. When the rival Southern Pacific Railroad lowered its own prices to remain competitive, real estate speculation in Southern California went into high gear and new boom towns sprang up nearly overnight.

17

Opinions on the *Californios* and Their Works

This book has followed the *Californios* over a period of 121 years, i.e., from 1769, when the Spanish first began to settle Alta California, to 1890, when Bancroft published the last volume of his *History of California*. During this era, many observers had opinions to offer on the *Californios*. Some of these will be mentioned here.

First, to set the record straight it is important to note an inherent friction between the *Californio* and the foreign ways of life. This friction gave rise to two stereotypes.

The first stereotype is that of the proud, rich, lazy, often-illiterate, "*mañana*-is-soon-enough" ranchero grandee. He is imagined as doing nothing more demanding than racing his horses under a blue sky and a mild sun. He dances half the night at balls, while during the day his hordes of Indian servants do all the hard or dangerous work. The second stereotype is that of the self-sufficient, literate, profit-motivated, expatriate settler who, thanks to his own hard work and technical skills, will soon displace the languid *Californio*.

Regarding the first stereotype, it must be understood that the vast majority of rancheros were neither rich nor lazy. Many did not own ranches at all or, if they did, they were probably only small spreads that were not very productive. It is certainly true that the ranchers themselves did not have to work hard every single day of the year (that was what their Indian servants were for), but their wives certainly did.

These *Californio* women usually had no choice but to oversee never-ending tasks of raising large numbers of children; keeping all the servants up to the mark; entertaining an endless stream of visitors; attending frequent religious celebrations; and, in general, making sure

17. Opinions on the Californios and Their Works

that their households were working as smoothly and as efficiently as possible.

Regarding the second stereotype, it is evident from historical records that not all the Americans or Europeans in California were saints. There was a great deal of violence and racism, especially in the gold fields. Men had to make sure that they were well-armed before venturing out onto California's trails. There was also much land-grabbing, both by outright violence and by self-styled "lawyers" and "financial experts" who were shysters at best. The Indians were kept in a dependent, subsistence state and were often murdered or abused, and foreigners not infrequently had Indian mistresses.

Having said all this, 11 examples—some negative and some positive—of how others saw the *Californios* and their works can be put forward here.

1. *A Russian commander comments on Californio soldiers (1816)*

An early and useful point at which to begin this review is James R. Gibson's 2013 compilation on *California Through Russian Eyes, 1806–1848*, which has already been quoted. This study introduces the reader to 32 contemporary documents which contain a great deal of unique firsthand information on the *Californios*.

In 1816, for example, Otto von Kotzebue, the commander of a Russian expedition sent to look for an Arctic seaway from the Pacific to the Atlantic, had this to say about the *Californio* soldiers he saw in San Francisco:

> ... the garrison consists of [only] one company of cavalry, whose head is the commanding officer, who has only one artillery officer under his command...
>
> ... we set off on our route with 10 cavalrymen in our convoy, themselves as fine and adept men as our Cossacks. They have acquired such skill from constant practice, for it is well known that the army in California serves only to protect the missions against attacks from the savages; moreover, they also help the clergy to convert the savages to Christianity and the converts to their new faith...
>
> The soldiers seem dissatisfied with both the government and the mission, and one cannot be surprised by this inasmuch as for 7 years running they have not received their pay and suffer much want, even of essential clothing; in addition, the residents do not have any European goods whatsoever, for trading vessels are not allowed to enter any harbor in California. It has to be regretted that this beautiful and fruitful country is not utilized at all.[1]

2. *U.S. Consul Larkin on the low value that Californios accorded to education (1845)*

In contrast to Oregon, where the early settlers made sure that every settlement had one or more schools, California did not have any organized public school system before the Americans came to power there in the wake of the U.S-Mexican War. The *Californios'* own relaxed ad hoc approach to education has been mentioned in earlier pages of this book. It formally came to an end only in 1849, when the Constitution of California established a public school system. From 1849 to 1851, Colton Hall in Monterey was the location of the state's first public school.

Before then, some small-scale but unsuccessful efforts had been made to found schools. In 1834–1836, for example, William Hartnell, a British expatriate, had opened a little school in Salinas but had to close it because he did not have enough students. Since there were no schools in Alta California,[2] some foreigners sent their sons to the eastern states for education, while some prosperous *Californios* sent theirs to schools in Hawaii.

U.S. Consul Larkin was very frustrated by the lack of newspapers and books. In 1845 he wrote to his friend Moses Y. Beach (grammar as in the original):

> There is no Books (excepting children first Books) for sale here ... but few would purchase if there were.... [In addition there were] no Newspapers in California, for which I attribute Four reasons. Either one may suffice. First there is no printer. Second no printing press. Three Editor [i.e., no editor]. Fourth there could no subscribers be obtained.[3]

The year before, in 1844, Larkin himself had tried to establish a private elementary school in Monterey to educate the sons of foreign expatriates and wealthy *Californios*. Toward this end, he circulated a subscription list among his friends and business associates in California and in September 1844 wrote to Alfred Robinson, who had previously done business in Alta California and was then living in New York City. Larkin asked him to recruit a schoolmaster to come out to Monterey. Robinson was at first enthusiastic about this project but for some reason he never followed up on it, so the idea came to naught.[4]

3. *An American businessman takes the Californios to task (1846)*

Alfred Robinson (1806–1895), one of the first Americans to do business in Alta California, is mentioned above. His own book, *Life in California*, first published in 1846, is important today because it gives the reader a generally sympathetic but often bitingly critical portrayal of *Californio* life. Here is an example of the latter:

> If Mexico, in her zeal for the welfare of her territories, had been more circumspect in the choice of officers for California [i.e., in the choice of governors for California], she would not have experienced the humiliation that she has borne, nor incurred the expense of so many expeditions to reconquer it. Her own people have in all cases been the fomenters; and here, as has been frequently done in Mexico, they

have aimed at the removal of certain governmental officers, not so much for the desire to reform, as the division of the spoils! This is the pretended patriotism of all Mexicans who have taken active part in revolutionizing their own country, and which has been disseminated by them amongst the Californians, till, like themselves, they have become "*Patriotas de bolsa*!" (Patriots of the pocket.)[5]

4. *Rev. Walter Colton on the Californios' enjoyment of life (1850)*

Writing in 1850 of his three previous years of service in California, Rev. Walter Colton, who has been quoted earlier, was so impressed by the pleasures the *Californios* got of life that it is worth quoting him here at some length. He wrote in his diary:

> There is no people that I have ever been among who enjoy life so thoroughly as the Californians. Their habits are simple; their wants few; nature rolls almost everything spontaneously into their laps. Their cattle, horses, and sheep roam at large—not a blade of grass is cut, and none is required. The harvest waves wherever the plough and harrow have been; and the grain which the wind scatters this year, serves as seed for the next. The slight labor required is more a diversion than a toil; and even this is shared by the Indian. They [the *Californios*] attach no value to money, except as it administers to their pleasures. A fortune, without the facilities of enjoying it, is with them no object of emulation or envy. Their happiness flows from a fount that has very little connection with their outward circumstances...
>
> Their hospitality knows no bounds; they are always glad to see you, come when you may; take a pleasure in entertaining you while you remain; and only regret that your business calls you away.... If I must be cast in sickness or destitution on the care of the stranger, let it be in California; but let it be before American avarice has hardened the heart and made a god of gold.[6]

5. *Richard Henry Dana, Jr., updates his famous book (1859)*

Beginning with the revised edition of 1869, Dana replaced the last chapter of his celebrated book, *Two Years Before the Mast*, with a new concluding chapter entitled "Twenty-Four Years After." In it, he recorded his impressions when he revisited California in 1859, contrasting what he saw then with what he had experienced 24 years earlier. A few of the many points he made can best be mentioned by condensing and paraphrasing them.

Dana wrote that as the *Golden* Gate, the elegant steamship on which he was a passenger, moored at a dock in San Francisco, many large clipper ships and high-pressure steamers were already clustered at the port; the city streets were there chocked with wagons. He was soon comfortably settled in the Oriental Hotel, which was located not far from the spot where he and his shipmates had beached their ship's boats on the sand (there being no dock then) 24 years earlier.

Los Angeles was also a large and flourishing town of about 20,000 inhabitants, now with blocks of stone or brick houses. It was a vibrant center for wine production, figs, olives, peaches, pears, and melons. San Diego, however, had not changed at all; Dana said that it was still, like Santa Barbara, predominately a Mexican town. He also visited Sacramento, which had grown to a city of some 40,000 people and was now served by fleets of river steamers and a thriving inland commerce.

Dana ends his account by noting that the *Alert*, a ship on which he had worked in Californian waters, had been a favorite vessel for all her owners, officers, and men. However, she was captured in 1862 during the Civil War by the Confederate steamer *Alabama* and was promptly burned at sea by her new masters.[7]

6. *Bancroft's interviewer Thomas Savage explores the Californio archives (1876)*

Both personally and professionally, the *Californios* themselves were not given to writing: as noted earlier many of them were illiterate. At the same time, however, they did not want to throw away official documents, even if these had not been consulted for many years. Bancroft understood the potential historical value of these old documents and took advantage of this fact by assigning to Thomas Savage the arduous task of sifting through them to see what they contained and, where appropriate, to have them safely rebound and conserved for study by future generations.

Savage had to use his own judgment in deciding what to preserve. Today there is no way of knowing whether a *Californio* editor (had there been one) would have chosen these or different documents. In any case, the end result of Savage's editing was his "Report of Labors in Archives and Procuring Material for History of California, 1876–9."[8] Aided by up to 12 assistants, in May 1876 he began abstracting 300 volumes of bound but disordered manuscripts in Spanish, ranging from 700 to 1900 pages each, plus a considerable number of unbound documents.

These archives, some of which dated from 1769, had been collected by the U.S. Government in 1851 but were now jumbled together in an extremely disordered state. Moreover, much of the writing was very hard to read, being faded by time and suffering from bad penmanship and worse grammar. Nevertheless, Savage and his helpers managed to complete their research within 10 months, producing 63 neatly bound volumes. Savage then continued his archival investigations in other parts of California, e.g., in Monterey, Santa Cruz, Los Angeles, San Diego, and Sacramento.

7. *Ramona: The novel and its descendants (1884)*

As mentioned earlier, *Ramona* is an American novel written in 1884 by Helen Hunt Jackson. It sketches out the life of Ramona, a fictional mixed-race Scots-Indian orphan girl who has to endure racial discrimination and much hardship. This novel has enjoyed remarkable popularity ever since publication, being first serialized in the *Christian Union* every week. Since then, it has been reprinted more than 300 times and has been adapted as a film four times. Well-known actresses who have portrayed Ramona on film include Mary Pickford in a 1910 silent movie, Dolores del Rio in a 1928 movie, and Loretta Young in a 1936 movie.

A play adaptation of *Ramona* has been performed outdoors every year since 1923.[9] Raquel Welch played Ramona at the Ramona Pageant of 1959. The canyon where this presentation takes place is located in Hemet, California in what has become known as the Ramona Bowl, a natural amphitheater in the foothills above the town of Hemet in Riverside County. The canyon was upgraded slightly in 1988 but many scenes are still played on the hillside and on the trails and clearings first created in 1920s and 1930s.

Ramona romanticizes the life-styles of the *Californios* and cannot be considered to be great literature. Nevertheless, it has contributed greatly to the memory of these unique men and women. Its sentimental and, indeed, semi-mythological presentation of Mexican colonial life coincided with the building of railroad lines into the area, with the result that many tourists wanted to see for themselves the places highlighted in the novel.

The pull of the novel became so strong, in fact, that some early visitors looking for "Ramona's birthplace" in San Diego or near the Ramona Pageant were bitterly disappointed to learn that Ramona herself was simply a figment of Helen Hunt Jackson's literary imagination and had never existed.

8. *María Ruiz de Burton's 1885 novel* The Squatter and the Don

The first female author with a Mexican-American background to write in English, María Ruiz de Burton has already been mentioned here in earlier pages. Her best-received novel, *The Squatter and the Don* (1885), was republished in 1992 in a new edition by Rosaura Sánchez and Beatrice Pita. It offers persuasive insights into many of the problems faced by the *Californios* after the U.S.-Mexican War.

The title page of this novel describes it as depicting contemporary events in California.[10] The book begins by recording the struggles of the fictional Alamar family against a group of squatters who settle on their ranch, kill their cattle with impunity, and force the family to flee from their ancestral land and move to San Francisco. In the second half of the book, the Alamars join forces with other San Diegans to lobby for a much-needed railroad terminus in their city. Alas, their hopes for a better future are shattered by government corruption and prejudice.

When she was writing this novel, Ruiz de Burton was herself, like the Alamar family, deeply embroiled in legal struggles over the title to her own ranch in San Diego County at Jamul, California. Squatters, suits, and countersuits involving this ranch would continue to be a burden for her until her death in 1895.

9. *"Fiesta Days" celebrations (1890)*

Beginning in about 1890, Anglo-American civic, business, and historical organizations in California finally began to pay close attention to the long-past and now "very romantic" *Californio* way of life, which in its heyday in about 1848 had never seemed romantic at all, either to the participants themselves or to outside observers.

These organizations' new interest in the *Californio* way of life, however, gave birth to the modern "Fiesta Days" celebrations, which feature floats showing romantic scenes imagined in pastoral California before the U.S.-Mexican War. Participants often include local businessmen, who ride fine horses and are dressed as *caballeros*, and local ladies who are decked out in period costumes. The annual Old Spanish Days Fiesta in Santa Barbara is probably the best known of these events.

This event was first held in 1924. Its modern version has been described on a website in these words:

> The Santa Barbara Old Spanish Days Fiesta Parade celebrates the history of the Santa Barbara area. Different cultural groups and time periods are represented in the parade, including entries from local Native American groups, Spanish Colonial re-enactors, Ranchero period revelers, and nineteenth century American settlers.
>
> The event draws thousands of visitors from around the world. Fiesta performers come from around the nation and Mexico to participate. Celebrities of international renown who have participated or performed at the Fiesta include Leo Carrillo, Will Rogers, Shirley Temple, Charles Lindberg, William Randolph Hearst, Don Wilson, Paul Whitman, and Delores del Rio.[11]

It seems fitting that the long-forgotten story of the *Californios* is now being remembered in such a positive and public—if semi-mythological—manner. For many decades after California had passed from Mexican to American rule, few Americans had any interest the *Californio* legacy itself, preferring instead to embrace the Mission Revival Movement (see below). This seemed to them to be much less "foreign" and therefore much easier to grasp.

10. *The California Mission Revival style of architecture (late 19th century)*

Rather than continuing to seek architectural inspiration from buildings in the eastern United States, by the late 19th century some American architects had fallen under the spell of the Spanish Colonial mission heritage of California.[12] They were motivated in part by California's own campaign in that era to restore these historic buildings, many of which had already fallen into ruin. Esthetically, these men and women were very favorably impressed by the mission chapels with their thick white stucco walls, red clay tile roofs, and bell towers. What became known as the California Mission Revival style became increasingly visible and popular across the West after the Santa Fe and Southern Pacific railways embraced it and began to use it in their new stations and resort hotels.

Remarkably, the American military was not slow to follow suit. In 1908 the U.S. Army established the San Francisco Port of Embarkation at Fort Mason. Instead of using standard building plans, the Army hired an architectural firm to design the port's buildings in the Mission Revival style. For example, Building C there had a hipped roof with clay tiles, overhanging eaves with brackets, and an undecorated concrete surface. The Fort Mason Chapel, built in 1942, contained many classic Mission Revival elements. Much better looking than the purely functional Building C, this chapel was covered in white stucco. It had red tile roofs, a bell tower, a projected arched entryway, a center quatrefoil vent, and deep narrow windows.

11. *Zorro, by far the best known Californio (1919)*

"Zorro," which means "fox" in Spanish, is a fictional character created in 1919 by the New York City-based pulp writer Johnston McCulley.[13] Zorro is, without doubt, now the best known of all the *Californios*. His story harks back to the Robin Hood legend, i.e., of a gentleman who steals from the rich to give to the poor. Zorro conceals his true identity behind a black mask and a flowing black cape. His famous symbol is the capital letter "Z," slashed with his rapier. In "real life" he is in fact Don Diego de la Vega, the noble son of a wealthy *Californio* landowner.

When Don Diego returns to San Diego from his studies in Spain, he finds that the city is now under the control of Capitan Monastario, an evil and corrupt army officer. Realizing that he by himself cannot hope to defeat Monastario and his troops, Don Diego resorts instead to foxlike cleverness to protect the common people against tyranny. In the process, he delights in making the soldiers look singularly foolish and incompetent.

The first Zorro story, *The Curse of Capistrano*, appeared in 1919 in *All-Star Weekly*, which later became *Argosy* magazine. More than 65 Zorro books and short stories followed, with an estimated 500 million readers around the world following the adventures of Zorro in 26 languages. In addition, there have been many filmed versions of Zorro, beginning with Douglas Fairbanks, Sr.'s portrayal in the 1920 silent movie, *The Mark of Zorro*.

In 1952–1953, Walt Disney obtained the film and television rights to Zorro. Early productions were filmed in black-and-white, but a later version in color won a new generation of young viewers. They were almost certainly already familiar with some the many products, e.g., playsuits, toys, watches, puzzles, games, and coloring books, that had long been licensed under the Zorro trademark. Later waves of viewers can now enjoy Zorro on computers and video games.

18

Three Young *Californio* Women

The following accounts are unique in the historiography of California. Sourced respectively to Maria Antonia Pico, Brigida Briones, and Amalia Sibrian, who were all members of the *Californio* gentry, these accounts initially appeared in the January 1891 issue of *The Century Magazine*.

As quoted here, they are drawn "from the old catalog" (no date given) of the *Californiana* section of the California Historical Collection's *Reminiscences and Memoirs of Gen. Vallejo, Gen. Bidwell, Gen. Fremont, and Other Early Pioneers of the Western Overland*, which is listed in the Bibliography.[1] The phrase 'Western Overland" refers to the activities in the American West of the individuals being studied. The accounts are too long to be quoted here verbatim, but excerpts will give the modern reader a very good flavor of *Californio* times.

Maria Antonia Pico

Maria's account was taken down by the American writer Charles Howard Shinn, who heard it from an old Mexican woman in Castroville, who in turn had often heard it related by Maria herself.

"A California Lion and a Pirate"

It was about the middle of November, 1818, and I was sixteen years of age. A vessel brought the report to Monterey that a whole fleet of pirates was coming. [This was the attack by the pirate Hipólite Bouchard, described in Chapter 7 above.] Everyone, in great fright, commenced to move [in ox-drawn carts] and hide the most valuable things.... About midnight we [i.e., Maria, her little sister, and little brother] reached a large, broken oak tree where our mother had told us to camp. We let the oxen loose to graze, and we crawled under the cart...

[Late at night, while her sister and brother slept, Maria heard a wild animal attack the oxen.] The morning was dawning when this happened, and in a few minutes I could see 100 feet down the cañon. An indistinct form began to be revealed here, and I hushed the children to watch and listen. There, as we soon saw, was a large California lion, or puma, pulling meat from one of our oxen.... I whispered to the others to lie still, because we had no place to hide, nor was it any use to try to climb a tree, for the California lion will climb like a cat. So we saw the lion finish his meal on our ox.

It grew very light, near sunrise, before he took any notice of us, where we sat under the ox-cart. As soon as he saw us he walked up very close, with a curious, wondering expression on his face, and went all about the cart, looking us over and making a purring sound. We sat close and held our arms abut one another, but did not say a word. He then came up so close that I felt his breath on me and finally he put his nose against my ankle. I had no stockings on, only home-made shoes, and his nose felt very strange, and made me expect to be eaten up at once. But I thought it best to lie still, and not cry out.

After what seemed a long time, the lion went back and lay down by the dead ox, about a hundred feet distance, keeping his eyes on us most of the time. He sometimes walked around the ox; then he went off a little way to a spring; then he came back and walked around the cart. At last he lay down again by the ox, shut his eyes, and seemed asleep.... We lay there under the cart all the morning.... Then about three o'clock mother and José, the peon, came down from the coast way [and understood the situation at a glance]. José ran forward and fired two shots, wounding the lion, but he got away in the rocks...

[Maria then volunteered to take her mother's horse and ride back to the ranch to obtain an important family book that her mother wanted. In the process, however, Maria encountered the pirates. There was gunfire nearby and her horse ran away because of the noise. She was determined to catch another horse, but then two men came out of the bushes and spoke to her.]

They were armed strangers, and very wild, so I fell on my knees and prayed them to do me no harm. One of them asked me my name, and why I was there; so I told him.... He laughed and said I was a good girl and sent his men to catch my horse. Then he dismounted while I still knelt there ... and he came up to me and kissed me on the forehead and called me Señorita, which frightened me very much. Then the man came up with my horse, and I looked at the leader of the two, and asked what he was going to do with me?

He looked at me and swore a great oath. "My girl," he said, "you are more brave than some of the people who were on the beach when we landed. [The *Californio* men on the beach ran away when the pirates attacked.] You shall go back." He put me on my horse, and kissed my hand, and said, "Ride fast; there are others of Bouchard's men who would not treat you so well." I thanked him briefly, and he added as he let go of the bridle that his name was Pedro Condré, and that he already had two wives aboard his ship, or he would have taken me there.

This last saying made me ride in great terror and with frightful speed down the gulches and up the hills. When I reached mother's camp I was crying, and so terribly excited that I could not say anything but "Hasten, hasten!" We left all our things hidden in the bushes, and went on to the Salinas [river].

[Later, at a Christmas church service,] the good padre called me out before the congregation and gave me a gold cross because of what he called my courage with the lion and with the pirate. It does not seem to me that I was very brave, for I only took things as they happened, but I was very much pleased with the cross and words of praise.

Selections from Two Articles by Brigida Briones

"A Glimpse of Domestic Life in 1827"

The ladies of Monterey in 1827 were rarely seen on the street, except very early in the morning on their way to church. We used to go there attended by our servants, who carried small mats for us to kneel upon, as there were no seats. A tasteful little rug was considered an indispensable part of our belongings, and every young lady embroidered one of her own.... Every woman in Monterey went daily to church, but the men were content to go once a week.

For home wear and for company we had many expensive dresses, some of silk, or of velvet, others of laces, often of our own making, which were much admired.... The rivalry between beauties of high rank was as great as it could be in any country, and much of it turned upon attire, so that those who had small means often underwent many privations in order to equal the splendor of the rich.

... most of the girls of the time had scanty educations. Some of my playmates could speak English well, and quite a number knew something of French.... The ladies of the province were born and educated here; and they lived and died, in complete ignorance of the world outside. We were in many ways like grown-up children.

Our servants were faithful, agreeable, and easy to manage. They often slept on mats on the earthen floor, or, in the summertime, in the courtyards. When they waited on us at meals, we often let them hold conversations with us, and laugh without restraint.

"A Carnival Ball at Monterey in 1829"

The first ball that I ever attended took place near Monterey about 1829, when I was Señora Brigida Cañes. I do not remember my age at the time, but I think I was about eighteen. I was invited by a friend in Monterey to visit her, as she had arranged a carnival ball, as was the custom of the country.

I left my home with the usual attendants at about eleven o'clock the day before, for our ranch was many miles distant. We met numbers of persons going to the party, all on horseback, and full of gaiety and youthfulness such as only a race that lives outdoors in such a climate as California, and without cares or troubles, can show.... Everyone could ride perfectly, and could pick up a leaf or a flower from the ground as he galloped past. Good riding was expected as a matter of course.

On this occasion they all had red, black, and green paint (for the most part colored earths, powdered) and *cascarones* (egg-shells filled with finely cut gold and silver paper), and vials of different colored liquids, all harmless. It was the great sport to ride against each other, each endeavoring to stain his opponent's face while himself escaping. As we neared Monterey the carnival spirit grew wilder, and the ladies' dresses and faces suffered, but we all took it in good part.

On our arrival at the ranch near Monterey where the festivities took place we found everyone already dancing. The assembled guests,rushing on us, lifted us from our horses and led us in, smearing our faces with more paint and breaking *cascarones* on our heads with much laughter. It was my first experience of so wild a scene, and the red, green, and black paint on my face made me uglier than a Yuma Indian. But as long as others were in as bad a case, I could not complain...

The annual carnival ball was a great feature of the social life of the time, and often lasted all night. The wild revel of the first part of the ball was succeeded by the most courtly behavior.

Amalia Sibrian

The following article shows how the *Californios* viewed the Americans; it thus reflects *Californio* values and attitudes. It also shows how "unworldly" some of the uneducated *Californios* were, who did not know that another language besides Spanish even existed.

"A Spanish [i.e., Mexican] Girl's Journey from Monterey to Los Angeles"

Early in the winter of 1829 my father, who had long expected an appointment under the governor, received a letter from Los Angeles saying that his papers were in the hands of the authorities there, and would be delivered only in person. [My father] decided to take my mother and myself with him and go overland [from Monterey], without waiting for the yearly vessel from Yerba Buena [San Francisco]...

A young American who had reached the coast from the city of Mexico heard of our plans and came to my father to ask if he might travel with us to Los Angeles, which was easily arranged. He did not know a word of Spanish, and I have often laughed at some of his experiences on the road, owing to his ignorance of our ways and speech.

At one house the señora gave him some fruit, whereupon he handed her two reales, which she let fall on the floor in surprise, while the old don, her husband, fell upon his knees and said in Spanish, "give us no money, no money at all; everything is free in a gentleman's house!" A young lady who was present exclaimed in great scorn, "*Los Engleses pagar por todos!* ("The English pay for everything.") I afterward told the American what they had said, and explained the matter as well as I could, but he thought it a foolish thing that no one, not even servants, could take money for services.

We several times met grown people, and heads of families, who had never heard any language except Spanish, and who did not know, in fact, that any other language existed. They were really afraid of our American, and once I was asked if there were any other people like him...

18. Three Young Californio Women

One day we passed a very ugly Indian woman, and he asked me to ask her [in Spanish] how old she was. Out of mischief I whispered, "*Yo te amor*" ["I love you"], which he said at once and she, poor creature, immediately rose from her seat on the ground and replied, "*Gracias, Señor, pero soy indio*" ("Thank you, sir, but I am an Indian"), which gave us sport long after.

The next day my companion gave me a lesson in English by way of revenge.... After mass all the men and boys assembled on horseback in front of the church, with the padre and alcalde at their head. They rode about in circles like a circus, fired guns, beat drums, and shouted. I thought it very fine, and by signs asked my American friend how he liked it, and he answered, "Dam-fools!" with such energy that I supposed they were words of praise. Indeed, I used the bad words as very proper English for a year or two, until I learned better, when I was of course much mortified.

Conclusion:
Six Calamities of *Californio* Life

The *Californios* often found themselves trapped in calamities that were not of their own making and that were far beyond their control. Six of these events have already been reviewed in this book but they can profitably be highlighted again here. In chronological order, they are as follows:

1. The failure, first by Spain and then by Mexico, to do anything about the well-known and long-standing American desire to extend the United States all the way from the Atlantic to the Pacific, i.e., including California itself. This desire was mentioned as early as 1758 in an American almanac published that year.[1]

2. The dismal military performance of the *Californios* during the U.S.-Mexican War (1846–1848), which contributed to their loss of California.

3. The flood of gold seekers and squatters into the foothills and valleys of Northern and Central California (after 1849), which spelled the ruin of the large-scale *Californio* ranches there.

4. The Land Law (1851), which plunged *Californio* ranchers into long, expensive legal battles that eventually deprived many of them of their land.

5. The great droughts in Southern California (mid–1860s), which laid waste to the *Californio* cattle herds of this region.

6. The impoverishment and barriozation of the *Californios* in the towns and cities (in the 1870s).

It was the last of these calamities that had the most lasting and most negative effects on the *Californios*.[2] These men and women were now

Conclusion: Six Calamities of Californio Life

considered by most Anglo-Americans as being indistinguishable from the broad mass of the Mexican-American community. As such, they, too, were reduced to the role of being the "others," i.e., poor, uneducated, Spanish-speaking, Roman Catholic "foreigners" who did not fit into the dominant Protestant Anglo-American mold and who were thus forced to create and maintain a new community for themselves.

By the 1860s, about half of the people living in Los Angeles were Spanish-speaking and had already begun to find themselves segregated in terms of the housing and land investments open to them. By the 1870s, except for a handful who had managed to retain some of their traditional wealth and social status, or those who had managed to win political positions, most of the *Californios* were now a dispossessed and impoverished minority. By the 1880s, Mexican-Americans had become even more segregated from the Anglo-American majority of the population. They were also losing their former political influence in Los Angeles, the location of the biggest barrio, because newly-drawn ward boundaries had divided the barrio. Almost half of the Spanish-speaking population now lived outside the original barrio and, perhaps for this reason, it no longer demonstrated a very high level of political involvement.

In fact, *Californios* could win only those elections where their families and friends took great pains to turn out and support them. By and large, the *Californio* candidates were already rich men whose interests were similar or identical to those of the most powerful Anglo-Americans. What is noteworthy here is how few Mexican-American voters there really were. In 1880, for example, fewer than 490 Mexican-Americans were eligible to vote in Los Angeles. The same family names cropped up, again and again, year after year, in the contests for local elections. The tragedy here was that the impoverished *Californios*—i.e., the people who needed the most help—were in effect excluded from the political process. As Richard Griswold del Castillo put it,

> Although superficially the Spanish-speaking did not appear to lack political representation, in fact they did. For practical purposes, the mass of laborers in the barrios remained politically inarticulate and unrepresented.[3]

But enough doom-and-gloom. Offsetting these calamities to some extent were the many positive qualities of *Californios*. To balance the historical books, as it were, they, too, need to be cited here.

The missions opened what would later become the great cornucopias of the California agricultural and livestock industries. As mentioned earlier, they cultivated wheat, corn, barley, beans, fruits, and grapes; made wine and brandy; and raised cattle, sheep, and horses. All this was possible due to the unremitting efforts of the friars, the *Californio* staffs, and the Indians of the missions. The livestock industry also owes a great deal to generations of ranchers and large landowners, many of whose forbears were *Californios*.

If these legacies are not enough in and by themselves, it must also be remembered that the *Californios* placed very high values on family ties, politeness, outdoor activities, respect for the aged, and religious observances. One of their greatest virtues was hospitality. The French lawyer, politician, and epicure Jean Anthelme Brillat-Savarin (1755–1826) was thinking of France when he wrote this, but it applies equally well to *Californio* life. According to Brillat-Savarin, "To invite someone is to take upon yourself the responsibility for his happiness all the time he is under your roof."[4]

The *Californios* were often described by both American and foreign observers as being an attractive, colorful, kind-hearted, uncomplicated, and very friendly people. Moreover, despite the adversities they suffered during and after the U.S.-Mexican War, as a group they remained unshakably cordial, long-suffering, and resilient in the face of the brave new world so suddenly thrust upon them by the American invaders. Their resilience is even more remarkable when one remembers that, as stated earlier, the adversities they faced were not of their own making and that there was little or nothing the *Californios* could do about them.

What, then, can be offered here, in closing, as a fitting epitaph for the *Californio* way of life? Perhaps here we can let General Mariano Guadalupe Vallejo speak for all of the *Californios*. Not long before his death in 1890 at the age of 82, Vallejo looked back on his own adventure-filled life with evident satisfaction and said: "I had my day. It was a proud one."[5] Many *Californios* would probably have agreed with him, as they looked back on their own admittedly more modest but still very colorful lives.

Annotated Chronology, 1510–1890

1510: The name "California" comes from a Spanish novel, *Las Sergas de Esplandián* (*The Labors of the Very Brave Knight Esplandián*), by Garci Rodríguez Ordóñez de Montalvo.

1521: The explorer Hernán Cortés gives the name *Nueva España* (New Spain) to the territories he had won for Spain in his conquest of Mexico. The Viceroyalty of New Spain, headquartered in Mexico City, will exert nominal political control over large chunks of the Pacific coastal region; the Southwest; the Gulf of Mexico coastal region; and Greater Florida, which included Florida and parts of seven other southern states.

1542: Juan Rodríguez Cabríllo is the first European to sail along and explore the California coast.

1697: As the first step on their colonization of Baja and Alta California, the Spaniards begin building missions in Baja California.

1715–1729 and **1733–1742:** Russian involvement in California stems from the expeditions of exploration and discovery under taken under the orders of Tsar Peter the Great.

1744–1848: Famously described as "the longest, crookedest, most arduous pack mule route in the history of America," the Old Spanish Trail links the northern New Mexico settlements near and in Santa Fe with those of Los Angeles and Southern California.

1758: An American almanac predicts that the United States will eventually extend all the way from the Atlantic to the Pacific, i.e., that California will become part of the United States.

1768: Two influential Spanish officials—*visitador general* (inspector general) Gálvez and Viceroy de Croix—put forward their reasons why Spain should occupy California. That same year, a royal order by King Carlos III directs that the occupation be undertaken, and Gálvez supervises the founding of a shipyard and naval depot at San Blas. In 1768 and 1769, Gálvez also grants

Baja California land to deserving Spanish soldiers to reward them personally and to encourage young men to join the military service.

1769: Fearing that if Alta California is not colonized, it will be taken over by the Russians or other powers, Spain begins a low-level program to colonize this region. The first step is an expedition from Loreto, Baja California led by Gaspar de Portolá and includes missionary friar Junípero Serra. During it, Sergeant José Francisco Ortega and a small band of men see San Francisco Bay for the first time. That same year, the Spanish build a presidio in San Diego and establish the first mission, San Diego de Alcalá, there.

1769–1823: The Spanish build a total of 21 missions which will ultimately employ 142 friars and will nominally baptize tens of thousands of Indians.

1770: Spain builds a presidio in Monterey.

1772: The Viceroy of New Spain assigns the Territory of Alta California to Franciscan friars.

1773: There are now only two presidios, five missions, and about 70 Spaniards in Alta California.

1774: The Spanish explorer and cartographer Miguel Constansó describes *Californios* as the *gente de razón*. This term means "people of reason" but "rational people" is a better translation. Constansó uses it to describe the European Spaniards, Creoles, and people of mixed blood—but not the Indians.

1774–1776: The de Anza expeditions establish an overland route north to San Francisco. It will later become the 650-mile-long track known as El Camino Real ("The Royal Road").

1776: Spain builds a presidio at San Francisco.

1777: The town of San José de Guadalupe is founded.

1781: Los Angeles is founded. Governor Filipe de Neve reports that the presidios of Monterey and San Francisco are now being "completely fed by the town of San José."

1782: Spain builds a presidio at Santa Barbara.

1784: In a typical petition and land grant, the San Diego presidio soldier Manual Pérez Nieto receives 150,000 acres from Alta California Governor Pedro Fages.

1790: Supply ships are no longer needed to carry flour, corn, or beans from San Blas to Alta California. During the 1790s, the population of Monterey, the capital of Alta California, varies from about 202 to about 400 people, many of them soldiers.

1798–1810: The port of San Blas goes into a rapid decline due to the growth of smuggling along the Alta California coast and to political instability in Mexico itself.

1797: The town of Villa de Branciforte is founded.

1799: The Russian-American Company is founded and will later trade with *Californios* in the San Francisco Bay area and along the coast north of San Francisco.

1810: Spain builds its fifth and final presidio at Sonoma.

1810–1821: The Mexican War of Independence ends the rule of Spain in its Viceroyalty of New Spain.

1818: An attack on Monterey by the pirate Hipólito Bouchard reveals how unready and how unwilling the *Californios* are to defend their homeland in the face of a foreign attack.

1821: Mexico wins its independence from Spain. *Californios* can now legally trade with foreign nations.

1823: There are so many wild horses in Alta California that great numbers must be slaughtered to preserve the pasturage for the *Californios'* riding horses and for their cattle.

1827: A European visitor describes San Luis Rey, the biggest and richest mission, as having "the aspect of a palace." Los Angeles is now the biggest town and is clearly on its way up.

1833: Juan Mariner, a 53-year-old Spanish ex-artilleryman, files a petition to be given a land grant known as Rancho Rincon de San Pascual. The "chain of title," i.e., the sequence of ownership of a given piece of land, of this ranch is a good example of this legal process.

1833–1846: The 21 missions of Alta California are secularized and about 770 grants of former mission lands are made to influential *Californios*. These grants are not based on formal land surveys but only on rough sketches known as *diseños* ("designs"). After Mexico loses the U.S-Mexican War, these sketches will not be accepted by the Americans as legal proof of land ownership. This will set in motion years of legal wrangling and mortgaging that, in the end, will bankrupt many *Californio* ranchers.

1834–1846: General Mariano Guadalupe Vallejo's Rancho Petaluma is the most prosperous ranch in Northern California.

1836–1837: Indian attacks in the San Diego area reach new heights, forcing the evacuation of ranches and even threatening San Diego itself.

1837: Andrés Castillero, an army officer, urges the minister of war in Mexico City to strengthen the defenses of both Californias, but no action is taken on his recommendation.

1840: In his famous book *Two Years Before the Mast*, Richard Henry Dana, Jr., describes *Californio* life in 1835–1836, especially the hide and tallow trade, which was the major economic activity in California before the Gold Rush.

1841: General Mariano Guadalupe Vallejo warns the Ministry of War about the threat posed by the Americans, but no action is taken on his recommendation.

1845: The final sale and lease of mission property ushers in a new social order based on the sudden prosperity and higher social status of major ranch owners. In that same year, Manuel de la Peña y Peña, the minister of foreign relations, sends to all the states of Mexico his own pessimistic analysis of Mexico's very poor prospects in any war with the United States. Yet again, however, no action is taken to strengthen Mexico's defenses.

1846–1848:
- In 1846, Americans in California stage the short-lived Bear Flag Revolt.
- That same year, the U.S.-Mexican War begins. In California, it will consist of a series of infrequent, small-scale, low-level incidents. The dismal military performance of the *Californios* during the war will contribute to their loss of California. The sole exception is the battle of San Pascual on 6–7 December 1846, where *Californio* lancers under Captain Andrés Pico defeat American soldiers under General Stephen Watts Kearny.
- In 1848, under the terms of the Treaty of Guadalupe Hidalgo, Mexico has to cede over 500,000 square miles of its land to the United States.
- This year is also the heyday of the big ranches of Alta California: there are about 455 of them, averaging nearly 19,000 acres each.

1848–1858: Gold is discovered in the foothills of the Sierra Nevada mountains in 1848. The subsequent flood of gold seekers and squatters into the foothills and valleys of Northern and Central California will spell the ruin of large-scale *Californio* ranches there.

After 1848: The term "barrio" is not used in California before the U.S.-Mexican War, but after the war it gradually comes to mean the region of a town or city where only impoverished Spanish-speaking people lived.

1849: It is estimated that 200 *Californio* families own 14 million acres of land.

1850: The Hacienda de Las Yorba has become the social and business center of the Santa Ana Valley in Orange County. It has about 50 rooms, arranged around a patio in the rear of the main ranch house, and more than 100 employees.

1850: California joins the United States as the 31st state. The remaining segments of Mexican rule in Alta California become all or parts of the American states of Arizona, Nevada, Utah, Colorado, and Wyoming.

1851: The U.S. Land Commission is established and will require *Californio* landowners to prove that they are in fact the legal owners of their ranches. This will subject them to many years of costly legal wrangling, which many of them will not be able to afford and will have to sell their lands.

1852: General Vallejo and his family move into Lachryma Montis, his home in Sonoma, and will live there for more than 35 years.

1854: There are now about 5,000 people living in Los Angeles.

1862–1865: Droughts of Biblical proportions in Southern California kill as many as 200,000 head of cattle.

1869: Richard Henry Dana, Jr., updates his famous book, *Two Years Before the Mast*, by contrasting the California he saw then with the Alta California he had known 24 years earlier.

1870s: The impoverishment of the *Californios* forces them to move into the barrios of towns and cities.

1874: The gifted but mercurial Henry Cerruti persuades General Mariano Guadalupe Vallejo to donate his personal papers to the historian Hubert Howe Bancroft.

1876: Bancroft's interviewer Thomas Savage dives into the *Californio* archives.

1880: Los Angeles now has a population of 33,000 people and a combined value of real estate and personal property of $16.4 million.

1881: Writing about life in Los Angeles 30 years earlier, the Los Angeles Ranger Horace Bell gives a vivid description of a large traditional house of that time, describing it as "an old-style angel habitation." Here Bell is making a play on the informal name of Los Angeles as "the City of the Angels."

1884: Helen Hunt Jackson's sentimental novel *Ramona*, which romanticizes both the life styles of the *Californios* and the plight of the California Indians, will have more than 300 printings and will be adapted four times as a film.

1884–1890: Bancroft's seven-volume *History of California* is a major scholarly contribution to the study of California history.

1885: María Ruiz de Burton, the first female Mexican-American author to write in English, publishes *The Squatter and the Don*. She argues that after the U.S.-Mexican War, Mexican-Americans remained a subjugated minority for many decades.

1886: An American reporter writes that Pueblo Viejo, the old barrio of Santa Barbara, has not changed much over the past 40 or 50 years.

1887: There are now about 12,000 Spanish-speakers in Los Angeles, but they comprise less than 10 percent of the total population.

1888: Bancroft's book *California Pastoral* is an elegy for the vanished *Californio* way of life.

1890: Bancroft finishes the last volume of his *History of California*. That same year, General Mariano Guadalupe Vallejo dies, and Guadalupe Vallejo, his nephew, writes movingly about the peaceful, happy way of life enjoyed by *Californios* before the U.S.-Mexican War.

Appendix 1: Notes on California Ports, 1769–1850

During this period, much of the 849-mile-long coast of Alta California was what contemporary mariners called an "iron-bound coast," that is to say, a rugged, rocky coast with very few ports. This appendix adds to what has been mentioned earlier about the ports that did exist, e.g., Monterey, San Pedro (the port of Los Angeles), San Diego, and San Francisco.[1]

Before discussing the various ports, it must be noted that many "phantom ships" were involved in the early days of the California trade, i.e., vessels that plied the coast engaging in illegal trading and therefore left no written records of their operations. Nevertheless, a paper trail has survived on legal fronts: ships' logs, ship registers, and Spanish or Mexican customs reports all offer insights into the complexities of recorded trade.[2] The following notes suggest the scale of this trade but do not purport to be a definitive statement on it.

In 1839, the Scottish merchant and explorer Alexander Forbes (1778–1862) published a book in London entitled *California: A History of Upper and Lower California from their First Discovery to the Present Time.* Much later, in his 1929 study *Seventy-five Years in San Francisco*, the California businessman and ship owner William Heath Davis (1822–1909) used Forbes and other sources to learn about early shipping in Alta California. He found that there had been a total of about 740 ship visits to California ports between 1774 and 1847.[3] These vessels called at different California ports at different times. The peak year of this coastal trade was 1834, when Davis lists 35 ship visits. Many of these ships, which were of varying sizes and nationalities, were engaged in the hide and tallow trade.

Monterey

The considerable difficulties the early Spanish explorers experienced when they were trying to locate, overland, what would become the port of Monterey arose from two facts. First, the considerable length and relatively unbroken coastline of Monterey Bay did not conform at all to their own expectations of what a promising port for Manila galleons should look like. Indeed, they did not even believe that they were then walking along the shore of a bay.

Second, the navigational instruments used to locate Monterey had been faulty and inaccurate. For example, Crespi's journal records in detail the Portola expedition's inaccurate readings of latitude. It was only when Serra told Portolá to look for the same giant oak under which Vizcaíno's Carmelite monks had said mass in 1602 that matters became clear. That advice turned out to be the key to the puzzle. In Crespi's final version of his 1770 journal all the facts began to fall into place, and thus the port of Monterey was "found again."[4] Writing in 1822, the foreign (probably British) ship captain John Hall had this to say about Monterey:

> On the 20th of June 1822], we weighed [from San Francisco] to Monterey, where we came-to on the 24th, saluting the fort with five guns [i.e., five cannon shots], which were returned by the same number. As a harbour, Monterey is extremely inferior to San Francisco; however it is quite protected from the South and S.W. winds; and by anchoring well under the point, a vessel may also be protected from the N.W., although the N.W. winds send in a heavy swell. Fish here also is plentiful, as are likewise provisions generally, including *good bread* [italics in the original].[5]

Some of the early days of the port of Monterey, which was the capital of Alta California, the only official port of entry, and the place where visiting ship captains were in theory required to pay stiff customs duties of about 100 percent on the goods they were importing, have already been described here.

Even before Mexico gained control of California in 1822, Spain's onerous rules prohibiting foreign trade had frayed very badly because the Spanish fleet simply could not hope to enforce these restrictions in far-off California. The underlying issue here was that, with no virtually industries of their own, *Californios* were very eager to trade for foreign merchandise.

With the demand for such goods far exceeding the supply, the inevitable result was widespread smuggling. Simply by evading customs duties, foreign ship captains could simultaneously lower the prices *Californio* consumers had to pay for imported goods and could also ensure high profits for themselves. When the Mexican government came to power, however, it welcomed foreign trade. Thus whereas between 1769 and 1824 an average of only 2.4 ships had called at Monterey annually, between 1825 and 1848 as many as 25 ships were now arriving each year.[6]

San Pedro

In 1542, while sailing off San Pedro Bay, the Portuguese explorer Juan Rodriguez Cabríllo saw smoke rising from the fires of Indians hunting game. For this reason, he named the natural harbor located here as the *Bahia de los Fumos* ("The Bay of Smokes"). Although he noted in his log that the bay "is an excellent harbor and the country is good with many plains and groves of trees," it was in fact then little more than a swampy marshland, and the Spanish made no effort to develop it.

Many years later, however, in 1769 Spanish officials and missionaries were attracted by its fine coastline, game-filled plains, and substantial Indian population. By 1771 the Spanish had established one mission at San Gabriel Arcángel, 40 miles inland from San Pedro, and by 1776 another at San Juan Capistrano, located about 45 miles southeast of San Pedro. Mission monks were therefore the first to make use of the harbor, delivering ox carts filled with hides and tallow to the water's edge to be picked up by ships carrying provisions from Spain.

During the colonial period, Spain restricted trade at San Pedro to only two ships a year carrying goods from Spain's House of Trades. Foreign ships could legally call there only for urgent repairs or to take on food and water. Because of these strict regulations, however, San Pedro and the nearby towns and missions that arose on the flats of San Pedro Bay actually prospered—thanks to their flourishing cargo-smuggling business.

As noted earlier, the city of Los Angeles was founded in 1781. The first American ship to call at San Pedro Bay was the brig *Lelia Byrd* in 1805 under the command of Captain William Shaler, who brought in sugar, textiles, and household goods, exchanging them for sea otter pelts and provisions. This transaction was almost certainly not authorized by Spanish officials and, indeed, it was not until an independent Mexico lifted Spain's oppressive restrictions in 1822 that trade could finally blossom. Under the new regime, San Pedro soon became a thriving commercial center and a desirable home for new settlers. By the time California became part of the United States in 1848, business in San Pedro harbor was beginning to boom.

San Diego

Between 1769 and 1835, about 83 ships are recorded as having called at San Diego. The peak year of this period was 1835 when nine vessels visited the port. These included[7]:

- *Pilgrim, Alert, Lagoda*, and *California* (American ships from Boston
- *Ayacucho* (an English brig from Callao)
- *Lorior* (an American schooner from Honolulu)
- *La Rosa* (an Italian ship from Sardinia)
- *Facio* (a Mexican brig from Guaymas)
- *Catalina* (an American brig, under the Mexican flag, from La Paz)

San Francisco

Before the Portolá expedition discovered San Francisco Bay in 1769, European ships had cruised the California coast for more than 200 years without ever discovering the fog-hidden entrance to the bay. Indeed, the Bay was first seen by Spanish explorers from the land, not from the sea. The first ship to enter the bay was the *San Carlos*, a two-masted 58-foot-long Spanish packet boat under the command of Captain Juan de Ayala. Packet boats were sturdy two-masted sailing vessels designed to carry mail, passengers, and freight in European countries and their colonies.

Built in 1767 at the Naval Department of San Blas and sent out by Viceroy Antonio de Bucareli to survey the waters of the bay, the *San Carlos* arrived at the Golden Gate on 5 August 1775 but the strong current soon pushed her back out to sea. However, by taking advantage of a tailwind she was able to make slow progress against the tide, which was probably ebbing by then. Under the dim light of a half moon, she finally passed through the Golden Gate at 10:30 p.m. The *San Carlos* anchored off what is now Angel Island and, over the next 47 days, her officers and crewmen used longboats (rowboats) to chart the various arms of the bay.

In mid–August 1776, the *San Carlos* returned with supplies and remained off what is now San Francisco until October 1776 in order to provide help in building a presidio and a mission there. In nautical terms, however, very little of note happened in San Francisco after that until 1835, when the English Captain W.A. Richardson, who has been mentioned here earlier, was designated as the port's first Harbor Master. At that time, the port was known as Yerba Buena and received a small handful of ships engaged in the hide and tallow trade and in whaling. Between April 1847 and April 1848, for example, only 11 ships called at San Francisco Bay. These included one barque (a three-masted vessel having her fore- and mainmasts rigged square and her mizzenmast rigged fore-and-aft); one brigantine; and nine whalers.

The Gold Rush brought a great upsurge of shipping to San Francisco Bay. In 1849 alone, more than 90,000 passengers arrived at San Francisco Bay aboard some 650 American and foreign vessels. Word soon spread in nautical circles that this bay was one of the best natural harbors in the entire world. Surrounded by navigable waterways, it was safe for vessels of any draught and big enough to accommodate ocean-going fleets.

The ocean mail service to the Pacific Coast began in the latter part of 1848 and continued in operation for the next 10 years.[8] It was the great link connecting the gold seekers and pioneers in California with their friends and relatives in other parts of the United States. The semi-monthly arrival and departure of the mail steamer was an important occasion in San Francisco. Its arrival was much more exciting than its departure.

As soon as it docked, for example, local journalists who were already on board (they had hired boats to meet the mail steamer in San Francisco Bay), hurried to their offices to print the news they had gathered in interviews. Month-old newspapers from the eastern states sold readily for one dollar apiece. To obtain a letter, it was necessary for a hopeful recipient to stand in a long line at the window of the post office. The line began to form the day or the night before the mail was actually received. Some men and boys made it their business to come very early and then to sell their places in line to late comers.

Long Wharf or Central Wharf, located on what is now Commercial Street, was therefore built in 1848–1850 and was the first major pier in San Francisco. It would eventually extend 2,000 feet out into the Bay over the shallow water and mud flats that had previously prevented ships from mooring, loading, and unloading at the shoreline. Other piers quickly followed, and San Francisco soon became the focus of oceangoing and river traffic for California.[9]

Appendix 2:
Rancho Camulos

Because of the flood of tourist dollars they were expected to bring in, rival locations all over Southern California publicized their alleged connections with Helen Hunt Jackson's blockbuster 1884 novel *Ramona*, which was instrumental in romanticizing the mission and rancho era of California's history. Two ranches in particular claimed that they had inspired her work: Rancho Camulos, near Piru in Ventura County, and Rancho Guajome in San Diego County. Jackson had visited both of them before writing *Ramona*. Even though she died in 1885 without defining where her novel was actually set, Camulos, which is now known as Rancho Camulos Museum and is a National Historical Landmark, became the most widely-accepted "House of Ramona."

By the 1880s, Rancho Camulos was not in good financial condition but it still managed to exude a deceptive air of prosperity. The annual July Fourth fiesta, for example, was a four-day affair with up to 75 invited guests, each of whom was greeted personally by Señora del Valle and then escorted into a comfortable room.[1] A servant summoned the guests to lunch, held in the garden where Ygnacio's eldest son, Reginaldo, was the host. The menu included roast pig, pickled olives, chilies, red and white wines, and coffee.

In the afternoon, the guests could amuse themselves by riding, singing, reading, conversation, and mountain-climbing. Watermelons and other light refreshments were available for the asking. The guests assembled for dinner at 7:00 p.m. around a table lighted by lanterns hanging from grape clusters; the main course was roast kid. Following an hour's stroll after dinner, they were then treated to music (piano, organ, and guitar), singing, and fireworks. On Sunday, Señora del Valle attended chapel with her Catholic guests and a fine lunch was held after the service.

Most of the guests were non–Hispanic Americans and for them such a celebration was a memorable new experience. Although it lacked the cockfights, bull baiting, horse racing, and patriotic Mexican songs that had been highlights of a classic July Fourth fiesta held in San Pedro in 1853, it still impressed the assembled guests.

Today this 1,800-acre working ranch is a fine example of an early *Californio* rancho in its original rural location.[2] It was the source of the first commercially-grown oranges in today's Ventura County. Ironically, despite its close association with *Ramona* and the Mexican-*Californio* way of life, the present ranch house was built only after California became a state, so the del Valle family never lived there under Mexican rule.

In addition to its literary importance, Rancho Camulos is also architecturally significant. The 10,000 square foot U-shaped Ygnacio del Valle adobe, with its two-foot thick walls and its long corridors, is one of the best examples of *Californio*-era colonial vernacular architecture in the United States. (Vernacular architecture is based on local traditions and construction materials; it does not use formally-trained architects.) Begun in 1853, this building evolved in a classic fashion by expanding to fit the needs of a growing family, financial constraints, and traditional *Californio* building customs. Outbuildings at Rancho Camulos today include a winery, barn, workers' housing, office, and chapel. The nearest urban development is now the village of Piru, located about two miles to the west. At the ranch itself there is an ancient and huge Black Walnut tree, perhaps the largest of its kind in the region, which dates from the early years of the ranch.

Appendix 3:
Jo Mora on the *Nuqueo*

Jo Mora (1876–1947) was a cowboy, writer, and illustrator whose 1949 book *Californios* is still memorable for its action-packed drawings and its vivid text. In the Foreword to this work he laid out his literary credentials. He wrote:

> More than forty-five years ago I had direct contact with many persons who had either lived through the latter part of the old ante-gringo regime in California themselves or who had known the people who had been part and parcel of the old life that extended back almost to colonial times. Their recollections were priceless to a researcher. Moreover, I was fortunately equipped for this work, both by my Spanish ancestry and consequent knowledge of the language of the range, and by my lifelong practice of vaquero ways.[1]

Mora was singularly well-equipped to review the unique lives and times of the *Californios*. For example, "*nuquec*" means "nape of the neck" in Spanish. As used here, it refers to the ability of a vaquero on horseback to kill a running steer with a single stroke of his knife. Because this was such a dangerous and unusual skill, it is worth describing here in detail. Mora made the following points in his book:

- The first step in the *nuqueo* was for a large crew of vaqueros to hold the cattle in a flat, clear, slaughtering ground known as the *matanza*. A smaller squad of riders known as *nuqueadores* (the knifemen) would then appear with knife in hand. They rode slowly up to a steer and then, with a quick stroke with the point of the knife between the vertebrae at the nape of the neck, they would, to use Mora's words, "drop a cow as dead as a doornail without a kick or a struggle."
- Since the cattle were used to mounted men, at first they took no

alarm. The knifemen could therefore kill a fair number of them as they rode quietly around the herd and gradually forced their way into it. Soon, however, the cattle realized the danger they were in and tried to escape. The knifemen then had to pick their victims on the run, as it were, riding alongside them and giving them the *coup de grace* at arm's length and at full speed.

- Mora ends the body of his account with these words:

  As the cattle grew more and more frenzied, the nuqueadores entered into the wild spirt of the occasion, and there was many a vaquero yell to split the welkin [i.e., to split the sky] and goad the victims to greater speed, the better to show off their own prowess.[2]

Appendix 4:
An Interview with the *Californio* Bandit Tiburcio Vásquez (1835–1875)

This interview, which took place on 15 May 1874 and appeared in the Los Angeles *Star* the next day, was reproduced by Robert Glass Cleland in his well-received 1941 book, *The Cattle on a Thousand Hills: Southern California, 1850–80*, on pp. 274–279.

Tiburcio remains controversial even today. Some Mexican-Americans see him as a folk hero who stood up against unjust laws and ethnic discrimination; many others regard him simply as a colorful outlaw. Before looking at some excerpts from the interview, however, a brief summary of his life may be of interest here.

Tiburcio was born in Monterey in 1835 to an old *Californio* family: his great-grandfather came to Alta California in 1776 with Juan Bautista de Anza's expedition. Unlike many of his contemporaries, Tiburcio was sent to school as a young boy and learned to speak, read, and write English. His criminal career began in 1852, when at the age of 17 he attended a local fandango with his older cousin, the outlaw Anastacio Garcia.[1] A fight broke out, and Constable William Hardmount was killed. Tiburcio and Anastacio fled the scene, but Tiburcio's friend José Higuera, who was also present at the fight, did not run away and was lynched by vigilantes the next day.

Hiding in the hills, Tiburcio soon became the leader of his own gang. Excusing his actions by claiming that he was only "punishing the whites" for their discrimination against people of Mexican and Spanish descent, he ranged up and down Central and Southern California as an accomplished horse thief. In 1857, he was caught after he had rustled a herd of horses in Los Angeles. Sentenced to five years in San Quentin, he briefly escaped in 1859 but was recaptured soon thereafter when he was caught stealing horses and was sent back to prison. Released in 1863, he made a short effort to stay on the right side of the law, but quickly fell back into a life of crime, now adding armed robbery to his list of offenses.

Arrested yet again in 1867 for a failed attempt to rob a store in Mendocino, he spent another short stint in San Quentin. As soon as he was released, he returned to Monterey and was badly wounded in a fight with Abelardo Salazar over a dispute involving Salazar's wife. He then fled to a Cantua Creek hideout in the Coast Range, but it was not long before he ran afoul of the law again.

In 1871 he and two other outlaws held up the Visalia stagecoach between San Jose and Pacheco Pass. They were soon pursued by a posse which wounded Tiburcio, killed one of his colleagues, and captured the third bandit. Tiburcio managed to escape and took refuge in his Cantua Creek hideout, but in 1873 he hit the outlaw trail again with his gang, holding up a store in Tres Pinos (now known as Paicines) in San Benito County. Some $200 in gold was stolen and three innocent bystanders were killed in the process.

This offense led to a $1,000 reward being offered for his capture, but he eluded his pursuers and found refuge in a steeply-sloped rock formation about 40 miles north of Los Angeles which is now known as Vasquez Rocks. In December 1873, Tiburcio and his men sacked the town of Kingston in Fresno County, stealing more than $2,500 from two stores and leaving some townsmen bound, face down, lying in the dust but otherwise unharmed. When news of this affront reached the governor of California, the reward on his head was gradually increased to $15,000. Local sheriffs organized posses to hunt down the gang.

Tiburcio was handsome, literate, charming, played the guitar, and was a good dancer. Women were attracted to him and he had many love affairs, several of them with married women. He enjoyed reading romantic novels and writing poetry for his many female admirers. Ironically, it was this fondness for women that brought about his own downfall.

When hiding at a cabin, Tiburcio seduced a local girl and made her pregnant. This so angered both the girl's family members and one of Tiburcio's own colleagues that they contacted the authorities and agreed to turn State's evidence against him. Armed with the information they provided, Los Angeles Sheriff William Roland finally captured him in the Arroyo Seco area of Los Angeles in 1874.

An Interview with the Californio Bandit Tiburcio Vasquez

At his trial, Tiburcio became a celebrity and a folk hero for his fellow *Californios*: hundreds of people came to visit him in jail, many of whom were women. Found guilty on two counts of murder, he was hanged in Santa Clara on 19 March 1875 at the age of 39. Some of the comments he made in his interview with the *Los Angeles Star* are as follows:

> My career grew out of the circumstances by which I was surrounded as I grew to manhood. I was in the habit of attending balls and parties given by the native Californians, into which the Americans, then beginning to become numerous, would force themselves and shove the native-born men aside, monopolizing the dances and the women. This was about 1852.
>
> A spirit of hatred and revenge took possession of me. I had numerous fights in defense of what I believed to be my rights and those of my countrymen. The officers [i.e., the law officers] were continually in pursuit of me. I believed that we were unjustly and wrongfully deprived of the social rights that belonged to us. So perpetually was I involved in these difficulties that I at length determined to leave the thickly-settled portion of the country, and did so.
>
> I gathered together a small band of cattle and went into Mendocino country, back of Ukiah and beyond Fallis Valley. Even here I was not permitted to remain in peace. The officers of the law sought me out in that remote region, and strove to drag me before the courts. I always resisted arrest.
>
> I went to my mother and told her I intended to commence a different life. I asked for and obtained her blessing, and at once commenced the career of a robber.... [At first] I made but little money by my exploits. I always managed to avoid arrest. I believe I owe my frequent escapes solely to my courage. I was already to fight whenever opportunity offered, but always tried to avoid bloodshed.
>
> [Summing up his most recent experiences just before his capture, Tiburcio ended the interview with these words:] For the past three weeks I have had my camp near the place where I was captured [i.e., Arroyo Seco], only coming to the house at intervals to get a meal. I was not expecting company at the time the arrest was made, or the result might have been different [in other words, he would have resisted arrest].[2]

Appendix 5:
A Recipe for *Puchero*, a *Californio* Beef Stew

At lunch or in the evening, the main dish in a typical *Californio* household in about 1848 might well have been a hearty, very heavily-spiced beef stew known as *puchero* ("stewpot" in Spanish). Such a dish was likely to be so strongly-flavored with chilies that a *Californio* diner could say, with evident appreciation, "Ah, this stew is capable of raising the dead!"[1]

Most foreign visitors to Alta California, however, found this dish much too hot for their own taste. The recipe given here is from a 1976 Time-Life book on *The Spanish West* and must be appreciably less fiery than its 1848 ancestor. For this reason, one optional ingredient—very hot *habanero* chili peppers, to taste—has been added here.

Ingredients

1 sun-dried beef or veal knuckle bone
½ teaspoon pepper
2 teaspoon salt
2 pounds cut-up veal
2 pounds cut-up beef
3 ears corn
3 sweet potatoes
1 cup *garbanzos* (chick-peas)
2 whole onions
3 dried tomatoes
2 green chili peppers
Optional: *habanero* chili peppers (very hot) to taste

A Recipe for Puchero, a Californio Meat Stew

1 pound green string beans tied in bunches
1 bundle turnip leaves
3 small green pumpkins or summer squash
1 hard apple
1 hard pear

Cooking Suggestions

Cover the knuckle bone and meat with cold water. Add the pepper and salt. Bring to a boil and skim scum from the water. Place all the vegetables and fruit over the meat in the order listed, the corn at the very bottom, the pear on top. Simmer for three hours. Do not stir. To serve, place the vegetables and fruit on one platter, meat on a second platter, and broth in a tureen. Serves 12.

Chapter Notes

Preface

1. Bancroft's written works include 27 books, many of them multi-volume works. He employed numerous research assistants in this process but revised much of their work himself. However, because neither he nor most of his assistants were academically-trained historians, his books do reflect some of his personal opinions and biases.

2. After Sánchez, *Telling Identities: The Californio testimonios*, p 6. By "testimonios" Sánchez means what she defines as "elicited dictations."

3. Some of these comments are drawn in part from Pitt, *The Decline of the Californios*, p. 14.

4. The modern historian Genaro Padilla has explained (in *My History, Not Yours*, p. 63) that, as General Mariano Guadalupe Vallejo wrote to his son, the goal of *Californio* memoirs was to construct a narrative of the past that would contend for authority over and against the many accounts that denigrated Mexican culture and social manners.

5. The classic study of the Indians of California is Alfred L. Kroeber's *Handbook of the Indians of California*, first published in 1919.

6. Not all the ranchos were huge. During most of the Spanish era, for example, the missions often had small plots of ground where crops were grown and where livestock was raised.

7. This phrase is the title of Leonard Pitt's 1966 book on the subject.

8. After Howard, *Sierra Crossing*, p. 14.

9. Quoted by Janin, *Claiming the American Wilderness*, p. 181.

Introduction

1. "Motives for Exploration," p. 2.

2. After Gibson, *California Through Russian Eyes, 1806–1848*, p. 15.

3. One of the best summaries of the Spanish settlement of Alta California is Weber's *The Spanish Frontier in North America*, pp. 236–265.

4. The length of a league varied, but a good approximation is 2.6 miles, which is the figure used in this book for computing distances.

5. After Gibson, "The Exploration of the Pacific Coast," pp. 348–349.

6. Quoted in Beebe and Senkewicz, *Lands of Promise*, p. 111.

7. After Rosenus, *General Vallejo*, p. 237 note 1.

8. After Clay and Troesken, "Ranchos and the Politics of Land Claims," p. 56.

9. After Cleland, *The Cattle on a Thousand Hills*, p. 21.

10. There seem to be no reliable statistics for the total number of Indians who worked at the missions, but "roughly 15,000" seems a good guess. This estimate was used by Pitt in *The Decline of the Californios*, p. 8. It should also be noted here that the role of the missions vis-à-vis the Indians has long been a very controversial one, with arguments ranging across the spectrum from "the Indians came to the missions voluntarily"

to "the Indians were virtually enslaved by the missionaries."

11. The Viceroyalty of New Spain embraced many far-flung and very different lands, for example: Mexico, Guatemala, El Salvador, Honduras, Nicaragua, Belize, Costa Rica, California, Texas, New Mexico, Arizona, Puerto Rico, Guam, the Mariana Islands, Nevada, Utah, Colorado, Wyoming, Florida, part of British Columbia, Cuba, the Dominican Republic, Hispaniola, Jamaica, Antigua, Barbados, the Philippines, and the Palau and Caroline Islands. The Viceroyalty was administered by a viceroy who was appointed by the Spanish king and who resided in Mexico City.

12. After Beebe and Senkewicz, *Lands of Promise and Despair*, pp. 313–315.

13. After Clay and Troesken, "Ranchos and the Politics of Land Claims," pp. 53–54.

14. After Beebe and Senkewicz, "Life on a California Rancho." In Beebe and Senkewicz, *Lands of Promise and Despair*. Berkeley: Santa Clara University and Heyday Books, 2001, p. 434.

15. After "Seventy-five Years in San Francisco," p. 20.

16. Quoted by Rosenus, *General Vallejo and the Advent of the Americans*, p. 198.

17. The U.S. Public Land Commission reviewed 809 cases involving private land grant claims. Of these, 604 claims were confirmed; 190 were rejected; and 19 were withdrawn. Many of these cases were appealed to the courts. The end result of this long, slow, expensive process was that 582 land claims were officially approved.

Chapter 1

1. This chapter draws heavily on my 2006 book, *Claiming the American Wilderness: International Rivalry in the Trans-American West, 1528–1803*, especially from the chapter on "The Spaniards: Children of the Sun," pp. 48–95.

2. After Golay and Bowman, *North American Exploration*, pp. 104–105.

3. After Janin, *Claiming the American Wilderness*, p. 75.

4. The first leg of the expedition consisted of four parts, all of which departed from Baja California. Two crews traveled by sea and two groups marched north on land. An additional supply ship was also dispatched from San Blas, Mexico, but she never reached San Diego and was presumed to have been lost at sea.

5. San Diego History Center, "Gaspar de Portola," p. 1.

6. Quoted in Golay and Bowman, *North American Exploration*, p. 233.

7. Quoted by San Diego History Center, "Gaspar de Portola," p. 1.

8. Quoted in "MissionTour," p. 1.

9. Quoted in PacificaHistory, "Portola Expedition November 4, 1769 Diaries," p. 2.

10. Quoted by Weber, *The Spanish Frontier in North America*, p. 245.

11. Quoted by Weber, *The Spanish Frontier in North America*, p. 246.

12. After Hafen and Hafen, *Old Spanish Trail*, p. 55.

Chapter 2

1. This chapter draws heavily on Beebe and Senkewicz, *Lands of Promise and Despair*, pp. 109, 111, 112, 114–116, 117, 294. The most detailed account of San Blas, however, remains Michael E. Thurman's 1967 book on *The Naval Department of San Blas*.

2. After Hardwick, "The Spanish Naval Department of San Blas," pp. 1–2.

3. Quoted by Beebe and Senkewicz, *Lands of Promise and Despair*, p. 111.

4. Quoted by Beebe and Senkewicz, *Lands of Promise and Despair*, p. 117.

5. Some of the following comments are drawn from Thurman, *The Naval Department of San Blas*, pp. 357–359.

Chapter 3

1. In *Lands of Promise and Despair*, p. 501, Beebe and Senkewicz list 27 missions in Baja California.

2. After Guadalupe Vallejo, "Ranch and Mission Days in Alta California," p. 1.

3. After Hackle, *Land, Labor, and Production*, p. 116.

4. Quoted by Time-Life Books in *The Spanish West*, p. 156.

5. Quoted by Cleland, *The Cattle on a Thousand Hills*, p. 57.

6. This photo is reproduced in Beebe

and Senkewicz, *Lands of Promise and Despair*, p. 312.

7. Quoted by Beebe and Senkewicz, *Testimonios*, p. xxv.

8. After Beebe and Senkewicz, *Testimonies*, p. 115.

9. After Pitt, *The Decline of the Californios*, p. 10.

10. After Clay and Troesken, "Ranchos and the Politics of Land Claims," p. 54.

11. Vallejo earned the title of General in 1836, when he was promoted to "Commandant General of the Free State of Alta California" after a revolt against Governor Juan Bautista Alvarado.

12. Guadalupe Vallejo, 'Ranch and Mission Days in Alta California," pp. 3–4.

13. Pitt, *The Decline of the Californios*, p. 10.

Chapter 4

1. After Camarillo, *Chicanos in a Changing Society*, p. 12.

2. Quoted by Cleland, *The Cattle on a Thousand Hills*, p. 7.

3. Quoted by Cleland, *The Cattle on a Thousand Hills*, p. 23.

4. Both the petition and the grant are from W.W. Robinson, *Land in California*, pp. 48–49.

5. After Beebe and Senkewicz, *Lands of Promise and Despair*, p. 279–280.

6. One of the best sources on land grants in Alta California is the book of that name written by Crisostomo N. Perez in 1996 (see bibliography).

7. After Cuts, *The Conquest of California and New Mexico*, p. 22.

8. After Robinson, *Life in California*, p. 223.

9. After Eisenhower, *So Far from God*, p. 200.

10. These two paragraphs are adapted from Perez, *Land Grants in Alta California*, p. 9.

11. Quoted by Cleland, *The Cattle on a Thousand Hills*, p. 17.

12. After Clay and Troesken, "Ranchos and the Politics of Land Claims," pp. 63–64.

13. After Monroy, "The Creation and Recreation of Californio Society," p. 174.

14. See Beebe and Senkewicz, *Lands of Promise and Despair*, pp. 434–442 for Lugo, and pp. 446–452 for Coronel. For Pico, see Botello's translation of Pico's *Historical Narrative*.

15. Dried meat, *carne seca* in Spanish, or "jerky," as Americans call it, was made as follows. When a steer was slaughtered, its hide was spread out on the ground, hair side down, and was used as a receptacle for the meat itself. This was cut into strips about one inch thick, five to six inches wide, and from one to three feet long. It was then dipped in brine, hung on a rope or a lasso in the hot sun, and turned every 24 hours. In four or five days, the meat became hard, black, dry, well-flavored, and very nutritious. *Carne seca* did not look very appetizing but when properly prepared it was full-flavored and very sustaining. A good way to cook dried beef is to pound it up fine; put it into a pan with some hot oil; and add a little water, boiled potato, fine-cut onion, red chili, and tomato pulp.

16. The following account is adapted from Amador, *Californio Voices*, pp. 141–143.

17. After Bowers Museum, "Portrait of Don Jose Andres Sepulveda, c. 1856 by Henri Joseph Penelon," pp. 1–2.

18. After Harlow, *California Conquered*, p. 25.

19. Quoted by Bancroft, *California Pastoral*, p. 282.

20. Quoted by Bancroft, *California Pastoral*, p. 279.

21. Pico, *Narration Historica*, pp. 149–150.

22. After Botello's translation of Pico's *Historical Narrative*, pp. 136–138.

23. After Cleland, *The Cattle on a Thousand Hills*, pp. 52–53, citing Don Meadows, "Bernardo Yorba Hacienda of Rancho Santa Ana." MS, Charles W. Bowers Memorial Museum, Santa Ana, California.

24. Drawn from Lisbeth Haas, *Conquests and Historical Identities in California 1769–1936*, p. 82.

25. After Sylvia Arrom, quoted in Lisbeth Haas's *Conquests and Historical Identities 1769–1936*, p. 82.

26. Quoted by Cleland, *The Cattle on a Thousand Hills*, pp. 30–31.

27. Quoted by California State University

Northridge, "Mexican California: The Heyday of the Ranchos, "p. 5.
28. After Dana, *Two Years Before the Mast*, pp. 211–214.
29. Quoted by Pitt, *The Decline of the Californios*, p. 14.
30. Quoted by Cleland, *The Cattle on a Thousand Hills*, p. 33. It is not clear where the 200 ounces of gold came from. Gold was not discovered in the Sierra Nevada foothills until 1848. Possibly this was gold salvaged from coins, ornaments, or other uses.
31. After Pitt, *The Decline of the Californios*, p. 10.

Chapter 5

1. Robinson, *Life in California*, p. 284.
2. Adapted from Honig, *The Presidios of Alta California*, p. 3.
3. Adapted from Honig, *The Presidios of Alta California*, pp. 4–5..
4. Dana, *Two Years Before the Mast*, p. 306.
5. Dana, *Two Years Before the Mast*, pp. 129–130.
6. Serra, "Trip to Mexico City," p. 174.
7. After *Find a Grave Memorial*, "Capt Jose Francisco Ortega," p. 1, and Bancroft, *The History of California*, vol. I, pp. 670–671.
8. Bancroft, *California Pastoral*, p. 304.
9. After Bancroft, *California Pastoral*, p. 304.
10. After Bancroft, *California Pastoral*, pp. 298–299, 302.
11. Adapted from Honig, *The Presidios of Alta California*, p. 7.
12. An Italian church known as Our Lady Queen of the Angels of Porciuncula was famous as the cradle of the Franciscan order.

Chapter 6

1. This and the next paragraph are drawn in part from Hackel, *Land, Labor, and Production*, p. 117-118.
2. Filipe de Neve, quoted by Beebe and Senkewicz, *Lands of Promise and Despair*, p. 223.
3. After Harlow, *California Conquered*, p. 86.

4. Quoted by Hafen and Hafen, *Old Spanish Trail*, pp. 36–37.
5. After Hafen and Hafen, *Old Spanish Trail*, p. 37.
6. After Griswold del Castillo, p. 8.
7. Brewerton, *Overland with Kit Carson*, pp. 36–37.
8. Bell, *Reminiscences of a Ranger*, p. 60.

Chapter 7

1. This chapter is drawn from a variety of sources, all of which tend to disagree on minor details. They include, listed in random order, Gutiérrez and Orsi, *Contested Eden*, p. 305; Harlow, *California Conquered*, pp. 33–34; Amador and Asisara, *Californio Voices*, pp. 71, 73, 75, 77; Beebe and Senkewicz, *Testimonios*, p. 36; Pitt, *The Decline of the Californios*, pp. 1, 2, 12; Osio, *The History of Alta California: A Memoir of Mexican California*, pp. 44–54, 260–268; Breschini, "Hipólito (Hypolite) Bouchard and the Raid of 1818," pp. 1–3; and The California State Military Museum, "Spanish and Mexican California: Hipployte de Bouchard and His Attacks on the California Missions," pp. 1–2.
2. Amador and Asisara, *Californio Voices*, p. 71.
3. Quoted by Pitt, *The Decline of the Californios*, p. 12.
4. Quoted by Beebe and Senkewicz, *Testimonios*, p. 36.
5. After Gutiérrez and Orsi, *Contested Eden*, p. 305.

Chapter 8

1. Many of the comments in this chapter are drawn from Digital-Desert: Mohave Desert, "The Old Spanish Trail"; Hafen and Hafen, *Old Spanish Trail*; and Janin and Carlson, *Trails of Historic New Mexico*, pp. 71–88, on "The Old Spanish Trail."
2. Hafen and Hafen, *Old Spanish Trail*, p. 19.
3. After Hafen and Hafen, *Old Spanish Trail*, p. 154.
4. Quoted by Rounds, *Mountain Men*, pp. 226–227.
5. After Hafen and Hafen, *Old Spanish Trail*, p. 171.

6. After Hafen and Hafen, *Old Spanish Trail*, p. 187.
7. After Hafen and Hafen, *Old Spanish Trail*, p. 362.
8. Brewerton, *Overland with Kit Carson*, pp. 56–59.
9. Brewerton, *Overland with Kit Carson*, p. 38.
10. Quoted by Hafen and Hafen, *Old Spanish Trail*, p. 268.

Chapter 9

1. After Harlow, *California Conquered*, p. 25.
2. Some of these comments reflect the views of Weber, "The Spanish Legacy in North America and the Historical Imagination," pp. 5–54, especially p. 11.
3. Bancroft, *California Pastoral*, pp. 273–274.
4. Twain, *Roughing It*, p. 197.
5. Dana, *Two Years Before the Mast*, pp. 131–132.
6. These comments have been drawn in part from Reyes, *Private Women, Public Lives: Gender and the Missions of the Californias*, pp. 93–94, 108, 148–149; and from Time-Life Books, *The Spanish West*, pp. 160–161..
7. Quoted by Reyes, *Private Women, Public Lives: Gender and the Missions of the Californias*, p. 148.
8. Quoted by Reyes, *Private Women. Public Lives: Gender and the Missions of the Californias*, p. 93.
9. Quoted by Reyes, *Private Women, Public Lives: Gender and the Missions of the Californias*, p. 108.
10. For the original transcript of this interview, see Beebe and Senkewicz, *Testimonios*, pp. 383–387; for explanatory comments on it by Beebe and Senkewicz, and their edited version of it, see pp. 17–29. The edited version is the one used here.
11. After Beebe and Senkewicz, *Testimonios*, pp. xiii–xvii, 165–169.
12. Unless otherwise sourced, all the information used here on Angustias de la Guerra is drawn from Beebe and Senkewicz, *Testimonios*, pp. 201–296.
13. Quoted by Beebe and Sankewicz, *Testimonios*, pp. 265–266.

14. After Beebe and Sankewicz, *Testimonios*, p. 295.
15. Sources used in this account include Kathleen Crawford, "Maria Amparo Ruiz Burton: The General's Lady," pp. 1–6; and Annenberg Learner, "Authors: Maria Amparo Burton (c. 1832–1895)."
16. After Carlos Hijar et al. in "Three Memoirs of Mexican Life," pp. 12, 13, 18, 23.
17. Robinson, *Life in California*, p. 254.
18. Vallejo, "Ranch and Mission Days in Alta California," pp. 1, 4.
19. Jackson, *Ramona*, pp. 10, 12.
20. After Janin and Carlson, *The California Campaigns of the U.S.-Mexican War*, pp. 10–11.
21. This account of Castillero's actions is drawn both from Castillero, "A Mexican Officer Urges Defense of Both Californias," pp. 406–409, and from Osio, *History of Alta California*, p. 320.
22. After Castillero, "A Mexican Officer Urges Defense of Both Californias," pp. 408–409.
23. Quoted by Hague and Langun, *Thomas O. Larkin*, p. 127.
24. Plummer, *Señor Plummer*, p. 194.
25. Plummer, *Señor Plummer*, p. 94.

Chapter 10

1. The information used here on the Russians in California is drawn from Watrous, "Russian Expansion to America," pp. 1–9; National Park Service, "Concepion Arguello & Nikokai Petrovich Rezanov," pp. 1–5; Schwartz, "Fort Ross California—A Historical Survey," pp. 1–26; Ogden, "Russian Sea-Otter and Seal Hunting on the California Coast, 1803–1841," pp. 29–51; and from selected documents in Gibson, *California Through Russian Eyes 1806–1848*.
2. After Gibson, *California Through Russian Eyes*," p. 24.
3. After Sánchez, *Telling Identities*, p. 207.
4. Dana, *Two Years Before the Mast*, pp. 297–298.
5. Unkovsky, "Voyage around the World," pp. 79–80.
6. Schabelski, "Visit of the Russian Warship *Apollo*," p. 7.
7. Zavalishin, "[Alta] California in 1824," p. 270.

8. Khlebinikov, "Notes about [Alta] California," pp. 338–339, 340, 341, 343, 345, 346–347.
9. These quotes are taken from Simpson, *An Overland Journey Around the World*, pp. 230. 233–234.
10. Some of the points made here are drawn from the chapter "Foreigners in California" in Janin and Carlson, *The California Campaigns of the U.S.-Mexican War, 1846–1848*, pp. 47–56.
11. Smith, *The War with Mexico*, p. 207.
12. Quoted by Gibson, *California Through Russian Eyes, 1806–1848*, p. 423.
13. After Gibson, *California Through Russian Eyes, 1806–1848*, pp. 423–424.
14. Markov, "Recollections of California," pp. 423–424, 426–427.

Chapter 11

1. Private communication of 6 June 2015 from Richard Griswold del Castillo.
2. Some of the comments in this chapter are drawn from the Monterey County Historical Society's "Spanish Governors of Alta California," pp. 1–2, and from its "Mexican Governors of Alta California," pp. 1–2. Other biographic information comes from Osio, *The History of Alta California*, pp. 315–342.
3. After Nuttall, "The Gobernantes of Spanish Upper California," p. 253.
4. After Nuttall, "The Gobernantes of Spanish Upper California," p. 262.
5. Cited in Osio, *The History of Alta California*, p. 317.
6. Pitt, *The Decline of the Californios*, p. 5. Sancho Panza was Don Quixote's squire in the novel by Miguel de Cervantes, which was published in two volumes in 1605 and 1615.
7. After private communications from Richard Griswold del Castillo of 6 and 8 June 2015, and from Albert M. Camarillo of 9 June 2015.
8. After Gregorio Mora-Torres, "Editor's Introduction," *Californio Voices*, p. 21.
9. After Osio, *The History of Alta California*, pp. 37–38.
10. Amador, *Californio Voices*, p. 117.
11. After San Diego History Center, "José María Echeandia," p. 1.
12. After Pico, *Historical Narrative*, p. 57.
13. Pico, *Historical Narrative*, p. 110.
14. Quoted in Pico, *Historical Narrative*, p. 66.
15. Quoted in Pico, *Historical Narrative*, p. 63.
16. After Pico, *Historical Narrative*, p. 66.
17. After Boggs, "Translation from Juan Bautista Alvarado's *Historia de California*," cited in "My Playhouse was a Concord Coach," p. 1.
18. After Pico, *Historical Narrative*, p. 48.
19. Pico, *Historical Narrative*, p. 79.
20. Amador, *Californio Voices*, pp. 171–172.
21. Amador, *Californio Voices*, p. 181.
22. This quote comes from the Foreword, by Martin Cole, of Pico's *Historical Narrative*, pp. 11–12.
23. *Historical Narrative*, pp. 144–146.

Chapter 12

1. Janin and Carlson, *The California Campaigns of the U.S-Mexican War, 1846–1848*, p. 8.
2. By modern highways, the distance between Fort Leavenworth and San Diego is 1,681 miles.
3. After Osio, *The History of Alta California*, pp. 239–240.
4. Quoted by Griswold del Castillo in "The U.S.-Mexican War in San Diego, 1846–1847," p. 5.
5. Quoted by Griswold del Castillo in "The U.S.-Mexican War in San Diego, 1846–1847," p. 5.
6. After Griswold del Castillo, "The U.S.-Mexican War in San Diego, 1846–1847," p. 5.

Chapter 13

1. After Pitt, *The Decline of the Californios*, p. 90.
2. When Robinson wrote this history of land titles in California in 1948, he was working as a Titleman for the Title Insurance and Trust Company in Los Angeles. A Titleman is a person trained to research and interpret land ownership and land titles.

3. Perfect Title Definition, p. 1.
4. In addition to these lands there are also (1) the public lands of the U.S., which were not conveyed under Spanish or Mexican authority, which lie outside the rancho and pueblo areas, and which passed directly to the U.S. with the cession of California by Mexico under the terms of the Treaty of Guadalupe Hidalgo in 1848, and (2) the state lands, which Congress granted to the State of California out of the public domain, to be used to fund education and reclamation in the state.
5. After Robinson's chapter, "Chain of Title," in his *Land in California*, pp. 73–90.
6. After Robinson's chapter, "The Land Commission," in his *Land in California*, pp. 91–109.
7. Quoted by W.W. Robinson, *Land in California*, p. 100.
8. After W.W. Robinson, *Land in California*, p. 92.
9. After W.W. Robinson, *Land in California*, p. 106.
10. After Perez, *Land Grants in Alta California*, p. 8.
11. W.W. Robinson, *Land in California*, pp. 112–113.
12. W.W. Robinson, *Land in California*, p. 106.
13. Quoted by Cleland, *The Cattle on a Thousand Hills*, p. 50.
14. Olmsted, "Mexican Land Claims—The U.S. Land Commission and The Burden of Proof, 1851–1854," pp. 3–4, citing Bancroft, *History of California*, vol. 4:576–577.
15. After Pitt, *The Decline of the Californios*, p. 119.
16. The following account is drawn in part from the Maritime Heritage Project, "VIPS in California in the 1800s," pp. 1–6.
17. Quoted by W.W. Robinson, *Land in California*, p. 237.

Chapter 14

1. Quoted by Paddison in *A World Transformed: Firsthand Accounts of California Before the Gold Rush*, pp. 116–117.
2. Quoted in Beebe and Senkewicz, *Lands of Promise and Despair*, pp. 388–389.
3. Bancroft, *California Pastoral*, pp. 408–409.
4. Dana, *Two Years Before the Mast*, p. 234.
5. Quoted by W.W. Robinson, *Land in California*, pp. 59–60.
6. Private communication of 12 July 2015 from Richard Griswold del Castillo.
7. After Hughes, "The Decline of the Californios: The Case of San Diego," p. 3.
8. Robinson, *Life in California*, pp. 191–192.
9. Colton, *Three Years in California*, p. 207.
10. After Osio, *The History of Alta California*, p. 21.
11. Osio, *The History of Alta California*, pp. 33–34.
12. Quoted by Mollins and Thickens (eds.) in Cerruti's *Ramblings in California*, p. 12.
13. Cerruti, *Ramblings in California*, pp. 87, 88.
14. Amador and Asisara, *California Voices*, p. 111.
15. Quoted by Beebe and Senkewicz, *Testimonios*, p. 303.
16. After Beebe and Senkewicz, *Testimonios*, p. xxxv.
17. These comments on *Californio* education are drawn from Bancroft, *California Pastoral*, pp. 493–525.
18. Bidwell, "Life in California," pp. 170–171.

Chapter 15

1. DeVoto, *The Year of Decision: 1846*, p. 223.
2. After Beebe and Senkewicz, *Lands of Promise and Despair*, p. 425.
3. A major source for this chapter is *The California Campaigns of the U.S.-Mexican War, 1846–1848*, by Hunt Janin and Ursula Carlson, pp. 41–46.
4. After PBS, "Mariano Guadalupe Vallejo," p. 1.
5. Bancroft, *California Pastoral*, p. 348.
6. Quoted by Sánchez, *Telling Identities: The Californio testimonios*, pp. 172–173.
7. Quoted by Beebe and Sankewicz, *Lands of Promise and Despair*, p. 426.
8. Quoted by Rosenus, *General Vallejo and the Advent of the Americans*, p. 41.

9. Quoted by Rosenus, *General Vallejo and the Advent of the Americans*, p. 169.
10. Colton, *Three Years in California*, frontispiece.
11. Much of the information about Vallejo's involvement in the state capital project and his later financial problems comes from Rosenus, *General Vallejo and the Advent of the Americans*, pp. 208–234.
12. Quoted by Rosenus, *General Vallejo and the Advent of the Americans*, p. 227.
13. Quoted by Rosenus, *General Vallejo and the Advent of the Americans*, pp. 227–228.
14. Some of the comments on Rancho Petaluma are drawn from the National Park Service article on Rancho Petaluma Adobe, pp. 1–3, and from California's State Park website article on "Petaluma Adobe State Historic Park," pp. 1–5.
15. National Park Service, "Petaluma Adobe California," p. 2.
16. Some of these comments are drawn from the Sonomaparks article on "General Vallejo's Home, " pp. 1–3.

Chapter 16

1. Some of the comments in this chapter are drawn from Griswold del Castillo, *The Los Angeles Barrio*, pp. 138–170..
2. Pitt, *The Decline of the Californios*, pp. 282–283.
3. After Hayes, *Historical Atlas of California*, p. 71.
4. After a private communication of 16 October 2015 from Jeff Lanzman of the Colton Hall Museum.
5. Camarillo, *Chicanos in a Changing Society*, p. 53.
6. Guinn, "The Passing of the Cattle Barons of California," pp. 1, 11.
7. Quoted by Los Angeles Almanac, "Pio Pico—Last Governor of Mexican California," p. 1.
8. After Sánchez, *Telling Identities: The Californio testimonios*, Preface, p. 1.
9. Quoted by Sánchez, *Telling Identities: The Californio testimonios*, p. 203.
10. After Camarillo, *Chicanos in a Changing Society*, pp. 128–129.
11. After a private communication of 3 June 2015 from Albert M. Camarillo.
12. After King, "Californio Families: A Brief Overview," pp. 1, 3.
13. After National Park Service, "A History of Mexican Americans in California: Post-Conquest California," p. 1.
14. After King, *Californio Families: A Brief Overview*, p. 3.
15. After Camarillo, *Chicanos in a Changing Society*, p. 10, and private communications of 3 August 2015 and 6 August 2015 from Richard Griswold del Castillo and Albert M. Camarillo, respectively.
16. Quoted by Camarillo, *Chicanos in a Changing Society*, p. 27.
17. Gutiérrez and Orsi, *Contested Eden*, p. 184.
18. Dana, *Two Years Before the Mast*, pp. 315–317.
19. After Santa Barbara Trust for Historic Preservation, "Casa de la Guerra," p. 1.
20. Quoted by Camarillo, *Chicanos in a Changing Society*, p. 56.
21. These two photos are reproduced in Camarillo, *Chicanos in a Changing Society*, p. 61.
22. Quoted by Camarillo, *Chicanos in a Changing Society*, p. 56.
23. Pitt, *The Decline of the Californios*, p. 104.
24. Pitt, *The Decline of the Californios*, p. 252.
25. After Pitt, *The Decline of the Californios*, pp. 252–253.
26. Adapted from Pitt, *The Decline of the Californios*, pp. 12–13.
27. After Pitt, *The Decline of the Californios*, p. 86.
28. After Plummer, *Señor Plummer*, pp. 56–60.
29. After Pitt, *The Decline of the Californios*, pp. 96–97, 100.
30. After Pitt, *The Decline of the Californios*, pp. 101–103.
31. After Pitt, *The Decline of the Californios*, p. 104.
32. After National Park Service, "El Clamor Publico Site," p. 1.
33. Bell, *Reminiscences of a Ranger*, p. 8.
34. Bell, *Reminiscences of a Ranger*, p. 7.
35. After Griswold del Castillo, *The Los Angeles Barrio, 1850–1890*, p. 42.
36. Bell, *On the Old West Coast*, p. 18.

37. Quoted by Richard Crawford, "The Great Drought," p. 1.
38. After Griswold del Castillo, *The Los Angeles Barrio, 1850–1860*, p. 42.
39. Bell, *On the Old West Coast*, pp. 82–83.
40. After Pitt, *The Decline of the Californios*, pp. 251–252.
41. After Cleland, *The Cattle on a Thousand Hills*, p. 112.
42. After Cleland, *The Cattle on a Thousand Hills*, p. 233.
43. After Cleland, *The Cattle on a Thousand Hills*, p. 233.
44. Quoted by Pitt, *The Decline of the Californios*, p. 255.
45. After Pitt, *The Decline of the Californios*, p. 270.
46. After Pitt, *The Decline of the Californios*, pp. 275–276.
47. After Richard Griswold del Castillo, *The Los Angeles Barrio, 1850–1890*, pp. 52–54.

Chapter 17

1. Quoted by Gibson, *California Through Russian Eyes, 1806–1848* pp. 88, 92.
2. At least seven men from the Spanish families that relocated from Baja California to Alta California before 1767 were literate, having learned to read in mission schools in Baja California. (Source: Crosby, *Antigua California*, p. 393.)
3. Quoted by Hague and Langum, *Thomas O. Larkin: A Life of Patriotism and Profit in Old California*, p 51.
4. Quoted by Hague and Langum, *Thomas O. Larkin: A Life of Patriotism and Profit in Old California*, p 53.
5. Alfred Robinson, *Life in California*, p. 150.
6. Colton, *Three Years in California*, pp. 222–223.
7. After Dana, "Twenty-Four Years Later," in *Two Years Before the Mast*, pp. 497–534.
8. See Beebe and Senkewicz, *Testimonios*, pp. 341–384, for the text of Savage's report.
9. After "Hemet, CA Ramona Pageant," pp. 1–2.
10. Some of the following comments are drawn from Warford, "An Eloquent and Impassioned Plea: The Rhetoric of Ruiz de Burton's *The Squatter and the Don*, p. 1.
11. "Old Spanish Days Fiesta," p. 1.
12. Some of these comments are drawn from National Park Service, "Mission Revival Style," pp. 1–6.
13. This account is drawn from Cotter, *Zorro—A History of the Series*, pp. 1–7.

Chapter 18

1. These accounts appear on pp. 467–470 of this volume.

Conclusion

1. Cited by Janin, *Claiming the American Wilderness*, p. 181.
2. Some of the following comments are drawn from Griswold del Castillo, *The Los Angeles Barrio*, pp. 150–170, and from Albert Camarillo, *Chicanos in a Changing Society*, pp. 117–141.
3. Griswold del Castillo, *The Los Angeles Barrio*, p. 160.
4. *Larousse: Traditional French Cookery*, p. 19.
5. Quoted in Time-Life Books, *The Spanish West*, p. 190.

Appendix 1

1. The information used here is drawn from the websites (listed in the bibliography) which cover the Port of Los Angeles; "The History of San Diego"; "Seventy-five Years in San Francisco"; the Port History of San Francisco; and the Spanish ship *San Carlos*.
2. After Pourade, "The History of San Diego: Vessels Touching at San Diego from 1769–1835," p. 1.
3. After San Francisco History, "Seventy-five Years in San Francisco, pp. 1–20.
4. After a private communication of 16 March 2016 from Dennis Copeland, Museums, Cultural Arts and Achieves Manager, City of Monterey.
5. Alexander Forbes quoting Captain John Hall in *California: A History of Upper and Lower California from Their First Discovery to the Present Time*, p. 329.

6. After San Francisco History, "Seventy-five Years in San Francisco, pp. 1–20.
7. After Pourade, "The History of San Diego: Vessels Touching at San Diego from 1779–1835," pp. 1–2.
8. This account of the ocean mail service is drawn from Hafen, *The Overland Mail*, pp. 44–46.
9. After San Francisco Port Department, "Port History," p. 4.

Appendix 2

1. The following account is drawn from Pitt, *The Decline of the Californios*, p. 253, who cites Lindley and Widney, *California of the South* (New York, 1896), pp. 205–206.
2. The following account is drawn from Triem and Stone, "Rancho Camulos," pp. 1–14.

Appendix 3

1. Mora, *Californios*, p. 9.
2. These points and quotes are drawn from Mora, *Californios*, pp. 157–161.

Appendix 4

1. This account is drawn from *Legends of America*, "Old West Legends: Tiburcio Vasquez—California Desperado," pp. 1–3.
2. These parts of the interview have been taken from Cleland, *The Cattle on a Thousand Hills: Southern California, 1850–1880*, pp. 274–279.

Appendix 5

1. This quote and the recipe itself, both of which have been very lightly edited, are taken from Time-Life Books, *The Spanish West*, p. 175.

Bibliography

"Alfred Robinson." San Diego History Center. http://www.sandiegohistory.org/bio/robinson/robinsonalfred.htm. Accessed 1 July 2015.

Amador, José María and Lorenzo Asisara. *Californio Voices: The Oral Memoirs of José María Amador and Lorenzo Asisara.* (Trans. and ed. by Gregorio Mora-Torres). Denton: University of North Texas Press, 2005.

Annenberg Learner. "Maria Amparo Ruiz de Burton (c. 132–1895)." https://www.learner.org/amerpass/unit05/authors-1.html. Accessed 6 May 2015.

Atreus, Stephen. "Russian Expansion to America." http://www.fortross.org/russian-american-company.htm. Accessed 7 March 2015.

Bancroft, Hubert Howe. *California Pastoral.* San Francisco: History Company, 1888.

_____. "Captain Ortega." In *The History of California.* 1884. Vol. 1, pp. 670–671.

Bandini, Juan. "A Statistical Description of Alta California." In Rose Marie Beebe and Robert M. Senkewicz (eds.), *Lands of Promise and Despair.* Santa Clara and Berkeley: Santa Clara University and Heyday Books, 2001, pp. 375–385.

Beebe, Rose Marie and Robert M. Senkewicz (eds.) *Lands of Promise and Despair: Chronicles of Early California, 1535–1846.* Santa Clara and Berkeley: Santa Clara University and Heyday Books, 2001.

_____. *Testimonios: Early California through the Eyes of Women, 1815–1848.* Berkeley: Heyday Books and the Bancroft Library, 2006.

Bell, Horace. (Lanier Bartlett ed.). *On the Old West Coast: Being further Reminiscences of a Ranger.* New York: Grosset and Dunlap, 1930.

_____. *Reminiscences of a Ranger or, Early Times in Southern California.* Washington, D.C.: Library of Congress, 1881.

Bidwell, John. "Life in California before the Gold Rush." In *The Century Magazine*, Vol. XLL, December 1890, no. 8, pp. 163–183.

Boggs, Mae Hélène Bacon. "My Playhouse was a Concord Coach: An Anthology of Newspaper Clippings and Documents Relating to Those Who Made California History During the Years 1832–1888." Library item number F 361, .B65, c. 2, Special Collections Department, Mathewson-IGT Knowledge Center, University of Nevada in Reno.

Booker, Margaret Moore. *The Santa Fe House: Historic Residences, Enchanting Adobes, and Romantic Revivals.* New York: Rizzoli, 2009.

Boozier, Virginia M. *Women and the Conquest of California, 1542–1840.* Tucson: University of Arizona Press, 2001.

Botello, Arthur P. (trans.) *Narración Historica: Don Pio Pico's Historical Narrative.*

Edited with introduction by Martin Cole and Henry Welcome. Glendale: Arthur C. Clark, 1973.
Bowers Museum. "Portrait of Don Jose Andres Sepulveda, c. 1856 by Henri Joseph Penelon." http://bowersmuseum.blogspot.fr/2007/10/object-of-the-week-portrait-of-don-jose.html. Accessed 10 October 2015.
Breschini, Gary S. "The Founding of Monterey." Monterey County Historical Society. http:www.mchsmuseum.colonization.html. Accessed 27 June 2015.
_____. "Hipólito (Hypolite) Bouchard and the Raid of 1818." Monterey County Historical Society. http:mchsmuseum.com/bouchard.html. Accessed 22 October 2015.
_____. "The Portolá Expedition of 1769." Montgomery County Historical Society. http:www.mchsmuseum.com/portola1769.html. Accessed 27 June 2015.
Brewer. William H. *Up and Down California in 1860–1864: The Journal of William H. Brewer.* (ed. Francis P. Farquhar, 4th ed.). Berkeley: University of California Press, 2003.
Brewerton, George Douglas. *Overland with Kit Carson: A Narrative of the Old Spanish Trail in '48*. Lincoln: University of Nebraska Press, 1993.
"Cabrillo's Legacy." Port of Los Angeles. https://www.portoflosangeles.org/history/cabrillo.asp.
California Historical Collection. *Reminiscences and Memoirs of Gen. Vallejo, Gen. Bidwell, Gen. Fremont, and Other Early Pioneers of the Western Overland.* Marston Gate: Amazon.co.uk, Ltd. Reproduction printed from a digital file at the Library of Congress; no date of printing is stated.
Camarillo, Albert. *Chicanos in a Changing Society: From Mexican Pueblos to American Barrios in Santa Barbara and Southern California, 1848–1930.* Dallas: Southern Methodist University Press, 2005.
"Casa de la Guerra: Social History." Santa Barbara Trust for Historic Preservation. http://www.sbthp.org. Accessed 10 August 2015.
Castillero, Andrés. "A Mexican Officer Urges Defense of Both Californias." In Rose Marie Beebe and Robert M. Senkewicz, *Lands of Promise and Despair.* Santa Clara and Berkeley: Heyday, 2001, pp. 406–412.
Cerruti, Henry. *Ramblings in California: The Adventures of Henry Cerruti.* Margaret Mollin and Virginia E. Thickens (eds.) Berkeley: Friends of the Bancroft Library, 1954.
Clay, Karen and Werner Troesken. "Ranchos and the Politics of Land Claims." In William Deverell and Greg Hise, *Land of Sunshine: An Environmental History of Los Angeles.* Pittsburg: University of Pennsylvania Press, 2005, pp. 52–66.
Cleland, Robert Glass. *The Cattle on a Thousand Hills: Southern California, 1850–80.* (2nd ed.) San Marino: Huntington Library and Art Gallery, 1951.
Colton, Rev. Walter. *Three Years in California.* New York: A.S. Barnes, 1850.
Cotter, Bill. "Zorro—A History of the Series." http://www.billcotter.com/zorro/history-of-series.htm. Accessed 27 September 2015.
Coy, Owen C. "The Battle of San Pascual: A Report of the California Historical Survey Commission with Special Reference to its Location." Sacramento: California State Printing Office, 1921. https://archive.org/stream/battlesanpascual00ocoy_djvu.txt. Accessed 21 June 2015.
Crawford, Kathleen. "María Amparo Ruiz Burton: The General's Lady." http://www.sandiegohistory.org/journal/84summer/burton.htm. Accessed 6 May 2015.
Crosby, Harry W. *Antigua California: Mission and Colony on the Peninsular Frontier, 1697–1768.* Albuquerque: University of New Mexico Press, 1994.
Crawford, Richard. "The Great Drought: Fickle Weather in 1860s led to Breakdown

of Cattle Industry." hppt://articles.latimes.com/1991-06-13/news/nc-780_1_cattle-industry. Accessed 30 July 2015.
Curnonsky. *Larousse: Traditional French Cookery*. London: Ebury Press, 1987.
Cutts, James Madison. *The Conquest of California and New Mexico, by the Forces of the United States in the Years 1846 & 1847*. Philadelphia: Carey & Hart, 1847.
Dana, Richard Henry, Jr *The Seaman's Friend: A Treatise on Practical Seamanship*. Mineola: Dover Publications, 1997.
_____. *Two Years Before the Mast*. New York: Penguin, 1986.
Davis, William Heath. "Seventy-five Years in San Francisco." http:www.sfgenealolgy.com/sf/history/hb75yap6.htm. Accessed 2 September 2015.
DeVoto, Bernard. *The Year of Decision, 1846*. New York: St. Martin's Press, 2000.
Dictionary of Canadian Biography. "Alberni, Pedro de." http://www.biographi.ca/en/bio/alberni_pedro_de_5E.html. Accessed 25 November 2015.
Digital-Desert: Mojave Desert. "Old Spanish Trail." http:digital-desert.com/old-spanish-triail. Accessed 20 August 2015.
Editors of Time-Life Books. *The Spanish West*. Alexandria: Time-Life Books, 1976.
Eisenhower, John S.D. *So Far From God: The U.S. War with Mexico, 1846–1848*. Norman: University of Oklahoma Press, 2000.
Eldridge, Zoeth Skinner. "General Mariano G. Vallejo (1808–1890)." http://www.sfmuseum.net/bio/vallejo.html. Accessed 15 June 2015.
Etter, Patricia. *To California on the Southern Route, 1849: A History and Annotated Bibliography*. Spokane: Arthur C. Clark, 1998.
Farnham, Thomas Jefferson. *Life, Travels, and Adventures in California, and Scenes from the Pacific Ocean*. New York: Wm. H. Graham, 1847.
Farris, Glenn J. (trans. and ed.) "Visit of the Russian Warship *Apollo* to California in 1822–1823." University of California Press, *Southern California Quarterly*, 1993, 75(1):1–13.
Find a Grave Memorial. "Capt Jose Francisco Ortega." http://www.findagrave.com/cgi-bin/fg.cgi?page=gr&GRid=67039081. Accessed 18 March 2015.
Forbes, Alexander. *California: A History of Upper and Lower California from their First Discovery to the Present Time*. Elibron Classics, Adamant Media Corporation, 2006 [a facsimile reprint of an edition published in 1839 by Smith, Elder and Co., London].
Frémont, John C. *Frémont's First Impressions: The Original Report of His Exploring Expeditions of 1842–1844*. (Introduction by Anne F. Hyde) Lincoln: University of Nebraska, 2012.
"Gapar de Portola." San Diego History Center. http://www.sandiegohistory.org/bio/portola.html. Accessed 18 August 2015.
Garavaglia, Louis A. and Charles G. Worman. *Firearms of the American West 1802–1865*. Niwot: University Press of Colorado, 1998.
"General Vallejo's Home." http:/www.sonomaparks.org/pub/place/4. Accessed 1 November 2015.
"General Vallejo's Home: Lachryma Montis." Sonoma/Petaluma State Historic Parks Association. http:www.sonomapark.org/pub/place/4. Accessed 24 June 2015.
Gibson, James R. (ed.). *California Through Russian Eyes, 1806–1848*. Norman: Arthur H. Clark Company, 2013.
_____. "The Exploration of the Pacific Coast." In Allen, John Logan (ed.) vol. 2. *North American Exploration: A Continent Defined*. Lincoln and London: University of Nebraska Press, 1997, pp. 328–396.
_____. *Otter Skins, Boston Ships, and China Goods: The Maritime Trade of the Northwest Coast, 1785–1841*. Seattle: University of Washington Press, 1992.

Golay, Michael and John S. Bowman. *North American Exploration.* Hoboken: John Wiley & Sons, 2003.
Griswold del Castillo, Richard. *The Los Angeles Barrio, 1850–1890: A Social History.* Berkeley: University of California Press, 1979.
_____. "The U.S.-Mexican War in San Diego, 1846–1847: Loyalty and Resistance" in *The Journal of San Diego History, San Diego Historical Society Quarterly.* Winter 2003, Volume 49, Number 1. https:www.sandiegohistory.org/journal/v49-1/war.html. Accessed 21 June 2015.
Guinn, J.M. "The Passing of the Cattle Barons of California." In *Southern California Quarterly,* Vol. 8, No. 1–2, 1909–1910 (pp. 51–60). http://archive.org/stream/jstor-41168654/4116854_djvu.txt. Accessed 21 July 2015.
Gutiérrez, Ramón and Richard J. Orsk. (eds.) *Contested Eden: California Before the Gold Rush.* Berkeley: University of California Press, 1998.
Hackel, Steven W. "Land, Labor, and Production: The Colonial Economy of Spanish and Mexican California." In Ramón Gutiérrez and Richard J. Orsk, *Contested Eden: California Before the Gold Rush.* Berkeley: University of California, 1998, pp. 111–146.
Hafen, LeRoy R. and Ann W. Hafen. *The Old Spanish Trail: Santa Fe to Los Angeles.* Lincoln: University of Nebraska Press, 1993.
_____. *The Overland Mail, 1849–1869.* Norman: University of Oklahoma Press, 2004.
Hague, Harlan. *Road to California: The Search for a Southern Overland Route, 1540–1848.* San Jose: Authors Choice Press, 2001.
_____, and David J. Langum. *Thomas O. Larkin: A Life of Patriotism and Profit in Old California.* Norman: University of Oklahoma Press, 1990.
Hardin, Garrett. "The Tragedy of the Commons." http://www.garretthardinsociety.org/articles/art_tragedy_of_the_commons.html. Accessed 29 November 2015.
Hardwick, Michael R. "The Naval Department of San Blas: Spain's Supply and Ship-building Center for Alta California and the Pacific Northwest, 1770–1810." http://californiamilitaryhistory.org/SanBlas.html. Accessed 25 August 2015.
Harlow, Neal. *California Conquered: The Annexation of a Mexican Province, 1846–1850.* Berkeley: University of California Press, 1989.
Harvard University Library Open Collection Program. "Immigration to the United States: California Gold Rush (1848–1859)." http://ocp.hul.harvard.edu/immigration/goldrush.html. Accessed 27 June 2015.
Haas, Lisbeth. *Conquests and Historical Identities in California 1769–1936.* Berkeley: University of California Press, 1995.
Hayes, Derek. *Historical Atlas of California.* Berkeley: University of California Press, 2007.
"Hemet, CA, Ramona Pageant." See California. http://www.seecalifornia.comfestivals/hemet-ramona.html. Accessed 20 November 2015.
Hijar, Carlos N., Eulalia Perez, and Agustin Escobar. "Three Memoirs of Mexican California." (As recorded in 1877 by Thomas Savage and translated by Vivian C. Fisher.) Berkeley: The Friends of the Bancroft Library, University of California at Berkeley, 1988.
"Hispanic Americans: Spanish Colonization and Californios (1769–1800s)." University of California. http://www.calisphere.universityofcalifornia.edu/calcultures/ethnic_groups/subtopic3a.html. Accessed 24 December 2014.
Honig, Sasha. "The Presidios of Alta California." California Mission Studies Association. http:www.californiamissionstudies.com/Research/Articles/The_Presidios.html. Accessed 8 April 2015.

Howard, Thomas Frederick. *Sierra Crossing: First Roads to California*. Berkeley: University of California Press, 2000.
Hughes, Charles. "The Decline of the Californios: The Case of San Diego, 1846–1856." *The Journal of San Diego History*. Summer 1975, Volume 21, Number 3. https://www.sandiegohistory.org/journal/75summer/decline.htm. Accessed 12 July 2015.
Hunter, Alexander. *Vallejo: A California Legend*. Sonoma: Sonoma State Historic Park Association, 1992.
Kroeber, Alfred L. *Handbook of the Indians of California*. New York: Dover, 1976.
Jackson, Helen Hunt. *Ramona*. Marston Gate: amazon.co.uk, n.d. (originally published in 1884).
Janin, Hunt. *Claiming the American Wilderness: International Rivalry in the Trans-Mississippi West, 1528–1803*. Jefferson: McFarland, 2006.
____, and Ursula Carlson. *The California Campaigns of the U.S.-Mexican War, 1846–1848*. Jefferson: McFarland, 2015.
____. *Trails of Historic New Mexico: Routes Used by Indian, Spanish and American Travelers through 1836*. Jefferson: McFarland, 2010.
"José María Echeandia." San Diego History Center. https://www.sandiegohistory.org bio//echeandia/echeandia.htm. Accessed 7 June 2015.
Juana Briones Heritage. "Juana's Life." http://www.brioneshouse.org/juanas_life.htm. Accessed 4 November 2015.
King, Alexander V. "Californio Families: A Brief Overview." http://www.sfgenealogy.com/spanish/calfam.htm. Accessed 12 September 2015.
Markov, Alexander. "Excerpt from Alexander Markov's Recollections of California [ca. 1845]." In James R. Gibson, *California Through Russian Eyes, 1806–1848*. Norman: Arthur C. Clark, 2013, pp. 421–451.
Mathes, W. Michael. "Some Reflections on California, 1776." http://www.sandiegohistory.org/journal/76fall/reflections.htm. Accessed 28 August 2015.
"Mexican California: The Heyday of the Ranchos." California State University Northridge. www.csun.edu/~sg4002/courses/4171/. Accessed 28 September 2015.
"Mission Tour: A Virtual Tour of the California Missions." http://missiontour.org/carmel/history.htm. Accessed 19 October 2004.
Monroy, Douglas. *The Borders Within: Encounters between Mexico and the U.S.* Tucson: University of Arizona Press, 2008.
____. "The Creation and Re-creation of Californio Society" in Gutiérrez, Ramón A. and Richard J. Orsi, *Contested Eden*. Berkeley: University of California, 1998, pp. 173–195.
Mora, Jo. *Californios: The Saga of the Hard-riding Vaqueros, America's First Cowboys*. Garden City: Doubleday, 1949.
"Motives for Exploration: Heading West and North." http://www.californiahistory.net/text_only/3.1.htm. Accessed 4 July 2004.
National Park Service. "Concepíon Arguello & Nikolai Petrovich Rezanov: A Presidio Love Story." http://www.nps/gov/prsf/learn/historyculture/love-story.htm. Accessed 24 May 2015.
____. "A History of Mexican Americans in California: Historic Sites—El Clamor Publico Site." http://www.nps.gov/parkhistory/online_books/5views/5views5h34.htm. Accessed 23 November 2015.
____. "A History of Mexican Americans in California: Post-Conquest California." http://www.cr/nps.gov/history/online_books/5views/5views5b.htm. Accessed 7 January 2015.

_____. "Mission Revival Style." http://www.nps/gov/goga/learn/historyculture/mission-revival.htm. Accessed 10 November 2015.

_____. "Petaluma Adobe California." http://www.nps.gov/nr/travel/american_latino_heritage/Petaluma_Adobe.html. Accessed 31 October 2015.

Nuttall, Donald. *The Gobernantes of Spanish Upper California: A Profile. California Historical Quarterly*, Vol. 51, No. 3 (Fall, 1972), pp. 253–280.

Ogden, Adele. "Hides and Tallow: McCulloch, Hartwell and Company, 1822–1828." In *California Historical Society Quarterly*, Vol. 6. No. 3 (Sept. 1927), pp. 254–264. http://www.jstor.org/stable/25177893. Accessed 8 January 2015.

_____. "Russian Sea-Otter and Seal Hunting on the California Coast, 1803–1841." In California Historical Society. *The Russians in California*. San Francisco, 1933. Special Publication No. 7. Reprinted from the Quarterly of the California Historical Society. Volume XII, Number 3. September 1933. Pp. 29–51.

"Old Spanish Days Fiesta." https://www.santabarbara.com/events/fiesta/. Accessed 13 November 2015.

"Old West Legends: Tiburcio Vasquez—California Desperado." Legends of America. http://www.legendsofamerica.com/we-tiburciovasquez.html. Accessed 17 October 2015.

Olmstead, Nancy J. "Mexican Land Claims—The U.S. Land Commission and The Burden of Proof." http://foundssf.org/index.php?title=Mexican_Land_Claims%E2%80%94The_U.S._Land_C... Accessed 11 June 2015.

Osio, Antonio María. *The History of Alta California: A Memoir of Mexican California*. (Translated, edited, and annotated by Rose Marie Beebe and Robert M. Senkewicz.) Madison: University of Wisconsin Press, 1996.

Padilla, Genaro M. *My History, Not Yours: The Formation of a Mexican American Autobiography*. Madison: University of Wisconsin Press, 1993.

PBS. "New Perspective on the West: Mariano Guadalupe Vallejo (1808–1890)." http://www.pbs.org/weta/thewest/people/s_z/vallejo.htm. Accessed 15 June 2015.

Perez, Crisostomo N. *Land Grants in Alta California: A compilation of Spanish and Mexican private land claims in the State of California giving pertinent data in relation to the United States of America's conformation and patenting of said claims, together with a compilation of legislation and litigation affecting each claim*. Rancho Cordova: Landmark Enterprises, 1996.

_____. "Ranchos of California." http://cluster3.lib.berkeley.edu/EART/rancho/html. Accessed 23 December 2014.

"Pio Pico—Last Governor of Mexican California." Los Angeles Almanac. http://www.laalmanac.com/history/hi05s.htm. Accessed 30 September 2015.

Pitt, Leonard. *The Decline of the Californios: A Social History of the Spanish-Speaking Californians, 1846–1890*. Berkeley: University of California Press, 1998.

Plummer, E.R. *Señor Plummer: The Life and Laughter of an Old-Californian*. Second edition. Hollywood: Murray & Gee, 1943.

"Portola Expedition 1769 Diaries." PacificaHistory. http://pacificahistory.wikispaces.com/Portola+Expedition+1769+Diaries. Accessed 17 August 2015.

Pourade, Richard F. "The History of San Diego." https://www.sandiegohistory.org/books/pourade/time/timevessels.htm. Accessed 2 September 2015.

Quaife, Milo Milton, ed. *Kit Carson's Autobiography*. Lincoln: University of Nebraska Press, 1935.

Regan, Geoffrey. "California and the Mexican War: The Battle of San Pascual." The California State Military Museum. http://californiamilitaryhistory.org/SanPascual.html. Accessed 21 June 2015.

Reyes, Bárbara O. *Private Women, Public Lives: Gender and the Missions of the Californias*. Austin: University of Texas Press, 2009.

Rezanov, Nicolai Petrovich and Georg von Langsdorff. "The Rezanov Voyage, 1806" in Paddison, Joshua (ed.). *A World Transformed: Firsthand Accounts of California Before the Gold Rush*. Berkeley: Heyday Books, 1999, pp. 95–99.

Robinson, Alfred. *Life in California During a Residence of Several Years in that Territory. Containing a Description of the Country and the Missionary Establishments, with Incidents, Observations, etc. With an Appendix; Bringing Forward the Narrative from 1846, to the Occupation of the Country by the United States*. San Francisco: William Doxey, 1891.

Robinson, W. W. *Land in California: The Story of Mission Lands, Ranchos, Squatters, Mining Claims, Railroad Grants, Land Scrip, Homesteads*. Berkeley and Los Angeles: University of California Press, 1948.

Rorbough, Malcom J. *Days of Gold: The California Gold Rush and the American Nation*. Berkeley: University of California Press, 1997.

Rosenus, Alan. *General Vallejo and the Advent of the Americans*. Berkeley: Heyday, 1999.

Rounds, Glen. (ed.) *Mountain Men: George Frederick Ruxton's Firsthand Accounts of Fur Trappers and Indians in the Rockies*. New York: Holiday House, 1966.

Russell, Carl P. *Guns on the Early Frontiers: A History of Firearms from Colonial Times through the years of the Western Fur Trade*. Lincoln: University of Nebraska Press, 1957.

Ruxton, George Frederick. "Wild Life in the Rocky Mountains." http://www.xmission.com/~drudy/mtman/html/ruxton.html. Accessed 28 May 2008.

"The San Carlos, First Spanish Ship to Enter the S.F. Bay." sfbaytimetraveler. http://sfbaytimetraveler.wordpress.com/about/the-san-carlos-first-ship-to-enter-the... Accessed 5 September 2015.

Sánchez, Rosaura. *Telling Identities: The Californio testimonios*. Minneapolis: University of Minnesota Press, 1995.

_____, and Beatrice Pita. eds. *The Squatter and the Don*. Houston: Arte Publico Press, 1971.

Schwartz, Harvey. "Fort Ross California—A Historical Synopsis." Fort Ross Conservancy. http://www.fortross.org/lib/html. Accessed 24 May 2015.

Serra, Junípero. "Trip to Mexico City." In Rose Marie Beebe and Robert M. Senkewicz, *Lands of Promise and Despair*. Santa Clara and Berkeley: Heyday, 2001, pp. 169–176. Accessed 12 July 2015.

Simmons, Marc. "Kit Carson and the Romance of the Old Spanish Trail." http://www.elpalacio.org/placeseries/winter07KitCarson. Accessed 20 August 2015.

Simpkins, Bill. "Los Angeles Biographies: Eugene Rafael Plummer." http://freepages.genealogy.rootsweb.ancestry.com~npmeltonlaplum.htm. Accessed 7 July 2015.

Shinn, Charles Howard. "Pioneer Spanish Families in California, With Special Reference to the Vallejos." In *The Century Magazine*, vol. XLI, no. 21, 1890, pp. 378–389; reprinted there in "Reminiscences and memoirs of Gen. Vallejo, Gen. Bidwell, Gen. Fremont, and other early pioneers of the western overland." California Historical Collection. Marston Gate: Amazon.co.uk, Ltd. No date of printing given.

Simpson, Sir George. *An Overland Journey Around the World*. In Joshua Paddison (ed. and introduction) *A World Transformed: Firsthand Accounts of California Before the Gold Rush*. Berkeley: Heyday, 1999, pp. 223–257.

Smith, Justin H. *The War with Mexico*. New York: Macmillan, 1919.

"Spanish and Mexican California: Hippolyte de Bouchard and His Attacks on the California Missions." The California State Military Museum. http://californiamilitary history.org/deBouchard.html. Accessed 22 October 2015.

Thurman, Michael E. *The Naval Department of San Blas: New Spain's Bastion for Alta California and Nootka, 1767 to 1798.* Glendale: Arthur C. Clark, 1967.

Triem, Judith P. and Mich Stone. "Rancho Camulos: National Register of Historic Places Nomination." http://www.scvhistory.com/scvhistory/camulos-nrph3.htm. Accessed 19 July 2015.

Twain, Mark. *Roughing It.* New York: Penguin, 1985.

Unkovsky, Semyon Yakovlevich. "Voyage around the World." In James R. Gibson (ed.), *California Through Russian Eyes, 1806–1848.* Norman: Arthur C. Clark, 2013, pp.75–83.

Vallejo, Guadalupe. "Ranch and Mission Days in Alta California." *The Century Magazine*, Vol. XLL, December 1890, no. 8. http://www.sfmuseum.org/hist2/rancho.html. Accessed 23 December 2014.

Vallejo, Mariano. "The Arrival of a North American Wagon Train." In Beebe, Rose Marie and Robert M. Senkewicz. *Lands of Promise and Despair: Chronicles of Early California, 1535–1846.* Santa Clara and Berkeley: Heyday Books, 2001, pp. 423–427.

"VIPS in California during the 1800s: Jose Yves Lemantour." The Maritime Heritage Project. http://www.maritimeheritage.org/vips/limantour.html. Accessed 5 December 2015.

Warford, Elisa. "An Eloquent and Impassioned Plea: The Rhetoric of Ruiz de Burton's *The Squatter and the Don.*" http://muse.jhu.edu/journals/wal/summary/v044/44.1.warford.html. Accessed 21 November 2015.

Weber, David J. *The Mexican Frontier, 1821–1846: The American Southwest Under Mexico.* Albuquerque: University of New Mexico Press, 1982.

_____. *The Spanish Frontier in North America.* New Haven: Yale University Press, 1992.

_____. "The Spanish Legacy in North America and the Historical Imagination." *The Western Historical Quarterly*, vol. 23, number 1 (Feb. 1992), pp. 5–24.

"Women Pioneers of Alta California." California Missions Resource Center. http://www.missionscalifornia.com/stories/women-pioneers-alta-california.html. Accessed 4 November 2015.

Zavalishin, Dmitry. "[Alta] California in 1824." In James R. Gibson, *California Through Russian Eyes, 1806–1848.*" Norman: Arthur C. Clark Company, 2013, pp. 243–279.

Index

Abiquiu, New Mexico 56
Adams, John H. 140
Aguardiente 32, 36
Aguirre, José Antonio 27
Alcalde 29, 43, 47, 101, 108, 110, 115, 119, 137, 157
All Star Weekly 151
Alta California 1, 2, 3, 4, 5, 6, 7, 8, 9, 13, 14, 15, 16, 17, 18, 19, 20, 21, 23, 24, 25, 26, 27, 28, 29, 30, 33, 34, 35, 37, 38, 39, 40, 41, 42, 43, 45, 46, 47, 48, 50, 53, 54, 56, 60, 61, 63, 66, 67, 68, 69, 70, 71, 73, 74, 75, 76, 77, 78, 79, 80, 81, 82, 84, 86, 87, 88, 89, 92, 93, 96, 99, 100, 107, 108, 109, 110, 111, 114, 115, 116, 113, 127, 144, 146, 161, 162, 163, 164, 165, 166, 167, 175, 178
Alvarado, Juan Bautista 89, 90, 91, 101, 125
Amador, José María 31, 32, 50, 87, 88, 92, 113
Anglo-American 56, 127, 135, 142, 150, 159
Argosy magazine 51
Argüello, Concepción 74, 75
Argüello, José 74
Argüello, Luis Antonio 74, 76, 88, 111, 117
Arnaz, José 61
Arrellanes, Teodoro 130
Arrillaga, José Joaquin 83, 84, 107, 134
Atchison, Topeka, and Santa Fe (ATSE) railroad 143
atole de pinole 31, 32

baile 49
Baja California 6, 7, 14, 16, 17, 20, 25, 59, 67, 70, 74, 86, 89, 90, 103, 161, 162
Bancroft, Hubert Howe 1, 22, 30, 44, 61, 63, 84, 90, 10, 108, 112, 113, 114, 116, 144, 148, 165
Bancroft Library 22, 116
Bandini, Juan 34, 45, 46, 47, 129
barrioization 126, 158
barrios 124, 126, 127, 128, 129, 159, 164, 165

Bear Flag Revolt 64, 91, 119, 122, 164
bear hunt 71, 110
beef trade 134; *see also* hide and tallow trade
Bell, Horace 49, 135, 136, 137, 165
Berreyesa, Antonio 134
Berreyesa family 133
Bidwell, John 115
Bidwell-Bartleson Party 115
Boston 8, 39, 110
Bouchard, Hipólite 153, 154, 163
Brewerton, George Douglas 49, 57
Brillat-Savarin, Jean Antheleme 160
Briones, Brigida 153, 155

Cabrillo, Juan Rodriguez 5, 161, 168
"California banknote" 23, 34, 36
California campaigns of the U.S-Mexican War (1846–1848) 95
California Mission Revival Movement 150
California Through Russian Eyes, 1806–1848 145
Californios' opinions of the Americans 63
Calle de los Negros 135
Callis, Eulalia 62
El Camino Real 16, 23, 84, 162
Cape Horn 8, 122
Carlos III (King) 14, 161
Carquinez Strait 119, 120
Carrillo, Carlos Antonio 85, 91, 107, 108
Casa de la Guerra 128, 129
cascarones 155, 156
Castro, José 44, 81, 87, 89, 91
Catala, Father Majin 24
Catholic Church 8, 11, 24, 32, 117
cattle 1, 3, 8, 11, 16, 21, 23, 25, 26, 30, 34, 36, 37, 38, 39, 45, 47, 48, 62, 68, 75, 77, 78, 79, 95, 101, 102, 105, 107, 110, 118, 119, 120, 125, 126, 127, 128, 131, 134, 136, 137, 138, 140, 142, 147, 149, 158, 159, 163, 165, 173, 174, 175, 177
cattle barons 126

199

The Century Magazine 115, 153
Cerruti, Henry 63, 64, 112–113, 165
chain of title 99, 100, 163
Chapman, Alfred B. 138
Chapman, Joseph 53
Chico, Marino 90
Chico, California 10, 26
cinnabar (ore of mercury) mines 140
Civil War 137, 141, 148
El Clamor Publico 135
clashes of cultures 2, 104
colonization of Baja and Alta California 13, 16, 20, 89, 100, 117, 161
Colton, Walter 4, 110–111, 119, 146, 147
Constansó, Miguel 14, 18, 162
Coronel, Antonio Francisco 29, 20, 33, 34, 108, 135
Cortés, Hernán 13, 161
Crespi, Fray Juan 14, 15, 167
crime 48, 63, 66, 140, 176
crop production at the missions 21

Dana, Richard Henry, Jr. 23, 38, 39, 42, 44, 61, 76, 109, 128, 129, 147, 163, 165
de Alberni, Pedro 84
de Anza, Juan Bautista 16, 30, 162, 175
de Borica, Diego 84
de Echeandía, José Maria 88, 89
de Gálvez, Joseph 6, 14, 17, 18, 25, 161
de la Guerra, Anita 128
de la Guerra de Hartnell, Doña Teresa 128
de la Guerra de Ord, Angustias 62, 66
de la Guerra y Noriega, José 127, 128, 129
del Carmen Lugo, José 29, 30, 32, 136
del Valle, Reginaldo 138, 171
del Valle, Ygnacio 27, 137, 138, 171, 172
de Mofras, Eugene 27, 48, 57, 105
de Neve, Filipe 46, 84, 85, 162
de Rivera, Fernando 14
de Solá, Pablo Vincente 50, 117
Díaz, Porfirio 94
Diseños 28, 29, 40, 163
Disney, Walt 152
Domínguez, Juan José 25, 26
Donation Land Claim Act of 1850 131
Drake's Bay 15

education (and lack of education) of the *Californios* 33, 34, 68, 70, 78, 79, 114, 115, 119, 140, 142, 145, 155
El Camino Real 16, 23, 84, 162
El Clamor Publico 135
El Refugio 33
El Tejon 27
Elizabeth I 13

Fages, Pedro 25, 26, 27, 43, 62, 83, 162
fandango 49, 129, 175
Farallon Islands 15, 80, 112, 115
farms 79, 109, 130, 141
Figueroa, José 89, 101, 117, 121

Flores, José Maria 93
foreign trade 63, 75, 167, 168
Franciscans 20, 83
Frémont, John C. 56, 64
friars 7, 16, 19, 20, 21, 36, 41, 52, 65, 68, 74, 76, 142, 160, 162

Garcés, Father Francisco 55
Garfias, Manuel 101, 102
Gaspar de Portolá 7, 13–16, 18, 43, 162, 167, 169
gente de razón 60, 69, 70, 71, 162
George, Henry 104–105
Gibson, James R. 145
Gillespie, Archibald 98
gobernante 83
Gold Rush 1, 10, 38, 58, 124, 128, 133, 134, 163, 170
Gonzalez, Mauricio 125
Great Droughts of 1861–1865 125, 137, 158
Griswold del Castillo, Richard 4, 82, 141, 159
Guinn, James M. 126
Gutiérrez, Nicolás 90, 100
Gutiérrez, Ramón 128
Gwin, William M. 102, 103

Hacienda de Las Yorbas 37, 164
Hall, Colton 4, 146
Hartnell, William 117, 146
Hawaii 140, 146
hide and tallow trade 8, 23, 33, 37, 38, 109, 134, 163, 166, 170
Hijar-Padrés colony 29, 67, 89
History of California 1, 144, 165
Hittell, John 26
horses 21, 27, 30, 32, 33, 34, 36, 37, 47, 48, 54, 55, 57, 58, 59, 61, 62, 68, 75, 76, 78, 79, 95, 96, 97, 101, 108, 110, 114, 115, 118, 119, 120, 128, 136, 144, 147, 150, 156, 159, 163, 175, 176
Hospicio de Pobres (Royal Hospice for the Poor) 65

Indians 3, 7, 8, 15, 21, 23, 24, 25, 26, 27, 28, 33, 35, 36, 41, 48, 53, 55, 56, 58, 59, 60, 66, 70, 76, 78, 79, 83, 84, 86, 89, 100, 108, 110, 116, 117, 118, 131, 136, 145, 160, 162, 163, 165, 168
Inter Caetera (1493) 13
irrigation 139, 141, 142

Jackson, Helen Hunt 60, 69, 70, 148, 149, 165, 171
Jones, William Carey 103

Khlebnikov, Kirill 77
"King of the Missions" (i.e., Mission San Luis Rey) 21
Kotzebue, Otto von 145

Index

Lachryma Montis 116, 120, 122–123, 164
Land Act of 1796 28
land claims 29, 99, 101, 102, 104, 105, 134
land commissions 99, 101, 102, 164
Land in California 99
land swindles 106
land titles 11, 99–196, 131, 132
Larkin, Thomas 39, 40, 71, 119, 125, 145, 146
Las Sergas de Esplandián 5, 161
lawyers 40, 103, 104, 105, 128, 132, 133, 134, 137, 138, 139, 142, 145
"leather jacket" soldiers 7, 14, 88, 113
Leese, Jacob 64
Leese, Rosalia Vallejo 63–64
Life in California 146
Limantour, Joseph Yves 99, 106–106
literacy (and illiteracy) 70, 132
Lorenza, Apolinaria 62, 65
Los Angeles 21, 22, 28, 29, 30, 33, 44, 45, 46, 47, 48, 49, 54, 55, 56, 57, 61, 71, 84, 85, 89, 90, 91, 92, 93, 101, 110, 115, 124, 131, 135, 136, 137, 139, 140, 141, 143, 147, 156, 159, 161, 162, 163, 165, 166, 168, 175, 176, 177
Los Angeles Directory of 1875 139
Los Angeles Rangers 135
Los Nietos 26
Lugo, Vincente 132, 137, 138

Manifest Destiny 2, 9, 94
Mariner, Juan 36, 100, 101, 163
Markov, Alexander 80, 81
McCulley, Johnston 151
mercury 133, 140; *see also* cinnabar
Mexican-Americans 159, 165, 175
Mexican Cession 9, 10
Mexican land grant policy 26
Mexican prestige system 141–142
Mexican War of Independence 7, 87, 163
Micheltorena, Manuel 27, 91, 92, 101, 105, 113, 120
missions in California 6, 7, 8, 14, 16, 17, 19, 20–24, 26, 27, 34, 36, 41, 43, 46, 48, 51, 55, 61, 65, 66, 68, 69, 74, 76, 78, 83, 84, 86, 88, 89, 90, 92, 93, 100, 110, 118, 145, 159, 160, 161, 162, 163, 168
Monterey (town, port, and bay) 4, 6, 7, 14, 15, 16, 18, 39, 41, 42, 43, 44, 46, 47, 48, 50, 51, 52, 53, 61, 62, 63, 65, 66, 77, 81, 84, 85, 86, 87, 88, 89, 90, 91, 103, 107, 109, 110, 112, 113, 115, 116, 117, 119, 121, 125, 126, 139, 146, 148, 153, 155, 156, 162, 163, 166, 167, 168, 175, 176
Mora, Jo 1, 173–174
mortgaging ranchos 126, 163
Mother Lode 10

Narración Historica 30, 92
New Almadén Quicksilver [mercury] mine 133, 140

New Archangel (Sitka, Alaska) 76
New Spain (*Neuva España*) 3, 7, 13, 17, 18, 19, 20,, 25, 43, 87, 161, 162, 163
Nicholas I (Tsar) 76
Nieto, Manuel Pérez 25, 26, 162
Northern California 10, 88, 89, 91, 110, 117, 118, 119, 122, 124, 130, 137, 163
nuqueo 131, 173–174

"old" *Californio* families 128, 134, 137
Old Spanish Days Fiesta 129, 150
Old Spanish Trail 4, 54–59, 161
Orange County, California 29, 37, 134, 164
orchards 41, 44, 142
Orsi, Richard 128
Ortega, José Francisco 15, 43, 44, 162
Osio, Antonio María 88, 96, 111
outlaws 135, 140, 176

Pacheco, Romualdo 140
Panic of 1873 139
Penelon, Henri Joseph 30, 33
peninsulars 88
Peralta, Pablo 134
Pérez, Eulalia 22, 62
perfect title 99, 104
Peter the Great 6, 161
Peyri, Father Antonio 36
Pico, Andrés 93, 95, 164
Pico, Maria Antonia 153–154
Pico, Maria Inocenta 113–114
Pico, Pio 127, 135
Pitt, Leonard 3, 24, 85, 125
Plummer, Eugenio 71, 72, 130, 131, 132
Point Reyes 15, 112
presidios 6, 7, 16, 17, 25, 26, 27, 31, 33, 36, 41–45, 46, 47, 52, 53, 53, 74, 75, 77, 81, 83, 85, 88, 91, 92, 108, 109, 110, 111, 112, 113, 117, 121, 162, 163, 169
proletarianization of Mexican working class 127
"Protestant Ethic" 2
Pueblo Viejo 129, 130, 165

quicksilver [mercury] 133, 140

Ramirez, Francisco P. 135
Ramona 69, 70, 148, 165, 171, 172
ranchos, rancheros, and ranch life of the
   Californios 2, 3, 5, 10, 11, 15, 21, 25–40, 41, 43, 44, 45, 46, 49, 52, 56, 61,, 65, 66, 70, 80, 83, 85, 87, 88, 99, 100, 101, 102, 103, 104, 113, 116, 117, 121, 122, 124, 125, 126, 130, 131, 133, 134, 135, 136, 137, 138, 140, 141, 142, 144, 163, 171, 172
Real Casa Espositos (Royal House for Abandoned Children) 65
recogida 21
Recuerdos Historicos 116
El Refugio 33

Index

Rezanov, Nikolay Petrovich 74, 75, 84
Rivera y Moncada, Fernando 14, 83
Robinson, Alfred 27, 41, 69, 109–110, 128, 129, 146
Robinson, W.W. 99, 100, 104
Roméu, José Antonio 84
Ruiz de Burton, Maria Amparo 62, 67–68, 149, 150, 165
Russia and Russians 4, 5, 6, 14, 15, 16, 17, 18, 19, 20, 41, 73, 74, 75, 76, 77, 79, 80, 81, 107, 117, 121, 145, 148, 161, 162; *see also* Russian-American Company
Russian-American Company 73, 74, 76, 77, 84, 163
Ruxton, George Frederick 54

Sacramento (valley, city, and port) 10, 28, 64, 79, 83, 86, 104, 109, 119, 120, 128, 148
sala 49
San Bernardino 29, 55, 57, 139, 46, 65, 161, 162, 169
San Blas 17–10, 20
San Diego (city and port) 4, 7, 14, 16, 18, 20, 25, 26, 27, 36, 39, 41, 42, 43, 46, 56, 65, 67, 83, 84, 88, 92, 95, 98, 99, 100, 110, 115, 126, 139, 148, 149, 150, 151, 162, 163, 166, 169, 171
San Francisco (city, port, and bay) 1, 7, 10, 14, 15, 16, 20, 30, 38, 41, 42, 43, 46, 47, 53, 56, 74, 75, 76, 77, 79, 80, 81, 83, 84, 85, 103, 104, 105, 106, 107, 111, 112, 113, 115, 117, 119, 121, 126, 141, 145, 147, 149, 151, 156, 162, 163, 166, 167, 169–170
San Jose 35, 36, 46, 56, 79, 84, 86, 128, 133, 134, 162, 176
San Luis Obispo 70, 83, 113, 139, 140
San Pascual, battle of 95, 96, 97, 164
San Pedro 33, 47, 49, 53, 105, 165, 168, 172
Sandwich Islands [Hawaii] 140
Santa Barbara 7, 41, 42, 43, 44, 53, 65, 66, 84, 115, 126, 128, 129, 130, 131, 136, 137, 139, 140, 148, 150, 162, 165
Santa Barbara Historical Society Library 130
Savage, Thomas 22, 30, 31, 32, 65, 66, 87, 113, 114, 148, 165
Schabelski, Achille 77
schools 68, 114, 115, 146
sea otters 14, 74, 78
Secularization Act of 1833 28
secularization of missions 8, 23, 27, 28, 48, 79, 84, 86, 89, 90, 91, 92, 100, 110, 117
Sepúlveda, José Antonio Andrés 29, 30, 33
Las Sergas de Esplandián 5, 161
Serra, Father Junípero 7, 14, 20, 43, 83, 84, 162, 167
sheep 21, 48, 58, 78, 118, 128, 137, 138, 139, 147, 159
Shinn, Charles Howard 153
"shotgun titles" 104

Sibrian, Amalia 153, 156–157
Sierra Nevada mountains 3, 10, 83, 164
Simpson, Sir George 48, 79
Sloat, John B. 66
Smith, Justin Harvey 80
Solá, Pablo Vincente 50, 51, 52, 53, 85, 87, 88, 117
Sonoma, California 16, 20, 41, 56, 64, 99, 100, 115, 116, 117, 119, 120, 121, 123, 163, 164
"Sonora Town" 124, 132
Southern California 10, 16, 25, 54, 56, 65, 70, 101, 102, 124, 127, 130, 134, 135, 136, 137, 139, 141, 142, 143, 158, 161, 165, 171, 175
Spain 3, 5, 6, 13, 17, 18, 19, 20, 23, 25, 27, 28, 32, 41, 43, 53, 61, 75, 77, 82, 83, 84, 85, 87, 100, 111, 117, 125, 151, 158, 161, 162, 163, 167, 168
Spanish-speaking population 128, 159
speculators 104, 105, 125, 141
The Squatter and the Don 67, 149, 165
squatters 63, 67, 80, 104, 120, 128, 130, 133, 134, 137, 149, 150, 158, 164

tallow 8, 36, 38, 39, 47, 76, 81; *see also* hide and tallow trade
El Tejon 27
Treaty of Guadalupe Hidalgo 2, 8, 9, 67, 82, 102, 104, 164
Treaty of Tordesillas 13
Two Years Before the Mast 23, 38, 147, 163, 165

U.S. Land Commission 99, 102, 164; *see also* land commissions
U.S.-Mexican War 2, 7, 11, 29, 39, 40, 56, 65, 67, 70, 71, 80, 89, 94–98, 99, 119, 124, 127, 131, 133, 134, 140, 141, 149, 150, 158, 160, 164, 165
U.S. Register of Historic Places 128
Unkovsky, Semyon Yakovlevich 76

Valenzuela, Jesus 130
Vallejo, Benicia 118
Vallejo, Mariano Guadalupe 24, 38, 51, 63, 64, 69, 112, 113, 116–123, 127, 160, 164, 165
Vallejo, Platon 121
vaqueros 9, 25, 30, 32, 55, 95, 110, 131, 138, 173
Vásquez, Tiburcio 140, 175–177
Ventura 128, 131, 139, 171, 172
Verdugo, Júlio 26, 138
Viceroy de Croix 6, 14, 161
Viceroyalty of New Spain 3, 7, 13, 19, 87, 161, 163
Victoria, Manuel 89
Vizcaíno, Sebastián 14,,15, 42, 167

Weber, David J. 60

Wolfskill, William 56

Yorba, Bernardo
Yorba family 33, 37, 134, 164
Yount, George C. 56

Zamorano, Agustin Vincente 89
Zavalishin, Dmitry 77
Zorro 151–152

www.ingramcontent.com/pod-product-compliance
Ingram Content Group UK Ltd.
Pitfield, Milton Keynes, MK11 3LW, UK
UKHW042006140426
5217IPUK00015B/1010